LIBYA

LIBYA ─────────────────

Jacob Mundy

Polity

First published in 2018 by Polity Press

Polity Press
65 Bridge Street
Cambridge CB2 1UR, UK

Polity Press
101 Station Landing
Suite 300
Medford, MA 02155, USA

ISBN-13: 978-1-5095-1872-2
ISBN-13: 978-1-5095-1873-9 (pb)

A catalogue record for this book is available from the British Library.

Library of Congress Cataloging-in-Publication Data

Names: Mundy, Jacob, author.
Title: Libya / Jacob Mundy.
Description: Cambridge, UK : Polity Press, 2018. | Series: Hot spots in global politics | Includes bibliographical references and index.
Identifiers: LCCN 2018002852 (print) | LCCN 2018012032 (ebook) | ISBN 9781509518760 (Epub) | ISBN 9781509518722 | ISBN 9781509518722(hardback)
| ISBN 9781509518739 (pbk.)
Subjects: LCSH: Libya--History--Civil War, 2011- | Libya--Politics and government--21st century.
Classification: LCC DT236 (ebook) | LCC DT236 .M79 2018 (print) | DDC 961.205--dc23
LC record available at https://lccn.loc.gov/2018002852

Typeset in 10.5 on 12pt Sabon
by Fakenham Prepress Solutions, Fakenham, Norfolk, NR21 8NL
Printed and bound in Great Britain by CPI Group (UK) Ltd, Croydon

For further information on Polity, visit our website:
politybooks.com

To Nolan

Contents

Figures

Acknowledgments

This book would not have been possible, first and foremost, without the insights provided by the various Libyan interlocutors who made my all-too-brief visits in 2012 and 2013 intellectually edifying. Those whom I can name publicly include Fawzi Abdesalam, Fathi Ali, Salah El Bakkoush, Wajdi Baraggig, Fathi Bashagha, Salim Beitemal, Salah Marghani, Taha Mohammed, Salah Ngab, Amal Obeidi, Mansour Ramadan, Taha Shakshouki, and the elders of Tawergha Camp Council in Janzur. Above all, I owe Sufyan Omeish, my research partner in 2012, a debt of gratitude for showing me aspects of the new and old Libya that I never would have seen. A band of others – journalists, officials, specialists, scholars, etc. – have also helped me navigate the thickets of Libya's politics before and after the 2011 revolution. Those who merit special recognition are Carlo Binda, Mietek Boduszyński, Peter Cole, Borzou Daragahi, Max Dyck, Mustafa Fetouri, Mary Fitzgerald, Ricky Goldstein, Dania Hamadeh, Salem Al-Hasi, Ahmed Labnouj, Aidan Lewis, Azza Maghur, Mansour Ramadan, Hanan Salah, Salwa Sheibany, John Thorne, Dirk Vadewalle, Mabrouka Al-Werfalli, and Yahia Zoubir. Additional forms of intellectual, logistical, and moral support for my research on Libya have been generously afforded by the American Institute for Maghrib Studies, Lindsay Benstead, Mary Casey and the Project on Middle East Political Science, Laryssa

Chomiak, Irene Costantini, John Entelis, Stephanie Fishel, Mia Fuller, Greg Gause, Hala Hweio, Osamah Khalil, Bill Lawrence, Dan Monk, Martyn Oliver, David Patel, Bobby Parks, Nancy Ries, Jean-Louis Romanet, and all of my family (old and new). The team at Polity Press, particularly Louise Knight and Nekane Tanaka Galdos, deserve recognition for their endless patience and refreshing efficiency. Production assistance from Neil de Cort and scrupulous copy-editing from Justin Dyer are likewise very much appreciated. Needless to say, none of these persons bear responsibility for any errors or (mis)interpretations that follow.

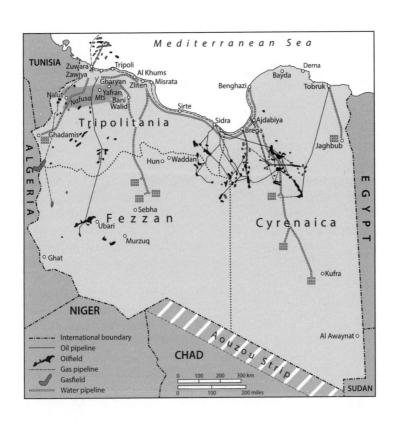

TUNISIA

Mediterranean Sea

Zuwara
Zawiya
Tripoli
Al Khums
Derna
Bayda
Benghazi
Tobruk
Nalut
Gharyan
Yafran
Zliten
Misrata
Bani
Walid
Nafusa
Mts
Sirte
Sidra
Ajdabiya
Brega

A L G E R I A

Ghadamis

T r i p o l i t a n i a

Hun
Waddan

Jaghbub

E G Y P T

Sebha

F e z z a n

C y r e n a i c a

Ubari

Murzuq

Ghat

Kufra

NIGER

International boundary
Oil pipeline
Oilfield
Gas pipeline
Gasfield
Water pipeline

CHAD

A o u z o u   S t r i p

Al Awaynat

SUDAN

0   100   200   300 km
0   100   200 miles

In the end, glorification of splendid underdogs is nothing other than glorification of the splendid system that makes them so.

Theodor Adorno, *Minima Moralia* (1951)

Introduction

For over half a decade, Libya has been ravaged by revolutionary violence, civil wars, and horrific acts of terrorism, all of which have further divided the polity, undermined the economy, fractured the state's sovereignty, and elicited repeated foreign interventions. These waves of political instability wracking the fragile mosaic of Libya's society were unleashed as the forty-two-year reign of Colonel Mu'ammar Al-Gaddafi came to its bitter and bloody end in 2011. Libya's anti-Gaddafi protestors, inspired by the successful revolutions in Tunisia and Egypt in early 2011, joined the Arab Spring in February, only to be dragged into an eight-month civil war that has irreparably fractured the nation. With military assistance from NATO and the Arab League, Libya's revolutionary militias, the *thuwar*, were finally able to depose the Gaddafi regime in the fall of 2011. Elections for a transitional government were soon held in the summer of 2012. Indeed, there was much hope and euphoria surrounding the possibilities facing a new Libya, a country with vast oil resources to finance its transition. Yet successive efforts to create a viable national authority only led to increasing social, economic, and political fragmentation across the country.

The primary question that drove the country back to civil war in 2014 was the extent to which Libya's new revolutionary forces should make any accommodation with the agents and institutions of the old regime. By the summer of 2014, Libya had two governments, both claiming electoral legitimacy and sovereignty over the country. Each was backed by unstable coalitions of militias representing a patchwork of ideologies and local interests. To make matters worse, a third government would emerge the following year. This one, however, would seek to extend the putative Caliphate of the Islamic State from the battlefields of Iraq and Syria to the scarred landscapes of Libya. In a desperate bid to hold Libya together, the North Atlantic powers backed the creation of a new interim national authority in late 2015 to lead the fight against the Islamic State and to stymie the flood of migrants and refugees leaving Libya's shores for Europe. Though there was some success with respect to the former, Libya's UN-backed Government of National Accord also complicated the already complex civil war that had erupted in 2014. By the end of 2017, questions continued to be raised as to whether or not Libya would become a failed state, if it were not already one.

The interesting thing about Libya, however, is the extent to which there often appears to be no relationship between political order in the country and the capacity of the central state that claims to rule it. Indeed, the Gaddafi regime was frequently accused of actively dismantling what few state structures Libya had either historically accumulated under Ottoman and Italian domination, or self-generated since independence in 1951. The historical weakness of the Libyan state was also one of the factors that allowed Gaddafi to seize control in the first place. The Gaddafi regime had easily come to power in a 1969 military coup that overthrew Libya's monarch, King Idris Al-Sanusi. Al-Sanusi had been a feeble and increasingly unpopular ruler, one installed by British and US administrators in a rush to give Libya independence after World War II. The Allied victory over the fascist armies of Italy and Germany on the battlefields of North Africa, a victory that was aided by Libyan partisans, had led to a tripartite French, British, and US administration over the former Italian colony, *Libia Italiana*. There were several reasons for the haste to give Libya independence in 1951.

Most Libyans would never accept a return to Italian rule and the United Nations would never abide an indefinite Anglo-American trusteeship. The occupying North Atlantic forces, keen to maintain their forward Mediterranean deployment in the emerging Cold War, found a willing partner in the Sanusi. Thus Libya managed to achieve independence under the Sanusi monarchy despite the absence of a strong nationalist movement or any state institutions outside of the colonial administration. Insofar as there was a Libyan polity to speak of, it was one that had yet to be woven together through the modern processes and technologies of state-building. The imposition of the Sanusi monarchy also served to retard the development of alternative political movements based upon republicanism, Arab nationalism, and Islamist modernization, all of which were viewed as antagonistic to Anglo-American interests in the region.

Prior to the establishment of an Italian colony in Libya (1911–43) and the installation of the Sanusi monarchy in 1951, Libya's Ottoman rulers (1551–1911) had done little to create modern institutions there either. For centuries, Istanbul's presence had been limited to extracting what little wealth it could from the dying trans-Saharan trade networks that terminated along the impoverished coastal lands between Cairo and Tunis. The autonomy of local Ottoman deputies to pursue their own economic activities, notably on the high seas, became a prominent feature in historical narratives of the period. In the final decades of Ottoman rule, Istanbul's grip on Libya merely served to thwart Franco-British encroachment as well as Italy's aspirations to be seen as a great European power through imperial expansion. The violence of the Italian occupation in the 1920s, which featured extensive ethnic cleansing and acts of genocide against various segments of Libyan society, helped to facilitate the creation of a plantation colony, one that could absorb large numbers of European settlers. Many Libyans did not sit idly by, yet they would pay a steep price in blood for their resistance to Italian fascism.

It is difficult to imagine how a country that had experienced such political ravages and natural disadvantages could become one of the most developed nations in Africa and the Middle East within a few short decades. But this is the magic of oil, and it transformed Libya beyond all recognition from the 1960s onward.

Oil has always been a blessing and a curse for those who rule the countries that possess it. This was certainly the case for King Idris, who had been granted one of the world's poorest countries in 1951, surviving on base rents from Washington and London for the first decade of his rule. Though the world was awash with cheap oil in the 1950s and 1960s, the quality of Libya's crude and the country's proximity to Europe worked to position it favorably in the geopolitics of the age. Libya was a dependable ally of the North Atlantic world and on the "right" side of the Suez Canal, so its entry into the international oil market flooded the state's coffers with easy money. Libya's rapid – almost unprecedented – economic development in the 1960s helped to alleviate the country's chronic poverty. But oil also resulted in significant social dislocation for many Libyans while the revenues buttressed the authoritarian tendencies of the Sanusi regime. In the end, the monarchy became a victim of its own success, as the modernization of Libya had created new socio-economic divisions and expectations, as well as a new international political consciousness among key segments of the population. The Free Officers' coup of September 1, 1969, had drawn deep inspiration from events unfolding across the Middle East and North Africa, as well as the Third World and Non-Aligned movements that had emerged during the tumultuous decades of decolonization in the 1950s and 1960s. On the whole, the people of Libya appeared to embrace the 1969 coup with cautious optimism.

What the September 1 revolution initially represented and what it would become in the years that followed radically diverged. Gaddafi and his followers could have simply enacted a political system based on military-backed single-party rule led by a charismatic and iron-willed figure, a system following the Egyptian, Algerian, Iraqi, and Syrian models. Had this been the case, Libya's history – and the ultimate fate of the Gaddafi regime – might have been quite different. Instead, Gaddafi set the country upon its own unique path, one in which a new kind of political system, a "state of the masses" or *Jamahiriyyah*, would be erected. The state would be governed from the bottom up without parties or a civil society. This order putatively adapted the best practices of traditional Libyan Islamic society and applied them to modern governance.

At the same time, the fledgling *Jamahiriyyah* had to be defended. A framework of revolutionary committees, courts, guards, and informants would extirpate the enemies of the regime wherever they existed, at home or abroad. Over time, these revolutionary organs and the *Jamahiriyyah* system came to serve themselves and the regime behind them, terrorizing and dividing a citizenry whose livelihoods grew increasingly dependent upon a centrally planned economy. Arbitrary detentions, political imprisonment, disappearances, invasive surveillance, and executions all became commonplace during the darkest phases of the revolution in the late 1970s and early 1980s.

All of this socio-political "imagineering" in Gaddafi's Libya was also made possible by the magic of oil. The global price of oil reached unprecedented levels from the mid-1970s through the early 1980s. During this period, Libya continued to pursue infrastructural development at a breakneck speed while also greatly expanding the size of its military apparatus. Growing tensions between the Gaddafi regime and the North Atlantic powers led Tripoli to embrace Soviet-made weaponry. Though Gaddafi would continue to profess his aversion to either the Western or Eastern blocs in the Cold War, Libya's oil-fueled military modernization would be used for territorial expansion into Chad and attempts to subvert the interests of Washington, London, Paris, Tel Aviv, and Riyadh through the deployment of proxy armies and terrorist groups around the world. The zenith of Gaddafi's international ambitions in the mid-1980s saw the disastrous defeat of Libyan forces in Chad and US military jets bomb Tripoli and Benghazi in an apparent attempt at regime change. Gaddafi's revenge – the downing of Pan Am 103 over Lockerbie, Scotland, killing 270 people – came in late 1988. United Nations sanctions and an embargo soon followed, cementing Libya's isolation and Gaddafi's status as an international pariah.

The Gaddafi regime was likewise increasingly isolated from the Libyan people. International sanctions coupled with depressed oil prices from 1986 onward had gutted the state's ability to buy political acquiescence through social spending and public employment. Efforts to liberalize the economy in the late 1980s were merely escape valves for pressures that were growing within the polity. Average Libyans, who had always trusted their immediate social environments far more than the various leaders in Tripoli, Benghazi, Rome, or Istanbul, continued to develop the local means to survive international isolation and the increasingly bunkered nature of the ruling elites. In the 1990s, the Gaddafi regime faced protest movements, military coups, tribal uprisings, and finally an Islamist insurgency that had gained experience in the Afghan campaign against the Soviets. The Gaddafi regime survived through increasing coercion as well as the traditional socio-political alliances and intra-tribal manipulations that had long underwritten its rule.

The regime's survival ultimately depended upon its willingness to concede to international demands regarding Libya's direct and indirect involvement with terrorism in the 1970s and 1980s. Accounting for Libya's efforts to develop weapons of mass destruction also helped the Gaddafi regime return to the international stage in the 2000s, as did increasing oil prices and the Libyan government's willingness to be a partner – albeit a discrete one – in the global war on terror launched after September 11, 2001. The Gaddafi regime also attempted to renew itself domestically by promising political reforms and enacting economic ones. The face of Libyan reform was Saif Al-Islam, Gaddafi's second son and the presumed *prince héritier* of the regime. Fluent in the international lingua franca of human rights and economic privatization, Saif Al-Islam helped to usher in a new age of neoliberalization that promised much but delivered little for most Libyans. It was a period in which the pretense of revolution and socialism was abandoned. In its place came the increasing visibility of the Gaddafi family's direct control over the state and the economy, as well as the nakedness of the plundering of public assets for private gain as oil prices climbed to record heights in 2008 ahead of the global financial collapse. The putative developmental success of Libya and its billions in cash reserves suggested the wherewithal to co-opt potential opponents or to coerce them with the regime's increasingly sophisticated and disciplined praetorian guards. In reality, a quarter of the population consisted of young men facing unemployment rates of over 30 percent. These young men would help launch their own revolution. And like Gaddafi's coup forty years beforehand, it was a revolution deeply inspired by international events, those unfolding in early 2011 to the west in Tunisia and the east in Egypt.

The Need to Rethink Libya After the Uprising

The narrative above, which is fleshed out in more detail in Chapter 1, gives us some sense of the conditions and trends that led to the 2011 uprising in Libya and why it became a full-blown, internationalized civil war (Chapter 2). The primary focus of this study, however, goes well beyond documenting Libya's place in the Arab Spring. The chapters that follow will first detail the aftermath of the 2011 conflict (Chapter 3) and will then examine the inability of Libya's transitional authorities to consolidate power effectively (Chapter 4). Lastly, this book will explain the myriad civil conflicts that followed this failed transition, conflicts that effectively divided the country's sovereignty between rival governments, that allowed the Islamic State to take root in central Libya, that precipitated a new round of discrete and overt foreign military interventions, and that created an international migration crisis along Libya's western coast (Chapter 5). With the advantage of hindsight, this study benefits greatly from the fact that several years have passed since the fateful events of 2011 radically altered the course of Libyan history. It is this perspective that makes this in-depth study of contemporary Libya both unique and warranted.

Needless to say, this study also builds upon the work of other scholars, researchers, and institutions that have attempted to understand post-revolutionary Libya, as well as the regional and international implications of its turbulent transition to a new political reality. In the final weeks of the 2011 uprising and in the months afterward, several excellent volumes and reports were assembled or reissued in order to explain the causes of the country's revolution. Other studies and collections soon appeared in the years that followed, providing new insights, context, and data on the events of 2011 and what significance those events held for the new Libyan polity taking shape. All of these works have had an immense influence on this book, as is made clear through frequent reference to their critical findings.

This study, however, is the first to reconsider the 2011 uprising in relation to the intractable political crises and armed conflicts that have for several years now inhibited Libya's transition to a stable post-Gaddafi order. Backgrounded by a chapter on Libya's unique history of state-making, state-unmaking, and state-evading (Chapter 1), the bulk of this text examines four distinct phases in the recent evolution of contemporary Libya: the significance of the 2011 uprising and the ways in which NATO's intervention shaped the course of the war and its aftermath (Chapter 2); the consolidation of opposing factions during and after the uprising from 2011 to 2012 (Chapter 3); the growing insecurity and political instability of the transitional period from 2012 to 2014 (Chapter 4); and finally the causes and consequences of the return to open civil war from 2014 onward (Chapter 5). An important effect of these final two stages was the emergence of an Islamic State affiliate in Libya, which would go on to claim the city of Sirte – the city where Gaddafi was born and later brutally executed in 2011 – as its North African capital in 2015. The failed transition in Libya and the return to open civil war would also allow for the flourishing of clandestine trade networks, notably in human trafficking, which contributed to the largest international refugee and migration crisis since World War II.

Though largely chronological in structure, this study aims to understand the various contexts, crucial decisions, and core stakeholders that generated the most fateful turning points in Libya's recent history. Given the ways in which the international community, particularly the North Atlantic powers, have problematically engaged with Libya's increasingly interlocking crises since 2011 (if not years and decades beforehand), the modest aim of this study is to step back and take stock of what has happened, reconsider the reasons for these events, and suggest – by way of conclusion – other ways of understanding the historical and geopolitical significance of what has happened in Libya since 2011. While this ultimate aim might seem lacking in any practical application, a driving concern behind this study is the extent to which modern Libya has always been caught up in the agendas of others who were looking for easy answers and comforting narratives. This study is not driven by the ultimate goal of arriving at lessons learned, actionable findings, or policy recommendations, but instead it seeks to understand Libya's recent history in relation to the larger forces that impinge upon it. These include those forces we often choose not to acknowledge and those that are beyond our ability to affect through existing social, political, and economic institutions. Just as there are no easy answers when it comes to rethinking Libya, little comfort will be offered to those who eschew responsibility for helping unmake modern Libya.

Uprising to Revolution, Civil War to Islamic State: Chapter Summaries

The process of rethinking Libya presented in this book begins by examining the emergence of Libya as a modern nation-state and the peculiar geopolitical trajectory it has followed. Contrary to most accounts, Chapter 1 presents Libya's consolidation as a nation-state as a contingent and relatively recent confluence of events, largely occurring in the years after independence in 1951. With the slow decay and collapse of the Ottoman Empire in the 1800s and early 1900s, its grip on Libya, Istanbul's last significant North African possession, finally gave way to Italian imperialism. Rome's conquest of Libya commenced in earnest over a quarter of a century after most of Africa had been claimed by the European powers in the 1880s. At the time of the Italian conquest, local ambitions for republican statehood existed among the Tripolitanian elites in Libya's western region. These ambitions contended with the dynastic claims of the Sanusi religious order in the eastern region of Cyrenaica. Both, however, were decimated as Rome embarked on its imperial project to annex and colonize the lands between French Tunisia and British Egypt from 1911 to 1943.

The idea that Libya was a modern nation-state – one land and one people, from Kufra to Zuwara, Sebha to Tobruk – was an idea that first had to be nurtured by the Sanusi monarchy when it was suddenly handed independence by the United Nations in 1951. The three pillars of King Idris's rule were the Sanusi religious order, the Anglo-American military presence, and finally the oil boom of the 1960s. Whereas the Sanusi monarchy variously refused to engage in statebuilding or only did so haphazardly, the Gaddafi regime would embark on a process of radical state remaking in the 1970s – or what many would consider an extended experiment in state *un*making. Though basic developmental indicators suggested that Libya had indeed made profound advancements from its dismal state at the end of World War II, this was largely the result of the country's oil wealth, which Gaddafi had also funneled into wasteful military adventures, international provocation, self-promotion across Africa, and questionable infrastructural projects like the Great Man-Made River, the world's largest – and perhaps most expensive – water-conveyance scheme.

In the early twenty-first century, after decades of misrule, Gaddafi's *Jamahiriyyah* had not created a new polity so much as it had created a terrorized populace well versed in the arts of political evasion through alternative social and economic networks rooted in their local environments. In the final decade of the regime, as global oil prices rebounded in the early 2000s, it seemed as if the Gaddafi family itself was engaging in an act of evasion. The neoliberalization of the Libyan economy and the increasing reliance on technocratic forms of governance allowed the regime to transcend the drudgery of rule by outsourcing it to experts while the Gaddafi family sought membership among the transnational political and financial elite.

Chapter 1 documents these and other contexts that help us understand the sources of furious anger that were unleashed in 2011 – the decades of repression, of social manipulation, of economic mismanagement, and of political disenfranchisement. Beyond the motivations driving many Libyans to take up arms against their government, these contexts also help us to understand how the 2011 uprising was organized at the local level. Networks for surviving the *Jamahiriyyah*, which had been both intentionally and unintentionally nurtured by the Gaddafi regime for decades, then turned on the regime, providing the socio-economic basis for its overthrow. Reviewing the regime's belligerent foreign policies and its reprehensible human rights record in Chapter 1 is also important because it helps explain why the North Atlantic powers resolved so quickly to intervene militarily in Libya's emerging revolution in 2011 despite these same powers having spent the previous decade rehabilitating Gaddafi on the international stage.

Chapter 2 examines how, when, and why various Libyan constituencies came together to oppose the Gaddafi regime – or to rally to its defense. The forces that would oppose the regime in 2011 were not exclusively the most marginalized social and political groups in country. In fact, the eventual success of the uprising partially rested in its ability to mobilize and redeploy many of the regime's own elites and institutions, as well as the social coalitions that had long supported Gaddafi's rule. Facilitating all of this was, as noted above, the *de jure* local politics of the *Jamahiriyyah* and the *de facto* local politics that had emerged alongside it as a result of the weaknesses, mismanagement, and imperfections of the Gaddafi state. These formal and informal forms of organization would not only empower the revolution to unseat the regime, they would go on to become the basic constituent elements of the various factions vying for control over the post-Gaddafi state (as Chapter 3 details).

While both sides in the 2011 uprising took precipitous measures that rapidly militarized the situation, it was undoubtedly the entry of NATO and the Arab League into the conflict in mid-March that had the greatest effect on the course of the civil war. The intervention, first of all, afforded the armed uprising and its international supporters time to reorganize and focus their efforts after the rapid collapse of the rebels' eastern front to Gaddafi forces. Secondly, the intervention sidelined other peacemaking initiatives, notably those of the African Union, as the participating international forces had essentially equated the ultimate destruction of the state's military capacity with regime change. Lastly, the intervention and other forms of covert assistance rendered to the rebellion provided the participating North Atlantic and Gulf states with an understanding of the forces they were assisting, those calling themselves *thuwar*. In some cases, this assistance would foster lasting alliances between specific Libyan constituencies and foreign patrons. With foreign special forces and intelligence agents deployed all across Libya by mid-2011 to assist with targeting and training, rebel fighters and NATO officers were working hand-in-hand to topple the regime. One location in particular, the western city of Misrata, which was subjected to a vicious siege by regime forces, would take these experiences of suffering and ultimate triumph into the post-revolutionary period. After all, it was Misratan fighters and not those who had launched the revolt in Cyrenaica who claimed the uprising's ultimate prize at the end of the fighting in October: Gaddafi himself. Unfortunately, the 2011 intervention represented the end – not the beginning – of direct international security assistance to Libya. Having morally legitimated and militarily supported Libya's *thuwar*, it would now be difficult for the uprising's North Atlantic partners to question, let alone confront, the political forces they had helped unleash and empower in Libya.

As Chapter 3 explores, the immediate post-revolutionary situation in Libya was a time of hope and fear. The end of the regime meant a new political reality could emerge across the country. Yet the reality that did emerge was one in which various stakeholders, particularly those claiming to have suffered the most at the hands of the regime – in the 2011 war and historically – were determined to prevent the reemergence of any semblance of the old order. Guiding the transition and navigating the society's old and new divides was the National Transitional Council, the body that had represented the revolution to the outside world but had little on-the-ground control over its various factions. The Council carried its structural incapacities and its own internal divisions into the post-revolutionary environment, a situation that had already outrun the Council's ability to affect it. Of the various parameters defining this new political reality, one of the most tense was the growing divide between those seeking radical change and those seeking accommodation with some of the institutions and agents of the former regime, particularly high-level officials.

In order to understand the growing political cleavages bisecting the Libyan polity at the local, regional, and national levels, Chapter 3 provides a geographical tour of the major sites in the 2011 uprising: the Tripolitania region, including the capital and Misrata; the Nafusa mountains to the southwest of the capital, home of the influential city of Zintan and Libya's Amazigh (Berber) communities; Libya's vast Saharan interior, notably its western region of Fezzan and its various ethnic communities; and finally the eastern region of Cyrenaica where the uprising began. The purpose of this survey is twofold: first, to introduce the major players in post-revolutionary Libya and, second, to understand the ways in which the old political system and efforts to overcome it were continuing to shape post-Gaddafi Libya. A year after the uprising, international attention was largely focused on the political campaigns and politicians running for Libya's interim parliament in the summer of 2012, arguably the country's first truly contested election in decades. Though this vote represented an important achievement, it falsely suggested that political power now rested in the hands of Libya's democratically elected authorities. An assault on US diplomatic and intelligence facilities in Benghazi on

September 11, 2012, by Islamist militants, which resulted in the death of the US Ambassador, was a stark reminder of who actually held power in the new Libya: the revolutionary militias.

The militia problem had metastasized beyond the control of Libya's frail central authorities. Indeed, Chapter 4 examines the proliferation of militias in Libya not as a mere symptom of the country's growing political dysfunction but as a key driver of the chaos. In the face of instability at the national level, the response of local communities was often to embrace militias as the only means of local-level protection. Regime loyalists and others targeted by the revolutionary militias formed their own counter-militias to defend themselves and their communities. In an effort to improve their position in the post-revolutionary struggle, militias representing weak and marginalized communities seized core state assets and held vital economic infrastructures hostage. Libya thus entered an insecurity trap, one in which efforts to achieve local security only reinforced insecurity at the national level. To make matters worse, this was a situation that Libya's interim leaders exacerbated by incentivizing more – not less – militia formation through compensation, salaries, and incorporation into formal military and security units. In effect, militias became a national jobs program for Libya's masses of unemployed young men. While it was easy to say that militias had become a threat to order in the new Libya, it was equally important to recognize that militias were the new order.

In this intensifying context that Chapter 4 attempts to document, those who would lead the new Libya adopted increasingly polarized attitudes. A growing alliance between moderate, orthodox, and radical Islamists would become the political front for those opposing accommodation with former regime elements. In the face of this campaign to purge the new Libyan state of all those who had collaborated with the former regime, an alliance of pro-accommodation interests formed, which included actors and groups whose social and political networks often had roots in the structures of the Gaddafi regime.

Elections for a new interim parliament in mid-2014 set the stage for the definitive rupture that would see Libya descend into its second civil war in less than four years. On one side of this contest was the nominally Islamist coalition called Libya Dawn, which maintained its grip on Tripoli owing in large part to the strength of Misratan forces and backing from states like Qatar and Turkey. On the other side of the civil war were the forces of Operation Dignity, led by Khalifa Haftar, a former officer in Gaddafi's armed forces. Haftar, having already launched a campaign to fight Islamist militancy in Cyrenaica, was backed by Libya's internationally recognized parliament, which had fled to Tobruk amid the growing violence and insecurity in Tripoli. Haftar's efforts soon boasted a growing list of international sponsors, including Egypt, Saudi Arabia, the United Arab Emirates, and, tentatively, Russia.

The final chapter of this book looks at this new civil war and the response of the international community. Both the war and the response of foreign interests were increasingly influenced by an altogether different development, one that few had seen coming but was, in retrospect, tragic in its predictability: the rise of the Islamic State in Sirte in 2015. Following the rapid, stunning success of the Islamic State in the Syrian civil war in late 2013 and its extension into western Iraq in the summer of 2014, Libyan and foreign jihadi fighters began to make inroads into Islamist factions in eastern, central, and western Libya. Their greatest success, however, was in the city of Sirte, which stood geographically between the Dawn forces in Tripolitania and the Dignity forces in Cyrenaica. At that time, Dawn and Dignity forces were in the process of consolidating their regional power bases before seeking a wider civil war with each other. With all eyes on Tripoli, Tobruk, and Benghazi, the city of Sirte, nominally under Misratan control, was of limited strategic concern to both sides. Islamic State activists also found a population in Sirte that had been collectively punished and marginalized for its close association with the former regime. Though the power of the Islamic State in Libya was limited, it nonetheless rested upon a political economy of rule employed by other militias across the country. The most visible aspect of this was the growing trade in human smuggling of international migrants, which became a lucrative source of funding for communities along Libya's coastlines, Saharan borders, and interior crossroads.

In taking control of Sirte away from Misratan militias and declaring an extension of Abu Bakr Al-Baghdadi's putative Caliphate to North Africa, the Islamic State in Libya sent shockwaves through the international community. The North Atlantic powers, which had increasingly retreated in the face of Libya's growing insecurity and civil violence in 2013 and 2014, found themselves compelled once again to launch an intervention in 2016. This time, however, the intervention was on a much smaller scale and had a much more limited objective: the eradication of the Islamic State from Libya.

At this point, the peacemaking efforts of the United Nations to reconcile the Dawn–Dignity divide were subordinated to the North Atlantic community's primary security interests vis-à-vis Libya: the Islamic State and the Mediterranean migration crisis. Progress on either agenda required the creation of a legitimate central authority that could liaise with foreign governments and, more importantly, consent to their interventions. The rush to create a Government of National Accord at the end of 2015 and to install a new executive body in Tripoli in early 2016 did nothing to achieve national reconciliation but it did allow the internationally supported campaign against the Islamic State to go forward. While Misratan forces bloodied themselves in a months-long fight to retake Sirte with US support, Haftar's Dignity coalition patiently consolidated and expanded its areas of control, eventually seizing almost all of Libya's core oil facilities and infrastructures.

With the Islamic State smashed and scattered at the end of 2016, Libya looked set for a final confrontation between Haftar's forces and his opponents in Tripolitania. Making matters worse, Libya's new internationally recognized head of government, Fayez Al-Sarraj, had effectively allied himself with elements of the Dawn coalition in order to take up residency in the capital. While most ordinary Libyans had long ago grown tired of the fighting and found ways to survive – and sometimes thrive – amid the uncertainty and violence, militias and local constituencies continued to hold most of the power in Libya through their abilities to act as political spoilers and economic saboteurs. Regardless of whether or not the impasse between pro- and anti-accommodationist elites could be overcome at the national level, Libya seemed to have truly become a state of the masses, one in which the people, now heavily armed, would never again let themselves be subjugated to any central authority.

1 | State of the Masses ——————

Since 2011, a series of political crises and violent conflicts have torn apart the Libyan state and fractured its polity. But the challenge of creating and sustaining political order in modern Libya has always been difficult. Those who have attempted to rule this vast and austere landscape, whether foreign empires or local leaders, have always faced an unforgiving territory.

Throughout history, the harshness of the environment has put severe limits on indigenous political and economic activity. Libya today is the world's sixteenth largest country by land mass and yet ranks among the world's least densely populated. Most of the land – 95 percent – is desert, and the desert is growing. In the center of the country, along the coastal edge of the Sirtica plain, the Sahara spills into the Mediterranean, effectively dividing the north of the country into two zones with small pockets of arable land in the west and even smaller ones in the east. Throughout history, these agricultural zones mainly supported semi-nomadic forms of pastoralism and limited amounts of plant cultivation. Agriculture was otherwise always a challenge; there are no perennial rivers in Libya to speak of and the annual rainfall is a quarter of that recorded in neighboring Tunisia. And while over 60 percent of Tunisian land is available for agriculture, Libya has only been able to raise that figure from 6.3 percent to 8.7 percent since independence, owing in large part to the industrial-scale exploitation of massive underground aquifers in the Sahara starting in the 1980s. Oil, however, is largely responsible for the rapid growth of Libya's population since 1960 by providing the state with the financial resources to import what could not be made domestically. The population of postcolonial Libya has climbed from 1.4 million to current estimates of over six million. This period also witnessed the rapid urbanization of the population, from below 30 to nearly 80 percent.[1]

While there are undoubtedly environmental factors that have inhibited local statebuilding enterprises in Libya throughout the ages, the country's modern history is one of near constant political and economic disruption. Libya's major population centers in Tripolitania and Cyrenaica had always lived in the shadow of their respective neighbors to the west and east, Tunis and Cairo, which were respectively seized by France and Britain in the late 1800s. Moreover, Libya's population declined in the 1800s during the late Ottoman period, coinciding with the collapse of trans-Saharan

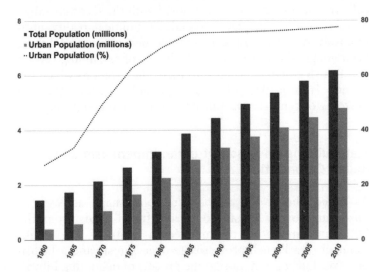

Figure 1.1. Population of Libya, 1960–2016.
Source: World Bank.

trade following the outlawing of slavery. Italian colonization from 1911 onward also left its mark on Libyan society. The country's indigenous population halved during the three decades that followed owing to migration, dispossession, conflict, and the genocidal policies of the Italian occupiers and their turn to fascist modes of rule.[2]

What also has to be recognized is that Libya's formation as a modern nation-state arose out of several geopolitical contingencies, notably the decline of the Ottoman Empire, the rapacious colonization of Africa by Europe's industrializing nations in the late 1800s, the global realignments of power during the 1914–45 period, and the new security imperatives of the North Atlantic states during the early Cold War. It thus makes little sense to ask why Libya never developed into a coherent nation-state prior to the establishment of its contemporary territorial boundaries, as well as the socio-political elaboration of its polity at the hands of competing external forces located in Istanbul (Constantinople), Rome, London, Paris, and Washington. Any insistence that Libya has always been impoverished, underdeveloped, and politically fragmented first has to contend with the fact that Libya never was a geographical, social, or political reality until relatively recently. The cartographic demarcation of Libya, beginning in the late 1800s at the hands of expanding French and British empires, brings into focus the extent to which the country is an artifact of modern geopolitics rather than an outcome of centuries or millennia of internal gestation.

Statebuilding on Sand: Ottoman Imperialism and Italian Colonization

As noted above, Libya's borders took shape as Western European powers began to seize African lands from the Ottoman Empire in the nineteenth century. The establishment of a French protectorate over Tunisia and a British one over Egypt set in motion the process of delimiting Libya's frontiers from the Mediterranean to the coastal interior. In the Sahara, however, Ottoman assertions of sovereignty were much more ambiguous.[3] It was not until after World War I that French ambitions in West Africa and British ambitions in the Sudan had formally delineated Libya's desert frontiers. By the time these were finalized in the 1930s, the country was under full Italian control. Rome's late entry into the game of North African imperialism had begun with the Italo-Turkish war of 1911, roughly fifteen years after Ethiopian troops routed Italian forces in East Africa. Having only recently unified as a modern nation-state, Italy pushed into Libya for obvious reasons: geographical proximity and geopolitical positioning vis-à-vis the other European powers. The rise of industrial capitalism has also created population surpluses that Italian leaders were eager to enlist in the national economy rather than see them go to the Americas. Those who harbored Italy's ambitions in Libya, which had been clear since the late 1800s, also attempted to marshal a new nostalgia for the lost greatness of the Roman Empire. Libya became the "Fourth Shore" of Italy, a reference to its Tyrrhenian, Adriatic, Ionian, and now North African coasts. The imposition of Italian rule also grew in parallel with the rise of fascism and the tyranny of Benito Mussolini's dictatorship, which was relentless in its persecution of Arab and Amazigh (Berber) resistance in Libya. The most infamous of these cases was Omar Mukhtar's eight-year insurgency in Cyrenaica (1923–31), which was met with horrific acts of ethnic cleansing and collective punishment by the occupying Italian forces.[4]

The initial success of the Mukhtar insurgency owed as much to classical tactics of indirect guerrilla warfare as it did to the social, economic, and political networks of the *Sanusiyyah*. Founded in the mid-nineteenth century by Sidi Muhammad Al-Sanusi (1787–1859), a prolific religious scholar from western Algeria, the *Sanusiyyah* was a Sufi order that originally developed in Saudi Arabia. The late eighteenth and early nineteenth century was a period of intense Islamic revivalism in the face of the decaying Ottoman Empire and increasing European penetration in the Middle East. Eventually settling in Cyrenaica in the 1840s, Al-Sanusi found a region relatively ungoverned by Ottoman authorities, as well as a population that was open to his brand of fundamentalist yet socially active mysticism. In the decades that followed, Al-Sanusi, his descendants, and his adherents – *Al-Sanusiyyah* – would create a network of dozens of lodges (*zawiyyah*) up and down the future Libyan–Egyptian border, eventually reaching into the Fezzan and as far as lake Chad. What Al-Sanusi's order networked together in these religious establishments was not simply an archipelago of centers for spiritual guidance and learning; these lodges were in fact sited in relation to the movement's growing economic influence on trans-Saharan trade. The *Sanusiyyah*'s economic power translated into political power as well, a fact that Ottoman administrators eventually came to understand and accommodate. Where *Sanusiyyah* power was its weakest was where direct Ottoman rule was strongest: in and around Tripoli. To the limited extent that urban classes, educated elites, and cosmopolitanism had developed in Tripolitania during the late Ottoman Empire, it was in Tripoli that modern notions of Arab nationalism and Islamic reform began to affect the thinking of future leaders of the Misratan and Tripolitanian republics. The *Sanusiyyah*, by contrast, began to look more and more like a hereditary dynasty by the time of the Italian occupation, with the leadership of the order having passed to Sayyid Idris Al-Sanusi, the grandson of the order's founder and the future king of Libya.

Following the Italian victory over the Ottomans in 1912, there were initial yet short-lived efforts by Rome to work with local authorities, particularly the *Sanusiyyah* and the leaders of the Tripolitanian Republic. By the time Mukhtar launched his insurgency in the early 1920s, Sayyid Idris was exiled to Cairo and the Tripolitanian Republic was void. Indirect Italian rule was in fact giving way to complete annexation, just as happened under France in Algeria. Like the Ottomans, the Italians had implemented successful strategies to divide the society and thwart resistance. In these new contexts of direct rule and settler colonialism, there was little room for the Libyans themselves, who were largely marginalized from what limited employment the colonial economy had to offer in terms of governmental administration, territorial security, or the plantation system.

Here it is important to note the extent to which outside powers continually interrupted the elaboration of indigenous state institutions in Libya, from the Ottoman dismantling of the Karamanli dynasty (1711–1835) to the Italian subjugation and eventual abrogation of the *Sanusiyyah* and the Tripolitanian Republic. Moreover, the modes of direct imperialism practiced in Libya during the late Ottoman Empire (1835–1911) and the Italian annexation (1918–43), if not the brief period of tripartite international administration from World War II to 1951, not only monopolized state power in the hands of foreigners, these foreign regimes often governed by creating or exacerbating divisions among Libya's traditional elites. Economically, Libya was extremely disadvantaged as well. Very little industrialization and urbanization had taken place under the Ottomans and the Italians. Libya's metropolitan working classes and mass-based political parties were anemic in comparison to those that had emerged in Tunisia and Egypt in the late eighteenth and early ninetieth centuries. Adding insult to injury, the battles of World War II caused extensive damage to what little civil and military infrastructures had been developed in Libya under the Italians. Upon independence in 1951, Libya was ranked as one of the poorest countries to enter the new family of nations created under UN auspices. As is frequently noted in the scholarly literature, its main exports at the time of its independence – that is, before oil – were scrap metal from World War II and a grass used for making paper.[5]

Direct Italian rule not only prevented the emergence of indigenous state institutions, it exacerbated the forms of political power that would be required to govern Libya in the absence of such institutions. By contrast, French rule in Morocco and Tunisia had relied heavily upon indirect forms of imperialism that worked with preexisting state structures. This mode of imperial rule was somewhat modeled after the British experience in India and, later, Egypt. Indeed, the contrast between Tunisia and Egypt, on the one hand, and Libya, on the other, is telling. In important ways, Tunisia and Egypt would emerge from European imperialism as they had entered it: with established bureaucracies, administrative classes, and disciplined armies, albeit more so. Libya, by contrast, had very little of these essential ingredients of modern governance when it was suddenly granted independence in 1951, several years ahead of its eastern and western neighbors, under King Idris.[6]

Libya was a polity largely created by international fiat. Over the course of the first half of the twentieth century, various social coalitions and ethnolinguistic groups increasingly found themselves either brought together in this new territorial entity called Libya or divided by the imperial borders being imposed. Among the latter were not only large communities in the Sahara, notably the Tuareg and the Tebu, but also peoples living along the northern border regions with Tunisia and Egypt. What these groups and coalitions all had in common was a shared historical marginalization from the dominant centers of power in the Mediterranean. Having long lived in the interstices of power, the constituent elements of the Libyan polity were all well versed in the art of manipulating, evading, and otherwise challenging central governance. Given the diffuse nature of political power in Libya and its centrifugal dynamics, its postcolonial history would be marked by struggles between those seeking to centralize state control and those resisting it.[7]

The United Kingdom of Libya

Not much changed with the arrival of the Sanusi monarchy, on the shoulders of the British and US military, in the 1950s. What few state institutions were developed during the monarchy's eighteen years of rule were largely created under the tutelage of advisors from London, Washington, and the United Nations, later to be followed by various kinds of economic, industrial, agricultural, infrastructural, and technological experts, particularly in the oil industry. As one of those development experts lamented in 1959, "Libya combines within the borders of one country virtually all the obstacles to development that can be found anywhere." He concluded, "If Libya can be brought to a stage of sustained growth, there is hope for every country in the world."[8]

Little did this UN economist understand how radically oil would transform Libya under the watchful eye of its North Atlantic patrons. In this way, the creation of state institutions and a national economy under King Idris would mirror the development of Saudi Arabia, where the Arabian-American Oil Company and US military power had been the cornerstone of the early Saudi state.[9] National defense and regime security in Libya were largely the responsibility of the United States and Britain, whose militaries represented the most competent fighting force in the country, even at the time of the 1969 coup.[10]

Another problematic feature of post-independence Libya was the gradual centralization, informalization, and personalization of power under the monarchy, which came at the expense of nurturing independent state institutions. The state was initially founded as a constitutional and federal monarchy, calling itself the United Kingdom of Libya in reference to its three main regions, Tripolitania, Fezzan, and Cyrenaica. This tripartite structure, with Benghazi and Tripoli as coequal capital cities, sought to empower the eastern and southwestern regions through federalism so as to counterbalance Tripolitania's demographic hegemony.

The most important developments, however, were those that enhanced the monarchy's power through the promotion of local and interpersonal politics over constitutional procedures and mass-based parties. The banning of all political parties in 1952, for example, set the tone for years to come. The regime preferred parallel yet informal institutions modeled after those of the precolonial *Sanusiyyah* order, ones that had relied heavily upon the extended royal family and Cyrenaican tribes allied to the dynasty. The system, however, was hardly stable. Governments rose and fell, and ministers rotated in and out on a constant basis.[11] By 1963, the federal system had been abolished in order to weaken the power of the three regions and to make oil concessions easier to negotiate with international firms. The Sanusi regime argued that national development priorities had been held hostage to regional interests. Nonetheless, as the Sanusi monarchy became more absolutist, regime-building – at the expense of statebuilding – seemed to take priority. The model of rule developing in Libya under King Idris began to mirror the system that had developed in Morocco after independence, where precolonial forms of socio-political organization and postcolonial constitutional institutions, albeit weak ones, had produced a hybrid regime. In both cases, the backbone of the regime's power was a "deep state" structure of elites loyal to the monarchy, known as *al-makhzan* in Morocco and increasingly as *al-diwan* (royal household) in Libya. These elites penetrated and manipulated official state institutions at all levels of governance while leveraging almost all means of economic productivity to the monarchy's gain. One of the beneficial effects of these arrangements was the forestalling of oppositional institutions and classes, whether in the government, the private sector, or civil society.[12] Though the Sanusi regime had a much later start than the centuries-old dynasty in Morocco, it had the added benefits of Anglo-American military protection and revenues from its collaboration with, among others, British and US oil companies.

Though geologists had known about Libya's oil for decades, it was not until ten years after independence that it began to flow. Development of Libya's oil sector had been inhibited by the fact that international markets had been awash with cheap oil after World War II, just as they had been for most of the early petroleum age. Maintaining prices at a profitable level while guaranteeing oil's free circulation had been the responsibility of a select number of international oil companies and North Atlantic states. Direct and indirect challenges to this system of price control, however, began to emerge in the 1950s, which threatened the energy supplies necessarily to fuel Western Europe's economic recovery after the war. As European imperialism crumbled across the Middle East and North Africa, newly independent states demanded more control over national resources.

The response of the North Atlantic powers to these demands revealed the seriousness with which they took the situation. For example, the Iranian effort to nationalize British Petroleum (BP) in 1951 was one of the factors that led the CIA to help orchestrate a coup in order to overthrow Iran's democratically elected leader and reverse the nationalization campaign. Another example was the Suez Crisis of 1956, in which an Egyptian initiative to impose domestic control over the Suez Canal led to a joint British, French, and Israeli military intervention to maintain foreign control over the canal. Both of these events and others contributed to the search for new sources of oil that could circumvent the growing geopolitical turmoil surrounding oil produced in Southwest Asia: that is, high-quality oil that did not have to transit through either the Suez Canal or vulnerable pipelines located near the Soviet Union. Given its proximity to Europe and King Idris's friendly relations with the North Atlantic powers, Libya was an alternative source of oil that could continue to feed the Marshall Plan. Libyan oil could also help weaken the growing power of the established producer states and those charging transit fees. The eight-year closure of the Suez Canal following the 1967 Arab–Israeli Six-Day War not only affirmed this logic, but it also helped make the Libyan state stupendously wealthy.

From 1961 onward, the revenues earned from oil in Libya quickly eclipsed the central government's primary source of funding: base rents paid by London and Washington. Key features of Libya's oil – its geological accessibility, its light-sweet character, and its low transportation costs – made it particularly desirable and profitable, back then as much as today. On the eve of Gaddafi's coup in 1969, an expert with the World Bank described Libya's stunning growth in the 1960s as unparalleled in development economics. Per capita income, for example, had grown from $50 in 1951 to $2,000 in 1969. Another telling fact was that Libya transformed overnight from an aid-receiving country to a major aid-donating country, notably providing assistance to Syria, Egypt, and Jordan after their defeat in the Six-Day War.[13]

The economic boom in Libya saw immense infrastructural and demographic changes, but not all of these changes were felt equally or equitably across the nation. The social dislocation of rapid development and urbanization, particularly around Tripoli and Benghazi, was matched by the economic frustration of growing wage inequality and inflation. The new Libyan economy had created obvious winners – the monarchy and those closely allied to it – and losers. To make matters worse, oil wealth only exacerbated the negative tendencies of the regime: its disdain for democratic consultation; its manipulation of regional and tribal politics; and its dependency upon Western governments, firms, and expertise. When the military coup finally happened on September 1, 1969, the people of Libya largely embraced the opportunity for change.

Gaddafi and His Global Revolution

Surprisingly, the initial response in London and Washington was to adopt a wait-and-see attitude toward the September 1 coup staged by the so-called "Free Officers Movement," led by a young and charismatic junior officer, Mu'ammar Al-Gaddafi. The primary concern of London and Washington seemed to be whether or not the monarchy would attempt to stage a counter-coup with military loyalists. For such to be realized, US forces stationed at Wheelus Airbase in Tripoli, one of the largest in America's global portfolio, would necessarily have to participate. Nearly twenty years after independence, the Libyan royal military was still utterly dependent upon US operational, technological, and logistical support, particularly its air force. At the same time, the extent to which the coup leaders, and the Libyan military at large, had benefited from British and US military training gave London and Washington hope that their new partners in Tripoli would more or less guarantee the continuity of their economic and security interests.

There were, however, reasons to be concerned. Heightened tensions across the Middle East and North Africa in the wake of the 1967 Arab–Israeli war had seen growing calls for pan-Arab unity, notably in the neighboring countries of Algeria and Egypt, with which the 1969 coup leaders in Tripoli seemed to align themselves ideologically. Whether this would become a moderate Arab republicanism in Libya or a militant one was the question. Though Morocco and Tunisia attempted to remain loyal to their NATO backers as best they could, Soviet arms sales were fueling the militarization of Algeria and Egypt. Moreover, international oil companies were facing increasing demands from the producer states for more equitable profit-sharing agreements, with nationalization of oil infrastructures being used as a threat. The "loss" of Libya would thus have been a significant blow to the North Atlantic's Cold War strategy in the Mediterranean, the Middle East, and North Africa.

The new regime in Libya, the Revolutionary Command Council, did not wait long to take actions that would reveal the country's new political direction. By the end of the year, it had nationalized some foreign properties, launched rhetorical attacks on representative democracy, promulgated an interim constitution, demanded a withdrawal of the Anglo-American military presence, and entered into an alliance with Egypt and Sudan. All of these policies would be intensified in the years to come, as would assaults on the political structures and social relations that had underwritten Sanusi rule. In a move that simultaneously disrupted the power of Libya's three regions and its tribes, the regime instituted a series of re-districting measures and administratively reorganized the state. In January 1971, Gaddafi began to propose some of the ideas that would be systematized in his *Green Book* and institutionalized as the *Jamahiriyyah*, starting with the idea of Popular Congresses. The only political association allowed in the country at the time was the Arab Socialist Union, a kind of single-party state. Civil society groups, trade unions, the press, entire professional classes, the education system, and religious organizations – including the Sanusi Sufi order – would find themselves either subsumed under these new political frameworks or suppressed by them. The putative final transformation of the Libyan revolution, from political to popular, was announced in 1973 as Gaddafi unveiled his alternative to liberalism and Marxism, the Third Universal Theory. Popular Committees were empowered countrywide to bring this new revolutionary phase into reality. Gaddafi himself, then only in his early thirties, ostensibly left formal politics the following year, acting as a self-appointed revolutionary sage, but also as one of the chief guardians of the September 1 revolution. Gaddafi's social, political, and economic critique of all forms of modernity heretofore, as well as his proposed alternative means of organizing cooperative and mutually beneficial human life, were presented in several works, starting in 1975. Collectively, these are known as *The Green Book*.

Dissent nonetheless emerged from within and outside of the regime in the mid-1970s, leading to a darker phase of the revolution in which special courts handed down numerous death sentences and lengthy prison terms against dissidents and coup plotters. The regime's security forces met protests in the streets and on campuses with violent repression and summary executions. Gaddafi then began organizing and mobilizing the dreaded Revolutionary Committees in 1977. These bodies, which he directly controlled, had surveillance and coercive capacities, and were embedded within social, political, and the military organizations. The purpose of these Committees was as much to protect the nascent *Jamahiriyyah*, which had been declared earlier that year in Sebha, as they were to protect the regime.[14]

In theory, the *Jamahiriyyah* devolved basic legislating to the lowest level possible, offering decision-making capacity to the people rather than to elected or imposed leaders. Its bodies were a series of committees and congresses through which grassroots initiatives could work their way to higher yet less powerful levels. Local, provincial, and national policy would be enacted not by elected officials but by committees of administrators and technocrats allegedly serving at the behest of popular congresses. In reality, this system of endless meetings and arcane procedures, all of which could be overridden, vetoed, ignored, or circumvented by the executive powers Gaddafi claimed not to have, unsurprisingly failed to elicit mass participation – to become the state of the masses.

The Green Book's reconceptualization of democracy as "the supervision of the people by the people"[15] also legitimated the regime's most paranoid tendencies, and equally empowered opportunists against their adversaries, all in the name of defending the sovereignty of the people. "Stray dogs" – a regime term for dissidents – could be variously punished, imprisoned, or executed with seeming impunity at home and, in a few cases, abroad. In the face of this overly elaborate governance system and the regime's growing repression, popular disengagement ensued, leaving the formal political sphere vulnerable to monopolization by loyalists and those seeking the regime's favor. Though the *Jamahiriyyah* allegedly drew inspiration from indigenous forms of social organization in Libya (e.g., tribal councils and the sovereignty of the local),[16] it failed to resonate with most of the population, whose basic needs were increasingly failed by the country's centrally planned economy.

Under the *Jamahiriyyah*, workers were said to be in control of their own workplaces, though this merely served to deny them the right to collective bargaining. Labor militancy, like all other forms of dissent, was punished for being anti-revolutionary. Cyrenaicans, in particular, were sensitive to the ways in which Gaddafi's state was deliberately seeking to undermine what limited social, economic, and political equality the Sanusi monarchy had attempted to establish between Libya's eastern and western regions. Whatever the *Jamahiriyyah* was meant to be in theory, it mainly functioned to divide the polity internally even more than it already was, forestalling what limited power could be generated against the regime through mass protest and action. In response to the uncertainty and violence produced by this system, Libyans turned to their immediate social environment to survive. Both tendencies within the polity – distrust of central authority and reliance upon local networks – would be successfully mobilized in the fight against the regime in 2011. Unfortunately, these tendencies would also work against the re-consolidation of the state in the years that followed.

The Making of a Petro-Pariah

The Gaddafi regime's attempt to impose such a fanciful, thoroughgoing reorganization of political life in Libya was made possible by the stupendous windfall of revenues the state earned from oil in the 1970s. These revenues not only financed massive infrastructural projects and the expansion of the welfare state, they also underwrote the accumulation of vast amounts of weaponry, a disastrous military intervention in Chad, and a series of escalating confrontations, both direct and indirect, with the North Atlantic powers, notably Britain and the United States.

From the end of World War II to the early 1970s, the real price of oil held relatively steady in the range of $2 to $3 per barrel. From 1973 onward, however, this skyrocketed, reaching almost $40 per barrel in the middle of 1980, the peak year of Libyan oil export revenues.[17] A major factor pushing global oil prices in this direction was a political and economic game of chicken being played between oil-producing states in the Middle East and the United States in the aftermath of the 1973 Arab–Israeli war. Attempting to use oil export restrictions against the United States vis-à-vis the question of Palestine, the so-called "Arab oil embargo" instead met with defiant policymakers in Washington who refused to succumb to such pressure. As oil prices soared, the producer states reaped huge windfalls, which were then poured into massive arms purchases encouraged by the Cold War powers. The results were the hyper-militarization of the Middle East and North Africa and, unsurprisingly, more insecurity, conflict, and violence across the region.[18]

Libya under Gaddafi would come to occupy a central role in this new geopolitics of the Middle East and North Africa as it emerged from the mid-1970s onward. Throughout the 1970s and 1980s, the Gaddafi regime repeatedly demonstrated its willingness to antagonize North Atlantic interests and to play the role of the eccentric and implacable Arab petrocrat. Political space had in fact opened up for Gaddafi to play this role in 1970 following the death of President Gamal Abdel Nasser in Egypt, who had been one of Gaddafi's greatest inspirations and an early mentor. Soon after the disaster of the 1973 war with Israel, Egypt under President Anwar Sadat pivoted away from Soviet influence and toward Washington, a move that eventually led to the 1979 Camp

David Accords with Israel. Awash with oil revenues, Gaddafi increasingly took it upon himself to champion the cause of defending the Palestinians, the Middle East, Africa, and, indeed, the entire Non-Aligned World from North Atlantic domination. Counterintuitively, Libya became quite useful to North Atlantic foreign policies toward the region precisely in Gaddafi's opposition to those policies. As a former head of Israeli military intelligence explained, "Qaddafi [i.e. Gaddafi] can be a kind of asset. Who else, in all his fanatic attempts to unite the Arabs, is keeping them divided to the extent Qaddafi is? He is a strategic threat, but perhaps a tactical asset; an agent of division in the Arab World."[19]

The Gaddafi regime's record of political hostility toward the North Atlantic world began with economic nationalization, which was later followed by direct military confrontation, indirect subversion, war with Western proxies, and finally support for terrorist organizations. In the oil sector, the regime's initial efforts in the 1970s to leverage a greater share of the profits through threats of outright nationalization eventually led to the takeover of BP's Libyan operations in December 1971. Other companies were forced to give Libya majority control over their joint ventures by 1973 and, in a clear act of political retaliation, the regime seized control over all US oil companies operating in the country because of Washington's support for Israel in the October War of 1973.

While high global oil prices meant that there was no shortage of businesses willing to work with the regime, tensions between Libya and Washington had been escalating as a result of Gaddafi's growing economic and political militancy, the latter resulting in the reduction and eventual withdrawal of US diplomatic personnel and the shuttering of the American embassy in 1980 for the next twenty-six years.[20] British relations with Gaddafi likewise reached a breaking point when Libyan embassy personnel in London shot at a crowd of Libyan dissidents from inside the embassy in April 1984, resulting in the death of a British police-woman. Militarily, US and Libyan forces often confronted each other over Tripoli's efforts to extend its claim of sover-eignty in the Mediterranean well beyond what was allowed under international law. In August 1981, the US navy shot down two Libyan jets that had been allegedly acting aggressively in international waters. Then, in April 1986, various sites in Libya were hit by the US military – what was widely believed to be a decapitation strike aimed at Gaddafi – in retaliation for a series of terrorist attacks tied to Libya's regime.

Indeed, the US government had placed Libya on its list of state sponsors of terrorism in 1979 shortly after it was first drafted. The reason for this was Gaddafi's ideological and – more importantly – material support for the international armed activities of non-state actors, notably various factions within the Palestinian nationalist movement and republican militants from Northern Ireland. For example, terrorists with the Palestinian Abu Nidal Organization attacked offices of El Al, the Israel national airline, in Vienna and Rome two days after Christmas in 1985, killing nineteen. While the Gaddafi regime denied involvement, the US government took further measures to isolate Libya economically.[21] A few months after the attacks in Vienna and Rome, a nightclub in West Berlin popular with US service members was bombed. Once evidence emerged tying the Gaddafi regime to the Berlin attack, the US military launched its April 1986 air raids on Tripoli and Benghazi. Gaddafi's escalating war with the North Atlantic world would finally lead the regime to conduct or otherwise facilitate two of the most infamous crimes in the history of civil aviation before September 11, 2001. The first was the December 1988 downing of Pan Am 103 over Lockerbie, Scotland, by a secretly placed explosive device. This was followed by the September 1989 bombing of a French passenger jet over the Sahara desert. All in all, these two acts claimed the lives of 440 passengers, crew, and persons on the ground. While the Lockerbie incident has been widely interpreted as revenge for the US attack on Tripoli and Benghazi in 1986, which the British had supported, the downing of UTA 772 over Niger appeared to target France for the support Paris had rendered to Gaddafi's rivals in Chad.

Libya's accumulation of oil wealth in the 1970s, which financed massive arms outlays, provides some insight into the reasons why Gaddafi felt capable of indirectly and directly challenging the North Atlantic powers through proxy wars, military adventurism, provocative alliances, and terrorism. It also helps explain the reasons for the regime's survival in the face of growing opposition, whether through the creation of a robust apparatus for the monitoring and repression of dissent or by diverting the nation's attention away from domestic failings and scapegoating others for Libya's growing international isolation.

It was not just Libya that experienced a massive buildup of arms in the 1970s; the entire Middle East and North Africa region saw military budgets balloon dramatically as the Arab–Israeli dispute intensified and global oil prices surged. Over the course of the decade, military purchases in the Middle East – not counting the countries of North Africa west of Egypt – had gone from under 20 percent of world arms imports to over 40 percent by 1982. That same year, the top ten countries with the highest ratios of military expenditures to central government expenditures were all in the Middle East. Annual military expenditures in the region went from under $2 billion in the early 1960s to over $10 billion per year in the following decade. Leading the pack at the end of the 1970s was Libya, which imported $2.1 billion in military goods in 1979 (or the equivalent of $17 billion in 2017 dollars). This figure was fifty-three times what the Sanusi monarchy had spent on military imports in 1969. While the Gaddafi regime maintained a diversity of armament suppliers in the early part of the decade (notably France), Soviet-made weaponry represented the majority by the end of the decade, followed by French and Italian arms.[22]

Beyond the regime's own security, these arms were put to use in proxy wars, support for terrorism, and the pursuit of the country's irredentist claim in Chad. Gaddafi's moral and material support for various kinds of rebel groups and insurgencies, from the anti-apartheid struggle in South Africa to radical urban terrorists in Europe, was ostensibly rooted in solidarity with national liberation struggles. But the various contradictions in support, reversals of policy,

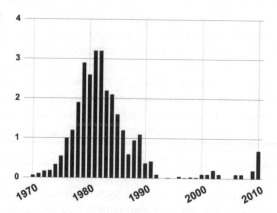

Figure 1.2. Libyan arms imports, 1970–2010 (billions of current US dollars).*
* Some years with zero imports have missing data. After 2000, imports below certain thresholds are not reported.
Source: US Department of State, Bureau of Arms Control, Verification, and Compliance.

ambiguities of purpose, and denials of responsibility made it difficult to identify either a political or a personal motivation behind Libyan foreign policy.[23] An example of this was Gaddafi's early yet limited support for Western Saharan nationalists, who began fighting Spanish colonial forces in 1973. Following the Moroccan and Mauritanian take-over of Western Sahara in 1975, Gaddafi continued to supply arms and aid to the Saharan rebels as they waged an insurgency against Moroccan forces in the late 1970s from bases in Algeria. Though the cause of Western Saharan nationalism resonated with Gaddafi's internationalist ideology, the Moroccan monarchy had in fact eagerly supported efforts by the ousted Sanusi monarchy to foment a coup against the Gaddafi regime in its early years.[24] To what extent Gaddafi's support for Western Sahara's struggle had been opportunistic or idealistic, or a mix of both, was upended by his surprising reconciliation with the Moroccan monarchy in a short-lived treaty signed in 1984. While the treaty fed Gaddafi's ambitions to unite the states of North Africa in a political union, it served Rabat's purpose of ending Libya's aid to the Western Saharan nationalist movement.

Gaddafi's efforts to forge military and political alliances across the Arab world in the 1970s and 1980s had largely failed to gain traction, a fact that owed much to his erratic and temperamental nature. On paper, the Arab Maghrib Union, a political and economic agreement signed by Algeria, Libya, Mauritania, Morocco, and Tunisia in 1989, is one of the most meaningful and long-lasting of Gaddafi's efforts at a multinational confederation, aside from the African Union, which was established in 2001. In reality, the Maghrib Union has been moribund since 1994, officially because of the ongoing Western Sahara dispute, though, up until 2011, the other member states were weary of Gaddafi as well. Indeed, Gaddafi's efforts to influence, subvert, dominate, and otherwise play a role in global politics left him with few friends in the Arab world and a growing number of skeptics among his allies, particularly in Africa, where he increasingly focused his foreign attentions in the 1980s and 1990s.[25]

Libya's War with Chad: A Quagmire in the Sahara

Among the most counterproductive of Libya's foreign adventures during the height of Gaddafi's power was the war in Chad. This series of conflicts stretched for over a decade, becoming the regime's millstone by the mid-1980s. Libya's claim on the Aouzou Strip in northern Chad, which was ultimately rejected by the International Court of Justice in 1994, was rooted in the social and economic networks that had existed across the Sahara for centuries as well as territorial exchanges between France and Italy during the 1930s.[26] A civil war in Chad, which began in 1965, afforded Libya the opportunity to advance its territorial claims and security interests through the Front de Libération Nationale du Tchad (National Liberation Front of Chad), a rebel group fighting the regime in the capital, N'djamena. In 1972, Gaddafi reached an alleged agreement with Chadian leaders that allowed Libyan forces to occupy Aouzou in secret. In exchange, Libya dropped its support for the rebels and provided aid to the Chadian government. A coup in N'djamena and a split in the rebel movement, both owing to continued Libyan meddling in Chadian affairs, led to a new stage in the conflict in 1978, one that saw Chadian rebels backed by regular Libyan forces making quick territorial gains deep into the country until they were driven back by a French intervention. Both the Chadian rebels and the government then fell into warring groups in which pro- and anti-Gaddafi factions largely defined each split.

Taking advantage of the chaos, the Libyan military mounted an impressive expeditionary operation in late 1980. Led by Colonel Khalifa Haftar, the incursion brought heavy armor and nearly 10,000 troops to staging points in central Chad. This became a temporarily successful bid to install a favorable regime in N'djamena.[27] By this point, Egypt and Sudan were likewise involved through proxy forces; Soviets provided indirect support to Gaddafi; and a Franco-American effort existed to back Hissène Habré, the future dictator of Chad. Surprisingly, Libyan forces withdrew from most of Chad in 1982 at the request of the Organization of African Unity, a body with which Gaddafi was keen to remain on good terms. Nonetheless, fighting continued in the north of Chad with a new Libyan offensive in the summer of 1983. Another French counter-intervention soon followed, tempering Libyan ambitions once again. Though both Libya and Chad agreed to a mutual withdrawal of forces, Tripoli consolidated its grip on the north in a bid to make the annexation of Aouzou a fait accompli.

A final Libyan effort to seize N'djamena in early 1986 was thwarted once again by government and French forces. The disintegration of rebel forces allied to Libya soon followed, leading to Gaddafi's definitive humiliation in the "Toyota War" of 1987. Going on the offensive, Chadian government forces in light pickup trucks routed Libya's conventional forces on the open battlefields of the Sahara and in the Tibesti mountains. Pushing into Libyan territory, Chadian forces captured large numbers of Gaddafi's troops, including Haftar. In the end, Libya's military barely held the Aouzou Strip.[28] By the time The Hague ruled in 1994 that Gaddafi's attempted annexation of Aouzou was unlawful, Libya was already under an extensive international sanctions regime, including UN sanctions enacted by the Security Council in 1992 for Tripoli's role in the Lockerbie bombing. Adding insult to injury, the Libyan economy was reeling from the 1986 downturn in global oil prices, as the average price per barrel hovered around or below the $20 mark until the late 1990s.

International Isolation and Internal Challenges

There were many fictions that defined life in the decaying *Jamahiriyyah* at the turn of the millennium. Above all was the fiction of the *Jamahiriyyah* itself. The more that the regime defended the idea and institutions of the revolution, the more that everyday Libyans were alienated from it. The schizophrenic nature of the system – allegedly empowered masses kept in a constant state of fear by an increasingly isolated and suspicious regime – forced Libyans to choose between a survival strategy of collaboration or evasion. The complex and esoteric decision-making processes of the *Jamahiriyyah* selected for those personalities and groups who were willing to tolerate its ambiguities and contradictions in order to advance their interests. The process of articulating and implementing national priorities was often hijacked by the provincial demands of local councils, numbering nearly four hundred, who used the inverted hierarchy of the *Jamahiriyyah* to serve the needs of their constituents. As Libyans disengaged from this system, power concentrated in two opposing sectors. Formally, the political system became an instrument of the regime through its praetorian guards and its allies in the congresses and the committees.[29] Informally, the power of parallel, clandestine, and localized networks also grew in strength as Libyans developed alternative means of surviving international isolation and domestic tyranny.

The *Jamahiriyyah* not only failed to create a new kind of polity, it failed to generate a new kind of economy. In fact, the government's attempts to control the economy inadvertently reinforced the informal networks that made political survival possible in Libya.[30] The state's abolition of private property and personal banking, as well as its effort to contain all professional and commercial activities within the public sector, instead generated parallel forms of economic activity that supported the widespread evasion of politics. The directly managed economy, ostensibly the only game in town, led to the expansion of alternatives to the state's dominance over banking and trade. The primary manifestation of this economic evasion was Libya's growing shadow economy and the power of black markets.

Two critical developments nurtured the growth of these informal networks in the 1980s and 1990s. One was the collapse of global hydrocarbon prices in the mid-1980s, which resulted in a contraction of the state-dominated economy. Some of this damage was self-inflicted. Libya had reduced its oil exports in the 1980s to extend its lifetime as an oil exporter. Lower Libyan output was also an aspect of a quota system established by the governments of the Organization of Petroleum Exporting Countries (OPEC). The cumulative effect on Libya was devastating for the economy. From a highpoint of $21 billion in oil exports in 1980, revenues fell to $6 billion by the end of the decade. As a result, the country's development budget was cut in half, though the state pressed ahead with some of its major industrial and infrastructural projects, like the Great Man-Made River. Military spending and lavish overseas assistance to various rebels and regimes likewise appear to have been curtailed, though the disaster in Chad and the end of the Cold War were also a part of this context. Efforts to change course economically in the late 1980s in the aftermath of the oil price collapse saw government investment in the private sector jump from under a tenth of all investment in the 1980s to nearly a quarter in the 1990s. Markets were allowed to reopen, regulations were relaxed, import controls were lifted, and some state ventures were privatized.[31] Nonetheless, the damage had already been done, and the international sanctions regime made recovery and reform all the more difficult.

The other critical development was Libya's international isolation, which peaked in the 1990s with the imposition of sanctions by the United Nations and other states. Estimates have suggested that, over the course of the sanctions regime, the economy lost tens of billions of dollars in potential revenues. While Libya was able to export oil at the level of its agreed OPEC quota, restrictions on imports saw its hydrocarbon sector fall behind other countries. New oil and gas fields remained unexplored or undeveloped; up-to-date technologies of extraction, circulation, and refining could not be imported. Nonetheless, the Gaddafi regime worked hard to maintain oil production and to complete the Great Man-Made River, both of which diverted revenues from other areas in need of investment such as agriculture, non-hydrocarbon industries, and social spending on education and health. International isolation also bred perceptions of scarcity among the population, which caused inflation rates to peak at 50 percent in 1994. The fact that the regime had somewhat liberalized the economy, starting piecemeal soon after the 1986 oil price collapse, meant that it was more difficult to impose price controls without alienating the established and emergent merchant classes. Toward the end of the 1990s, the government was still heavily subsidizing basic goods and providing food rations to families. Corruption, smuggling, and black markets proliferated, despite government efforts to punish such activities (e.g., the so-called 1994 "Purification Law") and to impose new immigration and labor regulations. Although a few Libyans thrived in this new economic environment, most fell behind. Indeed, the 1990s saw large-scale deportations of Palestinian, Egyptian, Sudanese, and sub-Saharan laborers to address Libyan unemployment. The growth of economic inequality was simultaneously a challenge and an opportunity for the regime. The challenge was containing its political ramifications; the opportunity was the rejuvenation of the regime through an alliance with Libya's business elites that would take the form of a neoliberal technocracy. On top of that, the regime began to capitalize on the society's growing religious conservatism, which had seemingly increased in the face of the economic uncertainty of the 1990s.[32]

As rulers across the Middle East and North Africa were discovering at the turn of the millennium, from the Gulf to Morocco, managed Islamist mobilization and capital accumulation were highly compatible and mutually beneficial strategies for regime survival. Economic liberalization and Islamist co-optation would not only allow for minimal political liberalization, it would also help to build a stronger foundation for the embattled Libyan regime as it went into its fourth decade.

The *Jamahiriyyah* lie

The regime's efforts in the 1990s and 2000s to find new ways of reconstructing its authority and control were not only a result of Gaddafi's international isolation but were also an effect of the domestically discredited *Jamahiriyyah* system. Perhaps nothing had discredited the *Jamahiriyyah* more than the violence that had been used to consolidate it. The outlawing of political parties and independent associations in the 1970s was matched by the regime's preference to let agitated crowds do the dirty work of identifying and punishing opposition (a tendency that would resurface thirty years later in February 2011). The public hangings of student activists in 1977 were only the most infamous acts of a regime that also orchestrated countless arbitrary arrests, torture, coerced confessions, deaths under custody, extrajudicial executions, prolonged detentions without trial, and the disappearances of critics, both real and perceived, throughout its rule. In 1980, the Revolutionary Committees dedicated themselves to the "physical liquidation" of any Libyan opposed to the *Jamahiriyyah* system, whether at home or in other countries. Foreign assassinations, attempted and successful, targeted the full range of dissidents, from students studying abroad to former politicians living in exile.

Responding to criticisms from human rights groups concerning state-sanctioned assassinations, the Libyan embassy (or "People's Bureau") in Belgium explained that Libya was only doing in the clear light of day what other countries did in the shadows. Gaddafi himself went so far as to oblige the citizens of the *Jamahiriyyah* to kill any Libyan opposition figures they might encounter while on pilgrimage (*al-hajj*) to Mecca. Similarly, special revolutionary courts often convened in secret to try political crimes. Executions by hanging or firing squad were often held in public (e.g., sports stadiums) and televised. A failed 1984 insurrection spearheaded by the National Front for the Salvation of Libya – a prominent opposition group led by exiled elites with secret cells in the country – notably led to a wave of detentions, trials, executions, and assassinations. By the mid-1980s, Libyan authorities were thought to be detaining hundreds, if not thousands, of political prisoners, many in secret locations that helped to hide the scope of the repression.[33]

The confluence of international isolation, military failure in Chad, the coming end of the Cold War, and low oil prices led to an economic "opening" (*al-infitah*) from 1987 onward. Politically, however, the regime proved reluctant to acknowledge past domestic abuses as anything other than the excesses of local authorities in the face of weak legal safeguards.[34] In this way, reforms to the judicial and private sector initiated by the regime in the late 1980s simply reaffirmed the power of Gaddafi to change the direction of the state at will.

To the extent that Libyans had found ways of evading the state and developing their own means of economic survival, the regime appeared to become more and more detached from the society. While his state withered, Gaddafi surrounded himself with a protective security apparatus and political acolytes, styling himself as an African wiseman to be dispatched in the service of conflict resolution across the continent. Some of this was choice and some of it was out of necessity. Low oil prices and economic stagnation in the 1990s had constrained the regime's ability to buy popular acquiescence through welfare programs and foreign ambitions, though overt forms of opposition were easily contained by the elite security and intelligence forces. The wider military apparatus, having failed Gaddafi in the deserts of Chad, withered in the face of poor training, funding cuts, and international sanctions.[35] From the height of the mid-1980s, military spending fell from over $2 billion per year to just over $420 million in 2000. Though the number of active duty soldiers held steady (circa 75,000),[36] the existing armaments and military infrastructures were in need of modernization by the end of the international embargo. Nonetheless, the incredible numbers of light arms the regime had accumulated during the 1970s and 1980s, and then after the lifting of sanctions in the 2000s, would become essential materiel with which the 2011 uprising would challenge the Gaddafi state.

The regime nonetheless continued to exhibit its repressive nature in the face of new challenges in the 1990s, opposition that notably took the form of sporadic protests, Islamist agitation, and tribal–military revolts. Not only did Gaddafi call for harsh punishments for minor crimes (e.g., amputations for thievery), laws were also enacted to allow for the collective punishment of crimes against the state. A variety of penalties and preventative actions could be taken against the relatives of suspected criminals, from housing demolitions to the detention of grandmothers, wives, and infant children.[37] Suspected participants in a 1993 Warfalla military coup plot, the activities of the National Front for the Salvation of Libya, and the guerrilla campaign of the Libyan Islamic Fighting Group were all subjected to arbitrary detention, torture, and, in a few cases, executions.[38]

The most infamous of the regime's abuses is undoubtedly the massacre of several hundred prisoners – perhaps as many as 1,200 – in the notorious Abu Salim jail in Tripoli in June 1996, which reportedly came in response to an uprising against poor living conditions and a lack of basic prisoners' rights.[39] The Abu Salim massacre would not only come to be understood as one of the most heinous crimes against humanity perpetrated by the regime, it would also become a rallying point for Libyan opposition groups in the years leading up to the 2011 revolt. Equally important was the fact that Abu Salim had become an incubator for the Libyan Islamic Fighting Group, an Islamist guerrilla organization that was mainly active in the latter half of the 1990s. By one account, nearly half of the group's core leadership were contained inside Abu Salim's walls at one point or another.[40] Many of them had participated in the jihad against the Soviet Union in Afghanistan in the 1980s and later joined the Al-Qaida network.[41] While the Libyan Islamic Fighting Group failed to assassinate Gaddafi or to organize a mass Islamist insurrection, an important consequence of their actions was the ability of the Gaddafi regime to claim it had been fighting its own war on terror before 9/11. Indeed, Gaddafi denounced the attacks on September 11, 2001. These facts allowed the regime to offer the West much more than oil concessions and other investment opportunities at the turn of the millennium. It allowed Gaddafi to sell fresh intelligence and hidden torture facilities to London and Washington.[42]

For all of the human rights abuses of the Gaddafi regime, Libya nonetheless presented itself as a developmental success story, having transformed from one of the world's poorest countries in the 1950s to one of the most successful in Africa and the Middle East at the turn of the millennium. On the eve of the revolt in 2010, the United Nations' annual *Human Development Report* ranked the *Jamahiriyyah* fifty-third on its human development index of 169 countries and territories, placing it among the second highest tier of development. This effectively meant that Libya was ahead of Saudi Arabia, Mexico, Russia, Brazil, and Turkey in terms of its overall development. The country had obtained this ranking largely through reported achievements in education, health care, sanitation, infrastructure, and social assistance.[43]

There were, however, reasons to think that the Gaddafi regime was overstating its developmental successes, as independent verification of basic indicators was either unfeasible or effectively prohibited. The status of women in Libya, for example, has been impossible to assess accurately for decades. Despite the ways in which Gaddafi applied a thin veneer of women's empowerment to his regime (e.g., female bodyguards and the prominent role played by his daughter, Ayesha, an international lawyer), the state's policies toward women and girls were founded in sexist and patronizing assumptions that were, on the whole, hardly more "enlightened" than any of its neighbors.[44]

The 2011 uprising itself revealed the extent of popular discontent with the system. The regime's efforts to maintain political order through economic liberalization had utterly failed, despite the fact that global oil prices had risen to unimagined heights and flooded the state with billions in reserves. The 2011 uprising also revealed the extent to which the *Jamahiriyyah* had been a phantom state. A 2014 investigation by Transparency International into the soundness of state institutions in Libya concluded, "The legacy from the Gaddafi regime with 42 years of dictatorship, informal structures and flourishing corruption has left little or no institutions upon which to build a well-functioning state. Most institutions, laws and regulations are either outdated or of very recent origin."[45]

The regime would in fact become a victim of its putative developmental successes, as well as its obvious failures. The hydrocarbon sector, which had singularly financed Libya's rapid transformation and underwrote the post-independence population boom, remained the dominant source of state revenues and exports, leaving the country incredibly vulnerable to price shocks. As the regime had cultivated a state–society relationship of asymmetric dependency, political tensions were simply regulated through coercion and government expenditures. But at the turn of the millennium, the Libyan regime entered a phase of promising too much and delivering too little, particularly with respect to a new generation that had come of age after the end of the Cold War. On the one hand, Libya's annual population growth rate declined, going from 2.9 percent during the period between 1975 and 2005 to a projected 1.9 percent during the following decade. On the other hand, the social dislocation of urbanization continued and accelerated during the Gaddafi period, going from over 57 percent of the population in 1975 to nearly 85 percent in 2005. Meanwhile an important effect of this population boom was the fact that a third of Libyans were under the age of fifteen in 2005.[46] The unemployment rate, meanwhile, was estimated to be one of the world's highest, particularly for younger strata. Though Libyan spending on all levels of education was purportedly strong, a large proportion of the labor force – perhaps 50 percent – was imported, both skilled and unskilled workers.[47] Indeed, upward of a quarter of the country's population prior to the revolution was foreign, mainly from neighboring Arab and African states. In response to social unrest, the Libyan regime would often expel large numbers of foreigners, though the investment and construction boom of the 2000s had seen their numbers rise.[48] Given high rates of youth unemployment, the reliance on foreign labor, and the regime's commitment to reducing the size of the state bureaucracy, formal avenues for socio-economic advancement were limited to non-existent. By 2011, there was no lack of unemployed fighting-age males in Libya, young men with few prospects for a better future.

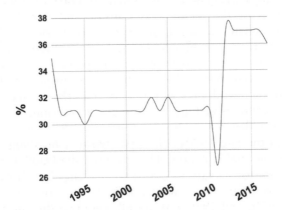

Figure 1.3. Unemployment rate of Libyan male youths (ages 15–24), 1991–2017.
Source: World Bank.

Libya on the Eve of the Revolt

Although international political concessions by the Gaddafi regime allowed it to shed some of the sanctions and isolation that had inhibited Libya's economic development during the 1990s, it was the resurgence of global oil prices in the first decade of the 2000s that propelled foreign interest in the country. This period witnessed a renewed effort by the regime to develop a neoliberal political economy of "enlightened" authoritarian rule and open markets, one spearheaded by Saif Al-Islam, Gaddafi's favored son. The 2003 appointment of a new prime minister, Shukri Ghanem, a technocrat with oil industry experience, likewise sent a message that Libya was open for business, a message that Saif Al-Islam took to the 2005 meeting of the World Economic Forum in Davos, Switzerland. This period of transition, reform, and reconciliation – how it was managed and mismanaged by both the Gaddafi family and the international community – arguably played an important role in laying the groundwork for the overthrow of the dictatorship in 2011.[49] Above all, this decade of growing domestic and global expectations of a better Libya brought a false sense of hope to critics and opponents of the regime, both inside and outside of the country. When the twin crises of high food prices and mass demonstrations hit North Africa in late 2010 and early 2011,[50] the violent and implacable response of the Gaddafi regime proved that such hope had been misplaced. It was replaced by new desires and dreams, ones that would propel the country to armed insurrection and revolution.

The Gaddafi regime began to articulate its new vision for Libya in the late 1990s. The first step was breaking out of its international isolation. This required the Gaddafi regime to account for its various efforts to challenge North Atlantic powers through proxy wars and state-sponsored terrorism in the 1970s and 1980s. Above all there was the question of Lockerbie. By 1998, Libya had already conceded to allow a trial of the key Lockerbie suspects under Scottish law, so long as it took place in a third country. A year later, the two defendants, Abdelbaset El-Meghrahi (an intelligence officer) and Lamin Fhimah (a national airlines employee), were handed over. Their trial in the Netherlands finally began in May 2000, resulting in an early 2001 conviction and life sentence for Meghrahi. Doubts nonetheless persisted as to whether or not the Gaddafi regime had handed over the agents most responsible for the bombing.[51] After the 2011 revolution, an independent investigation by a brother of a Pan Am 103 victim would identify more likely suspects behind the Lockerbie bombing, some of whom were being held and tried by revolutionary militias.[52] By that time, Meghrahi, who had been fighting cancer for years, had already been released from prison on compassionate grounds in 2009, a decision that was surrounded by controversy and accusations of BP having a hand in the release.[53] The Libyan regime's efforts to close the Lockerbie dossier also saw the victims' families indemnified with a fund of over two billion dollars from Libyan state coffers. Similar acknowledgments of responsibility and offers of compensation would follow, addressing the 1989 downing of UTA 772 over Niger and the 1986 nightclub bombing in West Berlin.

Other victims of the Gaddafi regime's violent internationalist phase, notably survivors of Libyan-supplied bombs to republican insurgents in Northern Ireland, would continue to press for truth and justice as well. A common sentiment shared by many within these survivors' organizations was not only a feeling that the Gaddafi regime was being far from forthcoming about its role in these acts of terrorism. There was also a growing sense that North Atlantic leaders and business elites were less concerned about holding Libya accountable and all too eager to develop political and financial relations with a revitalized regime. Indeed, the network of interests that were invested in the rehabilitation of the Gaddafi regime under Saif Al-Islam went beyond the US Department of State, the British premiership, the French presidency, and international oil companies. Elite academics at institutions of higher education like the London School of Economics and Harvard, and even critics of the regime like Human Rights Watch and Amnesty International, were all accused of turning a blind eye to the realities of the new Libya in order to gain access.[54]

Even more stunning than the praise and recognition being afforded to the new Libya in the first decade of the 2000s was the way in which the Gaddafi regime voluntarily collaborated with the North Atlantic world to advance the latter's core interests in energy security and counterterrorism. Once Libya agreed to render the Lockerbie suspects into custody, high-level meetings with US officials, the first in nearly two decades, began to take place. Additional steps were soon taken to mend or cement other bilateral relations, including Libya's participation with international organizations like the International Monetary Fund. United Nations, European Union, and eventually US sanctions were all eventually lifted.[55]

Early 2004 then saw Gaddafi visit the European Union's headquarters in Brussels followed by a visit to Tripoli by British Prime Minister Tony Blair. Libya's election to seats on the UN Human Rights Commission in 2003 (as chair), the Security Council in 2008, and as President of the General Assembly in 2009 were equally indicative of the country's new international standing. Indeed, nothing spoke to the reversal of Libya's fortunes more than the fact that the Italian government under the conservative leadership of Silvio Berlusconi agreed to offer $5 billion in compensatory investment in Libya in recognition of the crimes committed during the Italian occupation. Such outside investment continued to focus intensively on Libya's underdeveloped oil fields and aged energy infrastructures. Other reforms, however, targeted administrative districting, banking, public sector employment, the judicial branch, and state subsidies on imports and goods. These economic reforms were enacted to create new opportunities for private employment and foreign capital, reforms culminating in the creation of a Tripoli stock exchange in 2010.

What had made this all possible was not just the Lockerbie trial but a surprise announcement in 2003 that Libya was willing to work with the international community to account for, decommission, and remove all of its nuclear and chemical weapons capacities.[56] Five years later, the US Secretary of State, Condoleezza Rice, would cement US–Libyan ties with a visit to Tripoli (including the recently reopened US embassy) in the waning months of the George W. Bush administration. Less than a year later, Libyan national security advisor Mutassim Al-Gaddafi, one of Gaddafi's sons, reaffirmed these ties by visiting with Rice's successor, Hillary Clinton, in Washington.

Even after a decade of political and economic reforms, however, there was little doubt among Libyans who really controlled their country. Key Gaddafi allies such as the longstanding heads of the security establishment, Musa Kusa and Abu-Bakr Yunis Jabr, maintained their positions at the top of the hierarchy, even if titles and assignments were changed. While the world applauded Libya's changing political landscape, the country nonetheless continued to rank among those exhibiting the worst authoritarian tendencies in the world. Freedom House, an organization that monitors political liberties worldwide, consistently gave Libya its worst possible score throughout the "opening" of the 1998 to 2010 period.[57] Judicial reform likewise proved to be a sham. "In the last decade of Qadhafi's [Gaddafi's] rule, courts and trials remained a political tool in regime hands," wrote the International Crisis Group. "[C]orruption in their midst expanded."[58] The media, both state-controlled and newly created private outlets under Saif Al-Islam's initiative, continued to be tools of the regime as well.[59]

This strategy of regime re-consolidation also included efforts to co-opt Islamists. Saif Al-Islam spearheaded a reconciliation initiative between the regime and Libyan Islamists who had fought with Al-Qaida and the Libyan Islamic Fighting Group, as well as opponents associated with the Muslim Brotherhood and the National Front for the Salvation of Libya.[60] Though somewhat successful, these initiatives, absent any substantive national political reform, largely served to divide the Islamists from the rest of the opposition,[61] a division that would have lasting repercussions into the post-revolutionary phase after 2011.[62] Champions of a more progressive vision of Islam, particularly among Libya's liberal and technocratic elites, were just as silenced during the Gaddafi years, only to find their voices also drowned out in the cacophony of the post-revolutionary struggle for power.[63]

The multiplicity of competing revolutionary voices that emerged in 2011 had much to do with the intensely localized nature of social, political, and economic life that had developed to coordinate governance and as a means to survive the Gaddafi regime, tribes being a critical element of both. Indeed, the formal and informal roles of tribes and tribalism were not only an important factor in the articulation of the *Jamahiriyyah* system and the regime's desperate efforts to repress the revolt in early 2011, tribes also played key roles in the historical resistance to the Gaddafi state and the armed rebellion that finally deposed it.[64] Beyond tribes and tribalism, however, an important fact of life in modern Libya has been the centrality of various kinds of overlapping local and regional networks – geographical, social, religious, political, and economic. Ironically, the power of locally organized coalitions to manipulate, evade, or resist the state was both actively and passively reinforced by the *Jamahiriyyah* system. In this way, too, Gaddafi was a victim of his success.

But Libya after Gaddafi was nonetheless shaped by the architecture of the deposed regime. This is not to say that post-revolutionary Libya would come to represent "Gaddafism without Gaddafi," though a marginal constituency within the country would emerge after 2011 to demand a return to the old order. It is only to say that some of the most powerful alliances shaping Libya after the 2011 uprising either had been forged to underwrite the Gaddafi regime's power or had inadvertently emerged to resist it.

2 | Uprising and Intervention: Libya in Revolt

The arrest of lawyer and activist Fathi Terbil on February 15, 2011, in Benghazi is often said to have set in motion the events that led to the demise of the Gaddafi regime just eight months later. However, the dialectic of repression and resistance was already well underway before Terbil's arrest. By late January, both Libyan opposition figures and elements of the international community assumed that the ongoing wave of mass uprisings across North Africa and the Middle East – the Arab Spring – would inevitably target Gaddafi, the longest-standing dictator in the Arab world.

To the west of Libya, Tunisia's President of twenty-three years, Zine El-Abidine Ben Ali, had fled the country on January 14 amid sustained nation-wide protests. Though Morocco and Algeria would be spared similarly destabilizing movements, Western Sahara witnessed the territory's largest pro-independence demonstrations since coming under Moroccan occupation in 1975. To the east of Libya, tens of thousands of Egyptian protestors began their mass occupation of Tahrir Square in Cairo on January 25, an event that would eventually lead to the removal of President Hosni Mubarak on February 11 after nearly three decades in power. Around the same time, protest movements were gaining momentum in Yemen and Syria, though their ultimate trajectories would be less like the mass civil disobedience of Tunisia and Egypt and much more like Libya's – toward armed insurrection and civil war.

As the tumultuous events in Tunisia and Egypt unfolded in January, the Gaddafi regime took preemptive measures against known opposition figures and the country's new generation of activists. Resistance groups had already formed inside and outside of Libya,[1] and small demonstrations were taking place throughout the country. The regime dramatically escalated tensions on February 15, notably when its security forces killed several protestors in the eastern city of Bayda. For weeks, Terbil and other rights activists had been preparing for Libya's own "Day of Rage" (*yawm al-ghadab*), set for February 17. This protest was somewhat modeled after the events of January 25 that had seen Egyptians flood the streets of Cairo en masse. Libyans abroad were also helping lay the groundwork for an uprising. In Zurich, for example, some sixty exiled leaders of Libya's Islamist movement gathered late in the weekend of January 30 to see how they could mobilize support.[2]

While Libya's Day of Rage drew inspiration from the events in Tunisia and Egypt, the proposed date of the protests, February 17, was based on local histories of resistance as well. February 17 marked the fifth anniversary of protests in Benghazi that had been violently disrupted by security forces. The 2006 Benghazi protests had ostensibly been about cartoons in European newspapers that had variously depicted the Prophet Muhammad in offensive and provocative ways. Many regimes across the Middle East and North Africa had cynically tolerated and even manipulated the popular outrage that had been provoked by both the cartoons themselves and the support they received in the West as acts of free expression. In Libya, however, the regime used excessive and deadly force to disperse the crowd that had gathered in front of the Italian consulate in Benghazi on February 17, 2006. In the years that followed, Libyan activists attempted to organize memorial marches and demonstrations commemorating the events of that day, but these were repeatedly thwarted by the regime. One of the few groups that was able to successfully stage demonstrations in Libya were the families of victims of the June 1996 Abu Salim prison massacre. Terbil in fact worked with an organization representing Abu Salim victims and survivors, a campaign that had gained recognition from the Libyan legal system and the international community. The campaign for truth and accountability by Abu Salim families and victims had created a unique space of dissent in Libya by exploiting the regime's newfound rhetoric of reform and human rights.[3]

Tensions and repression had nonetheless been steadily escalating in Libya well before the arrest of Terbil and his colleague, Faraj Al-Sharani. With the resignation of Tunisian President Ben Ali in January and, more importantly, President Mubarak of Egypt in February, the Libyan regime, like many others across the region, was on high alert. For example, a military officer, Colonel Abdel Abdullah El-Gehani, disappeared at the hands of Libyan Military Intelligence on January 14 after making anti-regime comments online.[4] Then, in late January, writer and former prisoner of conscience Jamal Al-Hajji called for protests. He was arrested on February 1 on charges related to a suspicious automobile altercation. His arrest followed on the heels of two others, Ali Abdelounis Al-Mansouri in Tobruk and Safai Eddine Hilal Sherif in Ras Lanouf, both taken by the Internal Security Agency. Moreover, the final weeks of 2010 had already seen Libyan authorities also detain activists representing the Tebu and Amazigh minority groups.[5] Meanwhile, regime officials traveled the country in an effort to build a populist counter-movement against the growing dissent, promising jobs and housing while also making implicit threats and denouncing the Arab Spring. In a move that simultaneously revealed the seriousness of the brewing crisis and the utter intransigence of the regime, Saadi Gaddafi and interior security chief Abdullah Al-Senussi – two of the most feared and despised figures in the country – were dispatched to negotiate with the emerging February 17 coalition leaders in Benghazi.[6]

The regime's preemptive measures and clumsy outreach seemed to have little effect. On February 16, demonstrations were reported across the country, from Zintan to Tobruk. The regime also reached out to the country's domestic and exiled Islamists, particularly figures in the Muslim Brotherhood and former Libyan Islamic Fighting Group.

Among the latter were Islamists who had participated in Saif Al-Islam's national reconciliation and modernization initiatives in the first decade of the 2000s, people like Fighting Group veteran Noman Benotman, who attempted to steer the regime toward deescalation and dialogue with little success.[7] Other veterans of the Islamist insurgency, like Anis Al-Sharif, voiced support for the revolution by announcing the creation of a successor organization to the Libyan Islamic Fighting Group: the Libyan Islamic Movement for Change. Exiled leaders of Libya's Muslim Brotherhood also endorsed the uprising around the same time.[8]

Protestors took to the streets on February 17 in larger numbers than they had in the preceding days. Demonstrations often targeted the physical institutions of the *Jamahiriyyah* and associated cultural monuments of Gaddafi's revolution. Protestors even began flying the old tricolor flag of the Libyan Kingdom, not seen since Gaddafi's 1969 coup. In the coming weeks, communities in the northwestern mountain range of the Jabal Nafusa would soon begin flying the international flag of the Amazigh (Berber) movement as well.

The authorities' response was mainly to fall back on force. The crackdown in Cyrenaica was especially heavy-handed in Benghazi and Bayda. Over eighty protestors were reportedly slain as security forces fired indiscriminately into crowds in several cities.[9] In the hours after the news of the attempted crackdown broke, solidarity demonstrations followed in some of Libya's smaller and medium-sized cites, from Kufra in the deep southeast to the Nafusa mountains. Towns located near oil installations threatened to seize production sites, pipelines, and refineries. Protestors in Libya's third largest city, Misrata, joined the fray on February 19 and finally the capital, Tripoli, saw large-scale protests on February 20.

The protests in Tripoli initially emerged in the neighborhoods of those who had been on the losing side of the Gaddafi state, particularly those districts with crumbling infrastructure and overcrowded public housing, as well as old elite Tripolitanian families dispossessed of their power in the name of constructing the *Jamahiriyyah*.[10] As was the case in Benghazi and Bayda, the regime's response to the demonstrations in Tripoli was swift and merciless – and necessarily so, from the regime's perspective. As the protests in Tripoli grew, the demonstrators had attempted to occupy the heart of the capital, Green Square. If that occupation had been sustained, as it had been in Cairo's Tahrir Square and Tunis's Avenue Bourguiba, it would have been a symbolic catastrophe for the authorities. Preventing the occupation of Green Square, and dispersing solidarity demonstrations elsewhere in the country, became the primary objective of the security forces regardless of the human cost. As gangs of regime supporters roamed the streets of Tripoli shooting almost at random, Human Rights Watch tallied over 300 combined killings by government forces in Benghazi and Tripoli.[11]

The Libyan regime, however, appeared to be falling into a trap of its own making. The objectives of the protestors escalated as government repression intensified.[12] Around this time, reports indicate that demonstrators began using the same protest chant made famous in Tunisia and Egypt just weeks prior:

al-sha'b
yurid
isqat al-nizam!

"The people / want / the downfall of the regime!" In Misrata, eulogies for those killed in the February 19 demonstrations began to describe each of the fallen as a *shahid* – a martyr.[13]

A Recalcitrant Regime, a Radicalized Rebellion

Given recent events in Tunisia and Egypt, there were hopes that Gaddafi's inner circle would quickly come to its senses to avoid a similar fate, if not widespread violence. When it was announced that Saif Al-Islam Al-Gaddafi, the Colonel's oldest son and Libya's heir apparent, would address the nation on February 20, many expected that he would announce a conciliatory path forward, if not that his father had stepped aside.

The fact that Saif Al-Islam, and not Gaddafi, was the first to address the nation formally was in itself reason for hope. For over a decade, Gaddafi's British-educated son had cultivated a reputation – with much help from fawning international supporters – as the great hope for human rights in Libya, if not eventual political and economic liberalization. Indeed, his charitable organization had overseen the release of several long-serving political prisoners from the early 1990s as a goodwill gesture in early February. Moreover, the various elements of the Libyan opposition, from the remnants of the National Front for the Salvation of Libya and the Libyan Islamic Fighting Group to the domestic and exiled Muslim Brotherhood, frequently dialogued with Saif Al-Islam, even as the uprising was unfolding in the east.[14] Saif Al-Islam's February 20 speech, however, was regrettably unrelenting in its denunciation of the protests. Had he taken a more conciliatory stance, many rebel leaders felt that a negotiated transition could have been possible, perhaps with him leading the transition.[15] While Saif Al-Islam criticized the incompetence of the security forces and promised accountability, he made it clear that there would otherwise be no compromise with the more radical demands of the rebellion.[16]

Two days later, Gaddafi himself appeared on national television to give a lengthy and even more resolute address to the nation. Infamously, Gaddafi insisted that Libya would be purged of revolutionaries house by house, street by street.[17] In both speeches of the Gaddafis, the events of preceding weeks were blamed on degenerate citizens and outside influences, from Al-Qaida and the United States to drugs, alcohol, and satellite television. The condescending attitude and dehumanizing rhetoric of Gaddafi and his son were a cause for disgust and concern, as was their threat to raise an army of African mercenaries to conduct the counter-revolutionary campaign.

Beyond threats of future violence, the repressive actions of the regime in late February were already bad enough. In addition to using indiscriminate violence against the wildcat demonstrations, state forces deployed more selective violence against known dissidents and emergent revolutionary leaders, often holding them incommunicado in undisclosed locations. While some were high-profile opponents, others were everyday citizens, including minors, caught up in the maelstrom.[18] Allegations of torture and rape spread quickly. The population's access to the Internet was often impeded, and websites like Facebook, Twitter, and Al-Jazeera were deliberately blocked; cellular services were frequently disrupted; calls, particularly to the outside world, were being monitored. Journalists, foreign and Libyan, were also detained. During the war that followed the February uprising, several journalists would be killed in the fighting.[19]

From the start of the uprising, many within the revolution were convinced that the Gaddafi regime would not cede power without a fight. As a result, many Libyans were determined to seize the means of their own security, first and foremost. In Cyrenaica, the mass desertion of conscripted soldiers and officers reinforced an increasingly radicalized and armed opposition that was organizing itself around well-established social alliances.[20] The occupation of the military barracks in Benghazi on February 18 sent a very strong signal to the regime that the Libyan uprising would not necessarily follow the path of civil disobedience and mass nonviolent protest. Other localities followed Cyrenaica's example, raiding armories, driving out government forces, and equipping local militias.

The geography of the uprising and the evolving strategy of the revolutionaries played a large part in the rapid militarization of the revolt. The Tunisian and Egyptian revolutions had succeeded largely through nonviolent means when mass protests around the country emboldened coalitions of civic activists, labor, and youth to occupy the urban core of the capital city. In Libya, the regime quickly foreclosed this possibility through sheer force, taking extreme measures to prevent any occupation of Green Square, arguably the most valuable piece of political real estate in the country. As a result, the February 17 revolution became one of dispersion rather than concentration. If the urban masses could not render the capital ungovernable, then the entire state would have to be systematically disabled from the periphery to the center. Under these conditions, the Libyan uprising instead became a constellation of loosely coordinated and increasingly armed actors from the country's second cities, notably Benghazi and Misrata, as well as its neglected margins.[21] Yet the isolated nature of the simultaneous revolts challenging the regime rendered many of them vulnerable to repression, and so they armed themselves in response. This rapidly escalating dynamic quickly dashed domestic and international hopes for a peaceful revolution or a negotiated transition.

As the regime's monopoly over the legitimate use of force began to crumble, the strengths and weaknesses of the state's forces became clear. The regime had a number of formal and informal coercive institutions at its disposal. These included those already operating at the forefront of the anti-revolutionary effort. Chief among these were Military Intelligence and the Internal Security Agency, which were notorious for running torture centers, as well as various units that acted as the Gaddafi family's praetorian guard, notably the 32nd ("Khamis") Brigade, led by the youngest of Gaddafi's sons, Khamis. Within the *Jamahiriyyah*, popular security was ostensibly devolved to the grassroots via the Revolutionary Committees (the ideological police of Gaddafi's revolution), the Revolutionary Guard (a paramilitary force semi-autonomous from the army), and the Popular Guard (militias created in the 1990s to counter the Libyan Islamic Fighting Group).[22] Despite the density of state power that these overlapping layers of security suggested, the formal military numbered only 75,000 on the eve of the revolution, and a significant percentage seemed to be defecting to the rebels early on. Indeed, the state's security forces were far weaker than many imagined. A telling fact was the regime's frantic efforts to raise an army of volunteers from the country's Saharan communities and from sub-Saharan Africa. Though these efforts actually exposed the desperate situation facing the regime and the precariousness of its grasp on Libya, the belief that Gaddafi was outsourcing his atrocities to Saharan and sub-Saharan African mercenaries helped push the North Atlantic powers to intervene militarily in the name of humanitarian protection. However, subsequent investigations showed that very few, if any, mercenaries had answered

Gaddafi's call.[23] Indeed, representatives of Libya's Arab, Tuareg, and Tebu communities in the southern interior issued a joint appeal to their constituents to rise up against the regime on March 22.[24]

In the final years of the Gaddafi regime, the *Jamahiriyyah*'s defense, intelligence, and security forces had evolved to fulfill two functions: to monitor the society (and each other), and to quash any localized resistance. This arrangement, however, was poorly designed to confront simultaneous mass uprisings on several fronts. The security sector had in fact been managed in the same way that Libyan society was managed: through the diffusion of power and disaggregation of institutions so that no single force could constitute a realistic threat to the regime. This is why the rebellion quickly overran the state in several key locations (notably, most of Cyrenaica) and why the 2011 civil war took the shape it did. The Libyan air force and army were formidable on paper but in actuality they were undertrained, understaffed, and underequipped. The once mighty Libyan defense forces of the 1970s and 1980s had suffered greatly after the loss in Chad, the collapse of oil prices in the 1980s, and the international isolation of the 1990s, especially the sanctions regime. Events like the 1993 coup attempt and the Libyan Islamic Fighting Group insurgency only accelerated the regime's isolation and paranoia. Despite expensive upgrades and repairs to Libya's conventional land, air, and sea forces in the 2000s, the primary emphasis of arms and related purchases during the final decade of the regime was enhancing the capacity of the internal security and intelligence agencies that protected the regime.[25]

The 2011 civil war was thus shaped by the fact that the best military equipment was either in the hands of small, elite regime units or kept under lock and key in isolated arms depots, rendering much of it inaccessible to potentially loyal forces. This made it easy for the rebels to equip themselves with all kinds of weapons. It also allowed the air forces of NATO and the Arab League to eliminate most of Libya's conventional forces – e.g., armored vehicles, airplanes, command centers, and air defense systems – in the opening days of the joint military intervention in March. Instead of pitting a ragtag uprising against a fully armed petro-state, the Libyan civil war quickly became a symmetrical contest between two poorly coordinated coalitions of militias brandishing light arms and mobilized on "technicals" (modified civilian pickup trucks). One side, however, would soon be backed by the world's most powerful military alliance.

Toward Civil War

In the east of the country, the regime was quickly overthrown: government buildings were ransacked, sometimes set ablaze; weapons caches of the military and security forces were seized as local self-defense groups took up arms; state forces retreated, dispersed, or joined the rebellion; around the world, Libyan diplomats defected and exiles desperately tried to return for the fight. By the end of February, the mainstream opposition, both at home and abroad, had coalesced into a body calling itself the National Transitional Council. The Council claimed leadership of the movement yet had little effective military control over the armed revolutionary groups emerging throughout the country.[26] Much of its membership was secret, particularly its representatives in Tripolitania. The Council prominently featured several high-profile defectors from the regime, including the chair of the organization, Mustafa Abdul Jalil. Like other Council leaders, Abdul Jalil seemed an unlikely candidate to represent the rebellion given his longstanding ties to the governing authorities and his modest demeanor. He had most recently served as the *Jamahiriyyah*'s version of a Minister of Justice and as a cabinet member. Abdul Jalil, however, had been openly critical of the regime and even once resigned publicly out of frustration with the judicial system in 2010. Defecting soon after the massacres in Benghazi, he was joined on the Council by other high-level officials, including Mahmoud Jibril (a former planning and development official), Abdelfatah Younis (the Interior Minister, a former high-level military official, and one of Gaddafi's oldest allies), Omar Al-Hariri (a former military leader), and Ali Al-Issawi (a former foreign affairs official). At the United Nations, Libyan diplomats Abdel Rahman Shalgam (a former Foreign Minister) and Ibrahim Dabbashi (then Permanent Representative to the United Nations) had also defected on February 21 and began representing the opposition soon thereafter. Musa Al-Kuni, a Libyan Tuareg leader and consul in Mali, sided with the rebellion in March, calling upon his coethnics to join him in revolt.[27] Perhaps the most significant defections were those of Musa Kusa, Chief of External Intelligence, who escaped to Britain in March, and then Shukri Ghanem, head of the National Oil Company, in May. Given the number of high-profile defectors and opposition leaders, the uprising's domestic and international credibility grew rapidly.[28]

As the conflict deteriorated into an all-out civil war, the National Transitional Council began seeking international recognition in the early weeks of March 2011. One of the organization's strongest supporters, French President Nicolas Sarkozy, hosted several of the Council officials at the Élysée Palace on March 10. There Sarkozy recognized the Council as Libya's true government. Other acts of recognition followed, notably ones that allowed the Council to receive millions of dollars of cash ostensibly under UN embargo.[29] By the time the Council replaced the *Jamahiriyyah*, taking its seat in the United Nations on September 16, 2011, a majority of the world's states had already recognized it as Libya's legitimate authority. Beyond the symbolic value of such recognition, it also allowed the Council access to two other sources of tremendous value: billions of US dollars in embargoed assets and control over Libya's oil revenues. The Council successfully established itself as the new, if temporary, "core" of Libyan politics.

Support among the revolutionary forces for the Council's authority was tenuous at best. From the start, the Council's capacity to govern the factious Libyan polity was already being undermined by the proliferation of autonomous armed actors all across the country, notably the *thuwar* – the revolutionary militias.[30] These militias could range in size from 300 to 1,000 members, though they averaged between twenty and sixty men. Most were highly embedded in their communities, from which they drew moral and material support as local protectors.[31] Though all were dedicated to the powerful yet ambiguous notion of "the revolution," their loyalty to the Council was an entirely different question, a question that was mutually deferred by the Council and the *thuwar* until after the fall of the regime.

That the Libyan revolution was horizontally organized and effectively leaderless raised questions in North Atlantic capitals as to whether or not it could be hijacked by radical Libyan Islamists and transnational jihadists. The regime itself spared no effort to tar the rebels with the brush of Al-Qaida. It was also frequently noted that the small eastern city of Derna, with its reputation for Islamist militancy, had been one of the first to liberate itself from the regime in February 2011. Derna also fielded some of the most experienced and well-organized fighters in the revolution. Throughout the 1990s and 2000s, the city had been a hub for the Libyan Islamic Fighting Group and Libyans heading off to fight the US-led occupations of Afghanistan and Iraq. While Saif Al-Islam had worked hard to co-opt Islamists throughout the 2000s (even attempting to rally Fighting Group veterans and Salafi scholars to the regime's defense in 2011), the new generation of post-9/11 jihadists were viewed as a potential source of radical destabilization given the kinds of relentless, barbarous tactics that had been recently deployed in the Iraqi civil war. Regime efforts to emphasize the jihadi element in the revolution and the National Transitional Council's efforts to downplay it both obfuscated the complicated role of Islamists and Islamism in the 2011 revolution.[32] While the veterans of wars in Afghanistan, Iraq, and the Libyan Islamic Fighting Group made valuable contributions to the military campaign, there is little indication that any of the major actors or groups viewed the revolution as anything but a nationalist uprising.

The military campaign on the ground evolved rapidly in the early days of the uprising. The virtually instantaneous liberation of Benghazi and other key eastern sites was followed by another stunning rebel victory on March 3: the capture of

Brega. Located some 150 miles south of Benghazi, Brega is the center of Libya's major oil export facilities in the east. It soon became clear, however, that the regime would not cede this valuable region – the "oil crescent" – without a fight. As the revolutionary forces attempted to push westward from Cyrenaica and then the oil crescent, they met stiff resistance from regime forces. Simultaneously, armed rebellions in the Nafusa mountains and resistance cells in major coastal cities of Tripolitania, including the capital itself, also began to challenge the regime. The fall of Zawiya in the west, another key oil export zone, was another unthinkable loss for the regime.

Gaddafi's forces first went on the offensive to reclaim the capital region. The recapture of Zawiya and Zuwara, important coastal sites on the road to Tunisia, was followed by the encirclement of two major centers of revolt, Misrata along the coast and Zintan in the Nafusa mountains. Feeling confident that their grasp in the west was secure, regime forces then proceeded eastward from the Gaddafi stronghold of Sirte toward Benghazi, retaking rebel-held towns and oil infrastructure. As government troops approached Benghazi in mid-March, the rebellion appeared to be on the edge of a crushing defeat. Indeed, the Khamis Brigade's bloody recapture of Zawiya on March 11 was suggestive of the regime's resolve to smash the uprising regardless of the human cost. For many in the international community, the case for some kind of forceful response, one that would protect the people of Cyrenaica from the wrath of the Gaddafi regime, was now clear. And so, on March 17, the UN Security Council responded, authorizing NATO and the Arab League to take military action.

Negotiation or Intervention? Divergent International Responses to the Crisis

On the international stage, the first consequential actions to be taken against the Gaddafi regime was the Arab League's temporary suspension of Libya's membership on February 22.

The following day, the African Union condemned the government's use of violence. Soon thereafter, on February 25, the United States announced sanctions on key regime figures. The following day, February 26, the UN Security Council passed Resolution 1970, which included sanctions, an assets freeze, a travel ban on key officials, a total arms embargo, and referrals to the International Criminal Court. After an initial investigation found that crimes against humanity had been committed by the regime, the Court issued warrants for Gaddafi and his son Saif Al-Islam, as well as intelligence chief Abdullah Al-Senussi, on June 27.

Libya's membership on the UN Human Rights Council was suspended on February 25, and a UN commission of inquiry to investigate the regime's abuses was engendered soon thereafter. Two months later, an initial report of the International Commission of Inquiry for Libya found that government forces had indeed committed significant violations of international human rights and humanitarian laws, many of these abuses amounting to war crimes and crimes against humanity. These acts included the excessive and indiscriminate use of force, which was often lethal, as well as arbitrary and blanket detentions, disappearances, acts of torture, impeding medical personnel, attacking journalists, disrespecting safe spaces such as mosques and hospitals, and the use of unlawful foreign fighters. Controversially, the Commission also noted some of the abuses of the revolutionary forces.[33] Though initially smaller in scope and scale than the crimes committed by the regime, it was an early indication of the extent to which some of the *thuwar* were as lawless as Gaddafi's forces.

When it appeared that condemnations and sanctions were having little effect on the Gaddafi regime, proposals for an internationally enforced no-fly zone were put forward.[34] These grew out of early reports – few of them verified – that the Libyan air force was strafing and bombing civilians in rebel-held areas. Then, on March 7, the Libyan state forces launched what was said to be an all-out effort to take back Benghazi, punctuated by the recapture of Ajdabiya along the oil crescent soon thereafter. Though the Gaddafi regime's use of airpower against civilians was later proven to be overstated, voices in the international community nonetheless believed in early March 2011 that another siege of Sarajevo, if not a Srebrenica-scale massacre, was materializing before their very eyes.[35] Such concerns were in reference to the repeated failures of the international community to protect civilians from mass atrocities during the disintegration of Yugoslavia in the 1990s.

The idea of offering air protection to the Libyan rebellion gained steam on March 12 when Amr Musa, then Secretary-General of the Arab League, said his organization would support the imposition of a no-fly zone. Meanwhile, the African Union, which was also dealing with a simultaneous crisis in Côte d'Ivoire, engaged in a flurry of diplomatic activity to find a peaceful alternative to civil war and foreign military intervention in Libya. To that end, its Peace and Security Council created a High-Level Committee to Libya on March 10, composed of the heads of state from Mauritania, South Africa, the Republic of the Congo, Uganda, and the head of the African Commission. It aimed to gather in Mauritania just over a week later on March 19, and then fly to Libya to press Gaddafi to accept an AU roadmap to end the crisis. The roadmap envisioned a bilateral ceasefire, the deployment of humanitarian assistance, protection of civilians (particularly other African populations caught in the violence), and a negotiated political solution to the crisis.

The African Union's diplomatic approach was often dismissed as the desperate attempt of some of the continent's worst dictators to save one of their own. At the turn of the millennium, Africa was perhaps the last bastion of international support for Gaddafi. Publics across the continent adored the Brother Leader because of his social spending outside of Libya, his historical support for African liberation movements, and his open opposition to North Atlantic interests. Gaddafi had nonetheless done much throughout the 2000s to damage his relations with African leaders. Even towering African figures like Thabo Mbeki of South Africa, Yoweri Museveni of Uganda, and Robert Mugabe of Zimbabwe showed signs of exasperation with his political histrionics and meddling across the continent. Late in his tenure, Gaddafi continued to interfere in the affairs of African states, as he had done in the 1980s and 1990s, by offering support to rebel groups, often under the guise of peacemaking. Gaddafi's reputation as a founding member of the African Union was likewise undermined in the years that followed its creation out of the Organization of African Unity in 2001. Gaddafi had done little to enhance the profile of the African Union during his contentious tenure as its chair in 2009 and was otherwise a disruptive and unconstructive participant in the years before and after.[36]

While most of Africa's leaders were no longer enamored of Gaddafi, many feared the collapse of the Libyan state and the repercussions of an over-eager yet under-planned military intervention led by the North Atlantic powers. On a continent ravaged by insurgencies, civil wars, and foreign interventions, there were also concerns about the fact that the West was giving diplomatic, material, and military aid to an armed anti-government uprising. The African Union as a whole felt that the North Atlantic powers only seemed interested in peacekeeping in Africa when core interests were on the line, such as oil investments in Libya. Some AU members, notably President Idris Deby of Chad, cited more specific concerns. Like others, Deby was particularly frightened by the prospect of a destabilized Libya and the effects it would have on regional security in the Sahel.[37] Deby's concerns would prove frightfully prophetic: in 2012, Al-Qaida-linked militants, freshly awash with smuggled Libyan arms looted during the collapse of the *Jamahiriyyah*, seized large parts of Northern Mali and declared it an Islamic state.

The Intervention: A Responsibility to Protect?

On March 17, the UN Security Council passed a resolution (Resolution 1973) supporting the use of military power to protect civilians from Libyan state forces. Two days later, NATO and the Arab League launched their joint air campaign against the Gaddafi regime. The African Union's diplomatic efforts had been sidelined by the growing sense of urgency surrounding Libya's escalating violence as the regime's counteroffensive neared Benghazi in mid-March 2011. Yet the speed with which the North Atlantic leaders arrived at the decision to intervene militarily in the civil war was not simply a response to the real and imagined atrocities being committed against the Libyan people. The intervention was as much a response to decades of ambivalent and, more often than not, antagonistic relations between the Gaddafi regime and the coalition of North Atlantic and Arab states that sided militarily with the February 17 rebellion. Whereas the political abandonment of Ben Ali in Tunisia and Mubarak in Egypt had been difficult decisions for leaders in the Middle East and the North Atlantic world, the decision to intervene in Libya was far less agonizing. Gaddafi had been, at best, an ally of convenience on issues of energy and security during the final decade of his rule. More significantly, for over four decades, he helmed one of the most notorious pariah regimes to have emerged since World War II. Thus the decision to use military force against the *Jamahiriyyah* was not simply because of facts on the ground in early March 2011. In a way, the decision was years in the making.

All of that said, it was still surprising that an international coalition emerged as quickly as it did to respond to the crisis in Libya. Two of the countries that would lead the intervention, the United States and Britain, were particularly reluctant to get involved in such a large-scale military operation in the Arab world given the disastrous result of the 2003 Anglo-American invasion and occupation of Iraq, which was widely viewed by 2011 as an illegitimate, costly, and ultimately counterproductive political and military catastrophe. Not only were publics in Britain and the United States wary of getting involved in another civil war in the Middle East, President Barack Obama had arguably secured the White House in 2008 by promising to avoid the very kind of military entanglement that Resolution 1973 now authorized. Even in mid-March 2011, with Gaddafi's forces threatening to crush the Libyan uprising, over two-thirds of the US public still opposed the idea of intervening.[38] Even elements of the

US military establishment voiced opposition to the use of force in Libya. Part of the argument had to do with existing US military commitments in Iraq and Afghanistan. Obama had just withdrawn most US troops from Iraq despite the tenuous security situation there and, in Afghanistan, the Taliban seemed resurgent despite an increase in US troop levels.

Another aspect of opposition to an intervention in Libya within the US government was skepticism regarding the case for humanitarian action in the first place and whether or not it would do any good. While the Gaddafi regime had undoubtedly committed war crimes and systematic violations of human rights over the course of the previous month, the case for humanitarian intervention often rested on vague notions of an impending "genocide" that would occur unless the UN acted to stop it. Imposing a no-fly zone, it was furthermore argued, would be a meaningless gesture. Gaddafi's airpower was quite limited and the majority of the violence was coming from his irregular ground forces. To avoid a years-long quagmire, the war for Libya would have to be won on the ground, and that necessarily meant going well beyond passive measures like an arms embargo, sanctions, and a no-fly zone. Though the argument for humanitarian intervention was won by key figures in the State Department (notably Secretary of State Hillary Clinton and UN Ambassador Susan Rice) as well as in the White House (National Security Council member Samantha Power), the Secretary of Defense, Robert Gates, continued to voice concerns even as the war progressed.[39]

For the British government of Prime Minister David Cameron, also recently elected, the prospect of an intervention in Libya was fraught with danger and possibility. On the one hand, the British public was opposed to the idea of military interventions in the Arab world after costly invasion and occupation of Iraq in 2003, a legacy of the premiership of Tony Blair. On the other hand, there was also a British sense of responsibility for having helped resurrect the Gaddafi regime in the early 2000s, another legacy of Blair's leadership.

In fact, it was President Nicolas Sarkozy who was the most aggressive in his support for military action in Libya, despite the fact that France had been one of the strongest opponents of the 2003 invasion of Iraq on the UN Security Council. Sarkozy reportedly even threatened unilateral French action if his North Atlantic allies did not also rise to the challenge.

Whether or not Sarkozy's threat was real, an effective and overwhelming foreign intervention in the 2011 Libyan crisis necessarily meant that the operation would have to be led by the United States, the only global military power capable of launching, coordinating, and supplying a campaign of this magnitude – especially on such short notice. The Obama administration acceded to the idea of an intervention so long as it was multilateral, involved a regional partner, and did not involve any troop deployments on the ground in Libya. The participation of NATO and the Arab League respectively satisfied the first two conditions, whereas the third was satisfied by the fact that the National Transitional Council insisted that Libyans would do the fighting on the ground themselves.[40] This division of labor, Libyans fighting on the ground and their international backers supporting them from the air, was likewise an effect of the conflict that had torn apart Iraq after the 2003 invasion. A large-scale deployment of European and American troops in Libya would have been incredibly unpopular, and might have shifted many *thuwar* to Gaddafi's side.

Arab League support was also crucial in order to preempt objections within the UN Security Council, notably from China and Russia.[41] The mandate that was eventually given to NATO and the Arab League on March 17 by the Security Council was nonetheless a very weak one. Although no states opposed or vetoed the UN resolution, the Security Council saw telling abstentions from China and Russia, as well as a surprising abstention from a key NATO ally, Germany. They were joined by two important states from the global south: India and Brazil. Despite their traditional opposition to the alleged right of humanitarian intervention (or "the responsibility to protect"), the fact that China and Russia had not publicly threatened to veto the resolution was nonetheless viewed as a tacit approval of the air campaign's limited goals of imposing a no-fly zone, an arms embargo, and protecting civilians from immediate harm. China and Russia would later insist, however, that they had not voted for what the NATO–Arab League campaign inevitably became: a regime-change operation.

Even more surprising than the fact that the resolution had passed without a veto or an opposing vote was the support that Resolution 1973 received from the three African states then holding seats on the Security Council: Nigeria, Gabon, and South Africa. What few allies Gaddafi had left in the world tended to reside in Africa, and the African Union had been leading efforts to de-escalate the conflict through diplomacy. Another strong advocate of diplomacy had been Libya's neighbor to the west, Algeria, a country whose colonization by the French and its recent experience with protracted internal conflict in the 1990s heavily informed its foreign policy. Along with Syria, Algeria had been among the lone voices opposing the Arab League's support for a no-fly zone, suggesting that foreign involvement in the Libyan crisis would only make matters worse.

Arab support for the intervention was in fact not unanimous. It was being driven by the six members of the Gulf Cooperation Council, a coalition of petro-monarchs who had historically been challenged by the militant Arab republicanism of Gaddafi, as well as by Syria and Algeria to a lesser degree. The rest of the Arab League was likewise divided. Jordan and Lebanon supported the intervention, as did Morocco. Tunisia, Egypt, Sudan, and Mauritania, however, were reticent to support a Western military intervention in the Arab world.

Security Council Resolution 1973 – initially put forward by France, Great Britain, and Lebanon – had in fact offered a suite of policy options for the international community, not just military intervention. While the Resolution called for a ceasefire and an end to attacks on civilians, and offered support for the African Union's diplomatic efforts, the Council also imposed further travel bans and asset freezes on regime officials along with a total arms embargo, which included arms to the rebels. But by the time AU mediators were ready to go to Tripoli on March 20, a no-fly zone had already been imposed and military operations against the Gaddafi regime were well underway. Those imposing the no-fly zone told the African Union that the delegation's safety would be at risk if they tried to fly to Libya.[42]

Turning the Tide

The necessity – and thus the legitimacy – of the NATO–Arab League intervention in Libya would be subject to intense debate in the days, weeks, months, and years to come. Critics often cited reports that indicated the full compliance of regime forces with UN demands for a ceasefire, as well as the regime's stated willingness to pursue the African Union's roadmap to a negotiated solution. Proponents of the intervention countered by suggesting that such reports were inconsistent and that, more importantly, the regime was fundamentally untrustworthy.[43]

The reality of the situation on the ground in Libya, amid the thickening fog of war, was one in which neither side would have been able to enact a meaningful ceasefire had they even wanted to. On the one hand, the highly localized anti-Gaddafi forces largely operated autonomously from each other, desperately using what meager financial, human, and military resources they could muster. The Benghazi-based National Transitional Council had little direct control over the revolutionary militias, particularly Islamist cells and those fighting in Tripolitania. Even if the regime had enacted a meaningful and sustained unilateral ceasefire, many of the revolutionary brigades would have been unlikely to respect it, as there was little faith in the willingness of the regime to reciprocate and concede to the revolution's demands. Moreover, if the National Transitional Council had called for a ceasefire, it would have lost credibility with much of the armed uprising, and the fighting would likely have continued nonetheless. The Council's greatest asset was the international belief that it was a credible and broadly inclusive body representing most of the stakeholders in the revolution. As a governing institution, however, its capacities were limited. Calling for a ceasefire would have exposed this fact.

On the other hand, Gaddafi's forces, though sometimes backed by his well-trained and well-equipped elite units, largely deteriorated into a mirror of the uprising: a coalition of counter-revolutionary militias motivated by mixtures of self-interest, opportunism, anti-imperialism, and loyalty (familial, geographical, political).[44] This deterioration was exacerbated by the international aerial bombardment authorized by the United Nations. The initial goal of the NATO–Arab League intervention was to destroy the regime's ability to crush the rebellion, particularly by eliminating its conventional air and ground forces, as well as its communications and logistics. Within days, the Gaddafi regime had lost much of its heavy armaments and airpower along with its command-and-control capacity nationwide. An important effect of these initial NATO airstrikes against the regime was thus the

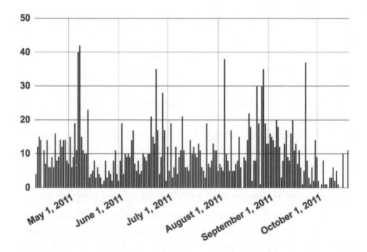

Figure 2.1. Daily totals of airstrikes conducted in Libya under NATO command, April–November 2011.
Source: "Nato Operations in Libya," *Guardian*, https://www.theguardian.com/news/datablog/2011/may/22/nato-libya-data-journalism-operations-country.

transformation of the civil war. Instead of conventional state forces facing off against irregular guerrilla armies, the conflict mainly consisted of militia-on-militia violence.

Even if it was not necessarily the policy of NATO and the Arab League to prevent a peaceful resolution to the crisis, the intervention nonetheless intensified the civil war by, first, morally legitimating the revolution and, second, physically degenerating the *Jamahiriyyah*'s forces. The less Gaddafi's forces looked like a regular army, the harder it would be for the forces of NATO and the Arab League to distinguish between loyalist and revolutionary combatants. Hence a small number of "boots on the ground," albeit highly covert, would in fact be necessary in order to minimize civilian casualties and to coordinate the air and ground campaigns against Gaddafi's counter-revolutionary militias.

The US Africa Command initially led the air campaign, with France and Britain working under its direction. While these three countries would go on to conduct the majority of strikes (with the United States providing the lion's share of munitions), the broader air campaign, consolidated under NATO control at the end of March, was eventually joined by Belgium, Canada, Denmark, Italy, Norway, Qatar, the United Arab Emirates, and, according to some reports, Jordan.[45]

The initial Anglo-American strikes sought to disable the regime's capacity to defend itself from aerial attacks while the French halted the regime's progress toward Benghazi. With the rapid elimination of the most visible and potent aspects of the regime's conventional air and land capacity, the forces of NATO and the Arab League could operate with almost total freedom. The problem was that they quickly ran out of targets. A telling trend was the shift from "deliberate" to "dynamic" strikes in Operation Unified Protector, as the joint campaign would be called. Deliberate strikes, which defined the early campaign, had intended targets. Dynamic strikes, by contrast, saw pilots flying over designated areas with no pre-planned objectives. They would instead be assigned targets identified by ongoing surveillance, those emerging from sudden developments on the ground, or other targets of opportunity. By the end of April, 90 percent of sorties were already of the dynamic variety.[46] While commanders would claim that NATO's ability to launch successful dynamic strikes improved as their overhead surveillance capacity improved (e.g., with the use of unmanned aerial vehicles), this was only part of the story. The crucial developments were happening on the ground.

With the destruction of their conventional capacity, Gaddafi's loyalist forces became increasingly irregular and militia-like, and also more and more embedded within civilian infrastructures. The goals of the NATO–Arab League intervention became more difficult to pursue without closer coordination with the rebels in order to distinguish friend from foe, civilian from combatant. The air campaign initially tapered off after its onslaught of cruise missiles and aerial bombardment. A lack of targets was not the only reason for NATO's caution. The transition in early April from a US-led operation to an Anglo-French-dominated one under NATO's authority was far from smooth. To make matters worse, there were also several "friendly fire" incidents in the early days of the intervention whereby rebel forces were mistakenly targeted in airstrikes. The targeting of arms depots also had caused civilian deaths, or "collateral damage," when exploded munitions landed miles away in nearby towns.[47]

Not understanding why the pace of attacks had slowed, rebel groups, often working in isolation and with limited communications, attempted to provide additional target information to NATO headquarters via the National Transitional Council and Libyans in the diaspora. In Misrata, rebel leaders had used a combination of GPS devices and the Google Earth mapping program to send target locations to the British military during the early weeks of the regime's siege of their city, though NATO rarely if ever used this information. Local commanders later discovered the reason why: the intervening forces did not trust much of the information being conveyed to them by the rebellion. Part of the problem was the close proximity of both sides to each other and to civilians. Another issue was the intervening forces' apprehension about their alliance with the rebellion. There were concerns that the revolutionary brigades might try to use NATO and the Arab

League for revenge attacks against loyalist civilian populations and for internecine rebel violence. Gaining reliable intelligence on the position of Gaddafi's loyalist forces thus required what had been ostensibly ruled out: boots on the ground.

In mid-April, several weeks into the siege of Misrata, French intelligence officers, traveling by sea, arrived to coordinate with the local resistance. After building trust with Misratan leadership, the French intelligence officials left, later returning in larger numbers with a handful of military personnel as well. They soon joined the Misratans on the frontlines of the fight against Gaddafi. The French used their own equipment to identify and locate loyalist positions, and passed that information via secure communications to commanders in Europe, to ships at sea, and even to pilots overhead in planes and helicopters. While these spotters helped direct the air campaign's targeting, British special forces arrived several weeks later to provide tactical advice to the *thuwar* on the ground in Misrata. Similar deployments of NATO and Arab League personnel occurred in the other main theaters of war, notably the Nafusa mountains, where Qatari and Emirati advisors were actively training and arming rebels.[48] These low-profile deployments helped the participating NATO and Arab League states coordinate with the rebels' ground forces while also working to prevent civilian casualties, friendly fire incidents, and misuse of the protective umbrella for ulterior motives. At the same time, these deployments also provided the intervening coalition with vital bits of information they had not yet received: who were the armed groups fighting Gaddafi, what were their motivations, and could they be trusted, particularly if they succeeded in their goal of toppling the regime?

The most controversial aspect of the coordination between the intervening forces and the revolutionary brigades were French arms transfers coordinated by the Qatari and, to a lesser extent, Sudanese governments. Though these transfers were a clear violation of the UN embargo, officials with the National Transitional Council began seeking arms soon after Resolution 1973 was passed. What began as clandestine and small-scale shipments of light equipment soon became, by the end of April, direct deliveries of arms via air cargo landings in Tobruk and Benghazi, as well as airdrops into the Nafusa mountains. Who would control these arms became a divisive issue within the rebellion, as eastern military officials like Abdelfatah Younis and Khalifa Haftar clashed with Islamists seeking to direct the equipment to their networks in Tripolitania via Sudanese intermediaries, Saharan trade routes, and the Nafusa mountains. Subsequent Tunisian acquiescence allowed arms, aid, fighters, and trainers to cross into western Libya to prepare the groundwork for the final assault on Tripoli. Not to be left behind, Misratan military leaders also pressed for aid and arms, using their sea access to facilitate the first transfers. Following the breaking of the siege of Misrata, Qatari and Sudanese shipments soon began arriving. All in all, some 20,000 tons of weapons would be delivered to Libya's rebels via these channels.[49]

A Question of Humanitarianism or Regime Change

The fall of Tripoli in August 2011 and the sudden collapse of the loyalist resistance in almost all other areas of the country caught many observers by surprise. In June, a prominent international think tank had erroneously concluded that only a diplomatic solution would spare Libya from years of civil war.[50] Efforts to find such a solution had in fact continued even after the NATO–Arab League intervention was launched. The African Union was the most prominent multilateral organization to pursue peacemaking efforts throughout the spring and summer of 2011. Its efforts to stop the Libyan civil war were initially interrupted when NATO launched its air campaign on March 19. An AU mission was finally allowed to visit Gaddafi on April 10, led by the Presidents of South Africa, Mauritania, the Republic of the Congo, Uganda, and Mali. It reported that the Gaddafi regime had, once again, accepted the principles of the AU roadmap calling for a bilateral ceasefire and negotiations with the opposition. African Union officials would later claim that Gaddafi himself had committed to stepping aside.[51]

As late as May 31, President Jacob Zuma of South Africa, who visited Tripoli once more, said that Gaddafi was still willing to discuss a truce and a negotiated transition. What followed were efforts by the African Union to bring representatives of the Gaddafi regime and the National Transitional Council to meet in Addis Ababa, but the latter refused to come.[52] Other peacemaking efforts were similarly rebuffed. Though the rebels harbored reasonable suspicions that the African Union was biased toward Gaddafi, the official UN mediator, Abdelelah Al-Khatib, a former Jordanian foreign minister, fared no better at getting the two sides to the negotiating table. A multilateral body called the Libyan Contact Group largely served to advance the interests of the intervening states and to help prop up the National Transitional Council. Turkey, which boasted good relations with the Gaddafi regime and elements of the rebellion, notably Islamists and Misratan elites, similarly offered to act as an intermediary but was simply ignored by the rebels and the intervening coalition.[53] The regime itself continued to make peace overtures to the outside world, even suggesting that Gaddafi, if not the entire family, would step aside to facilitate a democratic transition.[54]

These peace efforts seemed to have little effect on the National Transitional Council or the international powers backing the rebellion. Part of the problem was the demands for peace that had been imposed on the Gaddafi regime by the rebel leaders and the intervening states. The Council, emboldened by its growing domestic and foreign support, would only order a cessation of armed resistance once Gaddafi himself stepped down, a position outlined in its April "roadmap" for the future of Libya.[55] For the Council and its backers, regime change had become a precondition for a negotiated political solution to the Libyan crisis, rather than, as envisioned by the African Union, a possible outcome of such negotiations. The political leadership of the uprising also feared two other possibilities: that the regime would use negotiations to re-consolidate itself, or that it would use the existing battle-lines as a basis for a political solution based on territorial division between rebel Cyrenaica and "loyalist" Tripolitania and Fezzan.

The question of Gaddafi's role in any transition was further complicated by the insistence of NATO and the Arab League that, if the regime wanted to stop foreign military intervention, it would have to do much more than simply stop shooting. A credible ceasefire was defined as the complete withdrawal of all government forces from Misrata, Benghazi, and the key oil centers of Ajdabiya in the east and Zawiya in the west.[56] Given the high bar set by the rebels and their international backers, civil war and foreign military intervention had become inevitable in March and almost impossible to stop in the months that followed. The Gaddafi regime would never concede outright to such humiliating military and political demands, a fact that only the AU mediators seemed to understand. At the same time, the International Criminal Court's indictment of Gaddafi, Saif Al-Islam, and Abdullah Senussi on June 27 made internationally sponsored negotiations between the regime and the rebellion all the more difficult to imagine.

Critics of the intervention have often concluded that regime change – and not just humanitarian protection – was the actual agenda of NATO and the Arab League once the decision to use military force had been made, if not earlier. In reality, there was nothing secret about their intentions, which clearly linked protecting civilians with Gaddafi's removal. The pretense that the intervention was entirely humanitarian was implicitly undermined by President Sarkozy's decision on March 10 to recognize the National Transitional Council as Libya's legitimate government.[57] Behind the scenes, Qatar made arrangements in April to help export and process the crude oil under Council control.[58] More explicitly, Obama, Sarkozy, and Cameron issued a joint statement in mid-April about the coalition's aims. It said that the humanitarian objectives of the mission would be considered achieved once the Gaddafi regime was no longer in power.[59]

Since then, it has become even clearer that neither the National Transitional Council nor its international backers had ever really imagined any political accommodation with Gaddafi. In 2015, former British Prime Minister Tony Blair revealed that, with permission from the US and UK governments, he attempted to convince Gaddafi to step down in the lead-up to the UN vote on March 17. Blair had warned Gaddafi that there would be military intervention unless he left Libya.[60] Leon Panetta, the former director of the CIA who became Secretary of Defense in the middle of the 2011 air campaign against Gaddafi, later acknowledged that the goal of the intervention had been regime change, even if it was impolite to say so publicly at the time.[61] In the years that followed, North Atlantic leaders seemed powerless in the face of the collapse of the transitional process, the resort to civil war in 2014, the rise of the Islamic State in Sirte, and the exploding Mediterranean migration crisis. All of these developments combined to erode what little was left of the humanitarian façade of the 2011 intervention. The NATO campaign continued to stand as a military success of sorts but only when narrowly framed in terms of the very objective that had been denied – regime change. The relatively efficient, inexpensive, and expeditious ousting of Gaddafi was nonetheless a pyrrhic victory, one in which Libya's long-term security was sacrificed to meet the short-term political agendas of outside powers. The real tragedy, however, is the extent to which Libya's collapse could have been prevented, either by pursuing negotiations more aggressively at the outset or by deploying a more robust UN presence after the uprising. The intervention was sold to publics in both Libya and the North Atlantic world with the provision that there would be no foreign troop presence during or after the 2011 civil war. The international community's refusal to organize an international stabilization force after the fall of Gaddafi – a policy that Libya's new leaders were only too happy to support – meant that Libya's fate had been entrusted to the hundreds of angry, motivated, and empowered militias now ruling the country.[62]

The Downfall of the Regime

Regime change, however, proved to be more difficult than initially imagined. For months, the essential battle-lines hardly shifted. The main theaters of combat were the major port city of Misrata, which was choked off by encircling regime forces until mid-May; the vital eastern oil production centers near Ajdabiya, where movement on the ground had largely ceased between April and July; and in the west, along the coast, and in the approaches to the Nafusa mountains. When NATO voted to extend its mandate for another three months on June 1, regime and opposition forces were still deadlocked in the region of Brega and Ajdabiya; more progress had been made further west along the coast when the regime's stranglehold on Misrata was broken on May 15 with help from foreign military advisors working hand-in-hand with the Misratan *thuwar*.

As the war became increasingly protracted in the summer of 2011, there were several conflicting attempts to see if the rebels and the regime could be brought together. Owing to a lack of coordination and the inconsistent signals from the regime, these efforts – Russian–AU, Franco–Italian, US military and State Department, the Contact Group – never snowballed into anything substantive, and largely served to undermine the authority of Al-Khatib, the official UN mediator. Backchannel peace overtures from the Gaddafi regime to US officials, even as late as August, attempted to find a way to de-escalate the conflict by meeting international demands. As always, the regime did not help itself by continually sending mixed signals about the willingness of Gaddafi and his sons to step aside. There were additionally serious concerns about whether or not offers coming from anyone other than Gaddafi himself – Saif Al-Islam was the primary regime interlocutor during the war – were genuine and credible.[63] Efforts to settle the conflict peacefully also had little purchase with the rebellion as long as Gaddafi was allowed to remain in the country.

As the rebels had largely ruled out a political solution with the regime, the intervening coalition grew increasingly anxious to see the rebel leadership put forward credible plans to achieve military victory and to secure Tripoli after the collapse of the Gaddafi state, plans that would depend neither on NATO airpower for victory nor on international peacekeepers to stabilize the country. Fearing that the rebellion's international support would grow war weary, Mahmoud Jibril coordinated the Council's efforts, which involved Europe, the Gulf, and rebel groups in the Nafusa mountains and Tripoli, to deliver a quick victory and post-conflict stability on the cheap.[64] The rebels nonetheless became even more recalcitrant as momentum on the ground surprisingly began to shift in their favor during Ramadan, a time in which many had suspected the intensity of the war would diminish for the Islamic holy month that spanned most of August. Additionally, there had been concerns that the revolution might collapse into infighting following the mysterious July 28 assassination of Abdelfatah Younis, one of the most important regime defectors and rebel commanders. Throughout the war, the National Transitional Council continued to insist that it was in control of the situation and could achieve its objectives without foreign troops on the ground.

Though the international community had rallied to save Benghazi from a ruthless and bloody siege, this was in fact what Misrata experienced from March to mid-May as the partially occupied city suffered from pitched street battles, constant shelling, and sniper fire. As the regime withdrew some of its forces from Misrata to focus on different regions, it attempted to outsource and privatize the conflict by pitting Misratans against other communities in the area, notably the town of Tawergha. Misrata's major asset, its port, allowed aid, arms, and advisors to augment the capacity of the local militias, who soon spearheaded the assault on Tripoli in coordination with rebel groups in the Nafusa, though notably with little input from the National Transitional Council.[65] As in Misrata and the eastern front near Ajdabiya, military cooperation between rebel forces in the Nafusa mountains and their international supporters went well beyond mere aerial support and covert weapons drops. During the summer, Qatari personnel had helped Libyan Islamists from the capital establish military training camps in Nalut. These camps prepared special units from the Tripoli resistance to infiltrate the city and launch a coordinated uprising from within.[66]

By mid-August, Tripoli was surrounded. Rebel forces were converging from the liberated cities of the west, the mountains to the south, Misrata to the east, and even by sea from various destinations. Fighters from the Nafusa laid siege to Zawiya on August 13, liberating the city a week later. Then, on August 19, various resistance cells in Tripoli launched coordinated actions against the regime. Airstrikes hammered the city's defenses as well as Gaddafi's suspected hideout, the Bab Al-Aziziyyah compound, which rebel groups seized on August 23. Instead of a merciless house-to-house struggle to take the capital, one in which the regime's remaining chemical weapons might have been deployed, Tripoli fell to the rebels with very little fighting.[67] What was left of Gaddafi's security apparatus and loyalist militiamen was hardly enough to protect the leader's family, even less Libya's largest city. And to make matters worse for the Gaddafis, elite elements of their security apparatus had been conspiring with the opposition to betray the regime at the decisive moment of Tripoli's encirclement.[68] There was even a last-minute defection by Abdelsalem Jalloud, a former Prime Minister and once one of Gaddafi's closest allies. By September, Tripoli was secure enough for President Sarkozy and Prime Minister Cameron to make visits. They were followed by US Secretary of State Hillary Clinton, who met with National Transitional Council officials on October 18, two days before Gaddafi's bloody end.

What was left of the Gaddafi family began dispersing in almost every direction. Gaddafi's son Khamis, who had been directing regime forces in Tarhouna, was killed there on August 29. Gaddafi's wife Safia, along with his children Ayesha, Mohamed, and Hannibal, somehow slipped through rebel lines and fled west to Algeria. Both Saadi and Saif Al-Islam fled south, though in different convoys. While the former successfully crossed into Niger, the latter had sought protection, first, in Bani Walid, and then among the Tuareg of Libya's southwest. Saif Al-Islam was also reportedly attempting to escape the country through the desert when he was captured in the region of Ubari in November by Zintani militia members pursuing him. It has been suspected that

Abdullah Al-Senussi was with Saif Al-Islam yet somehow evaded capture. Senussi finally resurfaced months later when he was apprehended traveling to Mauritania via Morocco. Gaddafi and his son Mutassim, along with the remains of the regime's most elite guard units, fled to Sirte via interior routes that avoided the coast. Despite attempts by Gaddafi and Saif Al-Islam to open a dialogue with the rebels, these fell on deaf ears. Close relatives of the Gaddafi clan and hundreds of other key regime actors fled Libya, often to Tunisia and Egypt. Many even braved the long desert trek to Niger, such as Mansour Daw, a top security official. In some cases, it appears that the rebel town of Zintan facilitated the escape of several mid- and high-level officials, much to the dismay of Islamists and other hardline revolutionary groups.[69]

Though Tripoli had been largely spared the revolution's wrath, the same was not so for the loyalist strongholds of Bani Walid and Sirte as the noose began to tighten around Gaddafi and Mutassim. The revolutionary brigades' violent campaign to eradicate the last vestiges of the regime in September and October became increasingly brutal and indiscriminate, as did NATO's airstrikes in support of the hunt for Gaddafi.[70] Loyalist resistance in Bani Walid and Sirte proved to be more tenacious than expected, and so the revolutionary brigades were particularly reckless once they began attacking the towns' defenses in early September.[71]

Up to the very end, foreign airpower was central to the rebels' victory. The violent and unceremonious execution of Gaddafi in Sirte on October 20 – some of which was revealed in grainy cellphone videos posted to the Internet – was made possible by airstrikes from a US drone and French fighter jets, airstrikes that scattered and then disabled the convoy of trucks evacuating the Colonel.[72] Despite the fact that Cyrenaican forces had broken through Brega as far back as August 24, it was Misratan militias who would claim the war's final prize in Sirte. Amid the chaos of Gaddafi's last moments, it appears that he was unexpectedly shot dead by one of his captors, a young Misratan *thuwar*.

3 | State of the Martyrs ————————

Less than a year after Tripoli's liberation by rebel forces, there were clear indications that Libya's transition to a stable post-Gaddafi order was veering wildly off course.[1] The 2011 uprising had fragmented political power in the country and no single person or institution seemed capable of restoring competent governance at the national level. An important factor inhibiting the creation of an effective interim authority in Libya was the National Transitional Council's limited control over the militias that had toppled the Gaddafi regime, militias that, more often than not, answered to local authorities first and foremost. The Council was also riven by its own internecine violence. Although no other organization emerged to challenge its role as a figurehead, the Council's tenure was marked by opacity, internal clashes, and mismanagement, all of which exposed the numerous vulnerabilities of Libya's first post-Gaddafi government.

Politically, it was important for the National Transitional Council to insist that it was not a new regime nor would it become one. Truth be told, it could not have imposed itself on the new Libyan polity even if it had wanted to. Not only was the Council an incredibly weak institution, but various regional and local interests were also constantly outmaneuvering it. The cumulative effective of this constant rebalancing of power was to undermine the possibility of effective central governance. Indeed, this was often deliberate. The revolution, for many Libyans, now meant preventing the reemergence of an unaccountable central authority no matter the cost. For the thousands of young men organized within countless autonomous brigades, whose fluid allegiances and leadership were more local than national, the role they assigned themselves was that of protecting the spirit of the 2011 uprising and defending the memory of its martyrs.

The National Transitional Council mainly served to sell the Libyan revolution to intervention-wary leaders in the West by convincing them of its political legitimacy, military leadership, and democratic aspirations. The need for a coherent anti-Gaddafi front was also important in order to channel legitimate foreign aid – economic, humanitarian, and military – to the rebels and the population at large during the 2011 civil war. But here as well, the Council's record of successes was slim. It was frequently outflanked by entrepreneurial actors who found other ways of supporting the humanitarian needs of civilians and the military needs of the *thuwar* through informal social organizations and clandestine trade networks.

The National Transitional Council nonetheless succeeded in convincing its North Atlantic sponsors that it represented a competent body capable of guiding Libya to a new, peaceful, and democratic political reality. It also promised them a cheap and short war, followed by a smooth transition to a stable post-conflict order, one in which an international stabilization force would not be necessary. Why officials in Washington, London, and Paris were so quick to believe the Council's promises is unclear, especially given the international community's recent state-building failures following the US-led overthrow of regimes in Afghanistan in 2001 and Iraq in 2003. Indeed, the Council's April 2011 roadmap to constitutional governance in Libya, originally drafted in English, was clearly a piece of international public relations rather than an indigenous political manifesto. In retrospect, it seems as if all sides, amid the euphoria of the Arab Spring, were engaged in mutual acts of wishful thinking.[2]

Early Cracks in the Consensus: The National Transitional Council and the Uprising

As the Libyan uprising progressed, the disconnect between the National Transitional Council's technocratic leaders – many of them long-term exiles – and the revolution at large only widened. In fact, no single body or actor had control over what became a horizontally networked armed uprising consisting of autonomous resistance organizations. The Council had in fact recognized and made concessions to the highly localized nature of the Libyan polity. Its initial membership, numbering thirty-one, prioritized geographical representation over political notoriety. Most of the local Council representatives' names were kept secret during the first months of the uprising. This was to protect members and their families, particularly those representing areas under regime control in the west. After the fall of the Gaddafi regime, and as the Council expanded, its actual and evolving membership remained unclear.[3] Such opacity, though not necessarily intentional, did not augur well for more trans-parent and effective governance during the revolution and its aftermath. Nor did it bode well for women's advancement; there were never more than five women representatives on the Council during and after the 2011 uprising.[4]

Another factor inhibiting the Council from becoming an effective transitional authority was divisions within its top leadership. These divisions, which often pivoted on questions of military strategy and international diplomacy, also manifested as internal efforts to prevent the emergence of any single actor or group from gaining supremacy within the organization – an understandable reaction to Gaddafi's long tenure. The most high-profile clashes appear to have occurred between Abdul Jalil (whose authority as Council chair was frequently undermined), Prime Minister Mahmoud Jibril (who spent most of his time traveling between Europe and the Gulf representing the Libyan revolution), and Ali Al-Issawi (who ostensibly held the foreign affairs portfolio).

The rebel's military commanders were likewise divided and often accused of authoritarian tendencies as well. The Council's Minister of Defense, Omar Al-Hariri, had attempted to overthrow Gaddafi in the mid-1970s and subsequently spent many years as a political prisoner. His credentials within the opposition were seemingly impeccable. But the two leading commanders under him, Abdelfatah Younis and Khalifa Haftar, had more mixed records. Younis, a long-time Gaddafi ally and participant in the 1969 coup, was serving as the *Jamahiriyyah*'s Interior Minister at the time of the uprising. Upon defecting to the side of the February 17 uprising, Younis prevented the state's most effective units in Cyrenaica from crushing the revolt, earning him the title of commander in chief of the Free Libyan Army. Haftar, by contrast, had left the Libyan army in the 1980s to join the exiled opposition, living in the United States for many years. This happened after Gaddafi attempted to blame the disastrous war in Chad on Libya's military commanders. In the years following the February 2011 uprising, Haftar would emerge as one of the most polarizing figures in the Libyan political landscape, and he was often suspected of having had a hand in the murky July assassination of Younis, given their alleged rivalry.

Challenges to Younis's military leadership and his commitment to the revolution began to appear as the war in the east ground to a standstill.[5] An initial barrage of French bombs on March 19 stopped Gaddafi's forces from laying siege to Benghazi. This allowed the rebels to drive the loyalists back to the edges of Sirte by the end of the month. Yet in a stunning turnaround, regime fighters pressed the rebel army all the way back to Ajdabiya, reclaiming Brega. Insofar as the militias under Younis's command represented the bulk of the National Transitional Council's actual army, his failure to break past the regime's defenses along the Sirtican coast was threatening to isolate Cyrenaica's political and military leaders from the eventual battle for the capital. Meanwhile, the Misratan and Nafusa fronts were emerging as equally important and more dynamic zones of confrontation between the regime and the rebels. Younis's failure was all the more embarrassing given the extent to which his forces had benefited from extensive NATO air support and clandestine arms shipments facilitated by the Gulf states. Indeed, a sophisticated joint NATO–rebel offensive in mid-July failed to smash through the *Jamahiriyyah*'s forces, although loyalist troops were forced to retreat as far back to Ras Lanuf. As Cyrenaican forces became more isolated from the main fronts in the war, they were increasingly marginalized from the plans for decisive victory being worked out between various rebel groups in western Libya and their foreign partners. National Transitional Council commanders were entirely absent from an important July 20 meeting in Paris between Sarkozy, the heads of Misrata's Military Council, and other rebel leaders. It was there that the Misratans sought and won international support for a coordinated attack on Tripoli involving Nafusi and Misratan brigades, as well as resistance cells in Tripoli.[6]

Following the unsuccessful Brega offensive in July, the National Transitional Council recalled Younis to its headquarters. At some point along the way to Benghazi, unidentified assailants killed Younis and several of his deputies on or around July 28. Conflicting reports tell of an arrest warrant being issued for Younis, though some Council officials insisted that it had been a request for consultations. The Council also offered different and contradictory accounts of the killing and its putative authors. Much speculation has circled around the fact that Younis had served at various times as Libya's defense and interior ministers, and thus had been at the forefront of the regime's repression of Libyan dissidents. Libya's Islamists, above all, had suffered greatly in the prisons and torture centers of the regime. Older and younger jihadi veterans of Afghanistan, Libya, and Iraq were thus often accused of orchestrating what amounted to a politically motivated revenge killing against Younis. Other theories have held that Younis was still in contact with the Gaddafi regime, and so there were concerns that he might have been seeking a political solution with Gaddafi or Saif Al-Islam given the lack of headway on the battlefield and Cyrenaica's isolation from the heart of the conflict. An initial investigation by Libya's transitional authorities ultimately failed – or was unwilling – to unearth the actual network behind the slaying. Subsequent attempts found members Abdul Jalil and Mahmoud Jibril uncooperative with such investigative efforts, and one member, Ali Al-Issawi, was even directly accused of complicity in orchestrating Younis's assassination.[7]

Younis's assassination indeed came at a time that saw intense battles within the rebel leadership to define and control the revolution. In late July and early August, it was clear that the National Transitional Council had little control over the most important developments in the war, from the liberation of Misrata to the coming battle for Tripoli. Not only were the Council's mainline forces, the Army of National Liberation, mired in the Sirtica plain, its influence on the militias that would liberate Tripoli from without and within was minimal and indirect.[8] The Council leadership was also riven by internal debates over the strategy to take Tripoli and the question of who would ultimately control the capital. From the outside, critics demanded to know the extent to which former regime officials would be allowed play a role in establishing and maintaining the transitional order, from the technocrats of the *Jamahiriyyah* then dominating the Council to extremely polarizing figures such as Younis.[9] Facing the organization's seemingly imminent collapse, Abdul Jalil fired its executive body on August 8. Though Mahmoud Jibril was given the responsibility to form a new cabinet, events on the ground soon overtook the Council. Within days, Tripoli was liberated and the last elites of the Gaddafi regime were on the run, including the Colonel himself. It was not until October 3 that a new cabinet was announced. Notably, Abdul Jalil had given himself the foreign affairs portfolio.

In addition to these political and military challenges, the National Transitional Council also had to coordinate humanitarian initiatives in the regions under its control, and even some areas outside of it. Ali Tarhouni, an American-educated professor of business, was assigned the Herculean task of helping Libyans meet their basic needs. His initial work mainly involved restoring electricity and getting cash to the banks so people could buy food and other goods.

Tellingly, all kinds of commodities continued to flow easily into Libya throughout the 2011 uprising via the country's porous borders, though war premiums were high. Libyan traders already had years of experience thriving in the interstices of the *Jamahiriyyah*'s planned economy. These cross-border flows thrived because there were valuable goods that clandestine merchants could provide to Libya's neighbors in return, particularly smuggled oil.

Because of its international support, the National Transitional Council was able to skirt some of the restrictions on monetary flows and oil exports that had been enacted by the UN Security Council against the Gaddafi regime. The Council established its own central bank and national oil corporation. Procuring refined hydrocarbon products for energy, transportation, and cooking required foreign underwriting, which eventually came from Qatar. In addition to the energy crisis facing rebel authorities in Cyrenaica, which would have knock-on effects for water supply and the army's mobility, the Council faced a cash crisis as bank reserves dwindled in the summer of 2011. Again, its international backers came to the aid of the struggling revolution by creating mechanisms to allow access to funds otherwise frozen by the Security Council. Qatar and Turkey were the first states to come to the Council's rescue, with the latter literally flying $100 million in cash directly to Benghazi in July. Donations from key North Atlantic and Gulf members of the Libya Contact Group soon followed. An international disagreement over who owned hundreds of millions of freshly printed Libyan dinars, the rebels or the Gaddafi state, was only resolved after the fall of Tripoli. All in all, the National Transitional Council burned through $1.2 billion between July and November.[10]

Council member Ali Tarhouni arrived soon after the fall of Tripoli in late August to lead the transition in the capital. There he found Misratan and Nafusi brigades asserting themselves with little coordination and oversight. What leverage the Council thought it had over the revolutionary brigades from the Nafusa mountains, largely because of cash infusions flown into the region to help pay salaries,[11] was dwarfed by the spoils to be harvested from the fall of the regime, the occupation of the capital, and the rents – financial and political – to be earned from controlling state and private assets. There were also reports of systematic looting and other abuses conducted by the incoming militias in the capital and the loyalist areas in Bani Walid and Sirte. Despite the resources at the hands of the Council (e.g., control over Libya's national bank and oil company as well as support from international agencies and other governments), the occupying militias were busy establishing their own facts on the ground.

The local leadership of the armed and civil resistance in Tripoli, which had created its own parallel governance, aid, and security networks, also undermined the authority of the Council in the capital after the fall of the regime. An independent military command structure, the Tripoli Military Council, dominated by Islamists and led by Abdel Hakim Belhadj, a former commander in the Libyan Islamic Fighting Group, likewise attempted but failed to achieve hegemonic control over the city. Its hundreds of fighters were initially allied to the National Transitional Council but soon found themselves sharing the streets and infrastructure of the capital with various occupiers, Zintanis and Misratans chief among them.[12] The Supreme Security Committee, established in September 2011 by the Council, sought to regulate all the militias by bringing them under one command structure with the incentive of salaries. Its authority, however, was weakened by internal disputes and external challenges, as well as severe budgetary constraints. The regulation of militias also had the unintended effect of incentivizing more, not less, militia formation.[13] Meanwhile, neighborhoods throughout Tripoli took matters into their own hands to provide basic services, aid to the needy, and, most importantly of all, security. These forms of autonomous organization were not unlike the highly localized and privatized strategies of survival that Libyans had used to survive the failures and vagaries of the *Jamahiriyyah*. This time, however, they were doing much more than taking their economic needs into their own hands. They were meeting their own personal and communal security needs as well. And with the country now awash with more arms than the entire arsenal of Great Britain, personal and communal security was easily purchased or seized.[14]

Proliferating Centers of Power

There were several paradoxes that defined the political landscape in Libya at the end of the uprising. On the one hand, there was an immense sense of national unity that had propelled the rebellion to success. This nationalism continued to manifest as Libya's transitional authorities began the daunting task of building a new state. Behind this national consensus, however, was a patchwork of constituencies whose secondary and tertiary priorities, beyond the overthrow of the regime, likewise began to manifest in destabilizing ways. While most of Libya's new centers of power were committed to the revolution, understandings of what the revolution was and should be varied from location to location. How these centers of power – Tripoli, Misrata, the Nafusa, Cyrenaica, and the Sahara – experienced the 2011 civil war in different ways helps explain their shared failure to create a functional polity in the years that followed.

Tripoli

The emergence of distinct revolutionary identities across Libya owed as much to local and historical factors as to the ways in which the 2011 war affected each area differently. In Tripoli, countless resistance cells rapidly organized at the neighborhood level and among extended family members in February and March.[15] Alliances between militias eventually formed to represent and coordinate the revolution in the capital. Islamist networks, including the remnants of the Libyan Islamic Fighting Group, which had been most active in the 1990s, as well as a younger generation of Salafis, were particularly dominant in the capital. When Gaddafi fled at the end of August, there were 200 known resistance commanders representing a variety of locations and interest groups.[16] The most prominent umbrella organization in

Tripoli, the February 17 Coalition, was a union of traditional regime opponents (e.g., Islamists and long-time activists from the National Front for the Salvation of Libya) alongside a new generation of organized youth resistance. Defectors from the regime, notably intelligence and military officials, helped the Coalition form a military council.

As the war progressed, the Tripoli Military Council's goal was eventually to stage an urban uprising against the regime. Though Tripoli's resistance was well organized, disciplined, and had significant manpower, it initially lacked the material wherewithal to overwhelm the regime. Unlike the eastern and rural uprisings, which had benefited from significant defections of armed soldiers and quickly raided military installations (bases and depots), the urban resistance in Tripoli, where the regime's elite security forces were their strongest, had far less immediate access to weapons.

Arms were slowly and secretly brought to the capital via dozens of organizations and channels. Some of Tripoli's citizens reportedly volunteered to fight for the regime so as to obtain weapons they would use to overthrow it. Even a few state officials, working in secret with the resistance, were said to have used their access to remote stockpiles to smuggle weapons into the city. These arms were then distributed first among the networks that mattered most: the family.[17] Indeed, the risks facing these organizations were quite high. Though resistance leaders and cells took great precautions, the state's reaction to the discovery of these networks was often to "disappear" the apprehended person along with any known associates, including family members. Thus a culture of secrecy and autonomy developed among Tripoli's resistance cells out of necessity.

In Tripoli as well as elsewhere, the autonomy of the militias was often an effect of mistrust within the broader resistance, though this mistrust often had roots in the regime's decades of manipulating economic classes, social affiliations, and regional identifications. Islamists in particular were not always comfortable working with former persecutors who had defected to the revolution. Moreover, the Tripoli resistance often took issue with the National Transitional Council's military leadership for a number of reasons: the organization's decision-making was slow, circuitous, and significantly degraded after the assassination of Younis; its understanding of the realities in Tripoli was tenuous; and its plan to liberate the capital was overly reliant on foreign airpower.

When the time came for the rebel assault on Tripoli, the revolutionary forces converging from the south, west, east, and by sea found an armed and organized population already in revolt. Like the Nafusi and Misratan rebel groups that stormed the capital in August, the Tripoli resistance, led by the February 17 Coalition, would claim that they had liberated the capital in spite of – not because of – the National Transitional Council's alleged leadership. That said, the Coalition's claim of leadership was internally contested. It helped coordinate the various militias in Tripoli but had little direct control over all of them, particularly Islamists.[18] These internal disagreements within the Tripoli resistance were further complicated by the arrival of other militias who soon started seizing the capital's political, economic, and military assets. By September, Tripoli began witnessing armed clashes between the February 17 Coalition, Abdel Hakim Belhadj's Military Council, militias allied to the National Transitional Council, and other autonomous or nonaligned actors.

The power vacuum in Tripoli was further exacerbated by the National Transitional Council's initial reluctance to relocate to the capital of the *Jamahiriyyah* after the fall of the regime. Some Council members had hoped to restore Benghazi as the joint capital of Libya alongside Tripoli, as it had been under King Idris. However, it soon became clear that the fate of post-revolutionary Libya was being decided in Tripoli as fighting between the occupying militias intensified. An assertion of legitimate central authority was deemed necessary to stem the growing conflict between Tripoli's liberators, lest a powerful rival to the Council emerge.[19]

Misrata

As Tripoli became the epicenter of struggles over post-revolutionary Libya in late 2011, rival militia coalitions from

Misrata and Zintan managed to achieve a degree of dominance over all others, including the capital's own resistance cells. The city of Misrata was particularly well placed to assert itself in post-revolutionary Libya. The Misratan Military Council, for example, claimed to be in charge of coordinating over 200 different militias who served the interests of their city above those of the National Transitional Council.[20] The various other constituents that helped form the basis of Misrata's political and economic power appeared just as cohesive and just as motivated as its militias. With over half a million inhabitants, Misrata is Libya's third largest city, though very close in population to Benghazi. It is well known for its business activities and industry. Because of its deep-water port, Misrata is a major center for international trade and domestic commerce in Libya. Today, Misrata's port, the most important outside of the energy sector, hosts a free trade zone, though the city's commercial dominance was established long before the Gaddafi regime began pursuing neoliberal reforms in the early 2000s. During the months-long siege laid by Gaddafi's forces in 2011, the port was also a strategic lifeline that allowed Misrata to resist the regime. After the revolution, the city's international connections and economic independence helped it thrive when other major population centers, notably Benghazi and Tripoli, began to fall into conflict. It was also during the siege of Misrata that its civilian leadership and revolutionary brigades developed a level of military unity and a sense of political purpose that few other locales, cities, or regions obtained.[21]

A powerful resource that the city's revolutionaries drew upon during the 2011 uprising was their own history: narratives of Misratan resistance to Italian occupation, narratives of independent statehood led by Misratans, and narratives of Misratan marginalization during the Gaddafi era. This was not unlike the way in which the 2011 uprising in Cyrenaica reappropriated from the Gaddafi regime the image of Omar Mukhtar, leader of the guerrilla opposition to Italian colonization in the east in the 1920s. In Misrata, however, local histories of resistance to European subjugation had been suppressed during the Gaddafi period. This was particularly the case with the Tripolitanian Republic, a short-lived state that lasted from roughly 1918 to 1922. This Republic was led by a Misratan, Ramadan Al-Suwaihli, who has since become a local hero and icon of resistance to unjust rule. The recovery of these historical narratives helped to empower Misrata during the uprising as its leaders sought to restore their city's rightful place as a major force in Libya. It also re-forged a sense of shared identity in Misrata, whereas the capital strained under the fact that everyone was from somewhere else. At the same time, the Misratans' sense of purpose and shared identity had a dark side. Misrata's revolutionary brigades would become notorious for their abuses during and after the uprising. These abuses went beyond the violent excesses that marked the final hunt for Gaddafi and his grisly execution in Sirte. It included the widespread imprisonment, torture, and execution of suspected loyalists, as well as the wholesale ethnic cleansing of the neighboring town of Tawergha and its 40,000 residents.[22]

The excesses of the Misratan forces were often attributed to the weeks of terror the city experienced between March and May during the 2011 civil war. By many accounts, the battle for Misrata was the most ferocious and cruel of the entire uprising.[23] Starting on February 19, the city saw days of demonstrations in support of the country's growing anti-regime movement. The demonstrations, though mostly peaceful, were not tolerated by the local state forces. Dozens of protestors were killed in a vain effort to quell the uprising.

The regime's full-scale assault on Misrata finally began on March 6. Up until then, an understanding had been reached between the regime's forces, which were surrounding the city, and the local leadership: Misrata would not be subjected to further repression so long as it remained quiet. Allowing this period of respite proved to be a mistake on the part of Gaddafi's forces as the city's defenses were almost nonexistent when the uprising began. During these crucial weeks, Misrata developed its own revolutionary political leadership and nascent self-defense militias began to form. The city's revolutionaries soon aligned themselves with the National Transitional Council. And as with the Council, a respected judge, Khalifa Al-Zwawi, was chosen to head the organization. Other committees and associations were formed to administer the city and deliver services in the state's absence. As the regime continued in its efforts to suppress the revolt in the far west, in the Nafusa, and in Cyrenaica, clashes with Misrata's revolutionaries were almost inevitable as the city attempted to seize control of its own governance and security. Then, on March 6, regime forces entered Misrata to put the uprising down, only to find it was more than prepared to defend itself. In response, the regime dispatched Khamis Gaddafi and his dreaded 32nd Brigade – fresh from suppressing the uprising in Zawiya – to deal with the city.[24]

The regime's ruthless determination to retake Misrata can be understood in relation to the city's standing as the most significant rebel-controlled area in Tripolitania. For the National Transitional Council, supporting Misrata was equally important so as to keep its Tripolitanian base of resistance alive. The city's rebellion, alongside the resistance in the Nafusa mountains, countered any suggestion that the uprising was a mere east–west rivalry that could be solved on a territorial basis by granting Cyrenaica more autonomy yet with Gaddafi still retaining power in Tripolitania. Sustaining the rebellion on multiple fronts was also important for the National Transitional Council in order to divide the government's forces and offer the beleaguered Cyrenaican front some respite. For Misrata, however, survival, more than anything else, was the basis of its revolt. The Misratans put up a fierce resistance and eventually overcame the regime's forces, yet they initially faced steep disadvantages. Overcoming these disadvantages and breaking through the siege would transform the city. In February 2011, Misrata was merely one site of popular resistance. Nine months later, it emerged as one of the most powerful players in post-revolutionary Libya.

An initial lack of arms was one of the disadvantages facing Misrata's militias. Uprisings elsewhere in Libya benefited from the proximity of military bases and armories, as well as access to the outside world via Libya's western, eastern, and Saharan borders. The number of young men volunteering to fight for Misrata far outnumbered the weapons available to them. The Misratan resistance was able to collect a small number of arms from civilians and to steal others from the government (e.g., police and other internal security units). Given its encirclement and isolation in the center of the country, the city was dependent on itself and its port for survival. Some light arms were finally donated from the National Transitional Council in Benghazi in mid-March, which were smuggled into the city via small fishing vessels.

The regime forces occupied strategic points in the city, using snipers, mortars, and other indiscriminate ordnance to terrify it into submission. Misrata's urban guerrillas, however, were supported by an impressive network of civilian volunteer organizations providing everything from food to medical aid. By May, this coalition of resistance succeeded in turning the tables on the regime's forces by blocking their access and escape routes – effectively putting the occupiers under siege until they surrendered or starved.[25]

From mid-May onward, the way in which the battle for Misrata evolved holds the key to understanding how the city obtained its exceptional military coherence. Though Gaddafi's forces lost their hold on the city center, they still had Misrata surrounded as more troops and volunteers came from Tripoli and elsewhere to maintain the blockade and bombardment from the west. To the southeast, the siege was maintained through the occupation of Tawergha, where regime fighters, largely from Sirte, embedded themselves among the town's buildings and civilian population. In this new context, the battle for Misrata was no longer an irregular conflict pitting an occupying force against an urban insurgency. It was now a more symmetrical contest. The defense of the city simultaneously on three fronts required more sophisticated and robust forms of military organization. The rapid enhancement of Misrata's forces was facilitated by increased access to arms via the seaport. The assistance of NATO advisors on the ground and airpower up above also contributed to the rapid qualitative and quantitative growth of Misrata's brigades during the summer of 2011. Once the airport was recovered at the end of May, arms from Sudan and Qatar were flown directly into Misrata, which gave the city a distinct advantage in the final push to liberate the rest of Tripolitania in August. By the time of Gaddafi's death, Misrata not only boasted one of the most professional militia coalitions in Libya, it was also one of the largest, with over 30,000 registered fighters belonging to over 200 distinct brigades.[26] These brigades would go on to promote their city's interests in the name of the hundreds of Misratan *shuhada'* – martyrs – who had already died in its city's defense.

The Nafusa: Zintan and the Imazighen

After the fall of Gaddafi, the unlikely challenger to Misrata's political and military dominance in Tripolitania was Zintan, a small mountain town of approximately 20,000 inhabitants with a reputation for loyalism to the Gaddafi regime. Located in the middle of the mountain range known as the Jabal Nafusa, Zintan sits among a constellation of highland towns and villages that arc from the Tunisian border to the outskirts of Tripoli. South of the range, the mountains give way to arid plains and then the Saharan desert. This geography gave the Nafusa a distinct advantage during the rebellion. Unlike the major coastal cities that were either assaulted or occupied by the regime's forces in 2011 (e.g., Zawiya, Misrata, Ajdabiya, and Benghazi), most of the towns of the Nafusa were easily defended from the state's efforts to retake them. Moreover, the Nafusa was able to sustain its resistance to the regime given its access to Libya's borders with Tunisia, Algeria, and Niger. These routes afforded the Nafusi rebels access to international lines of financial, humanitarian, and military support. As the Italians had learned a century before, confronting a popular insurgency in the Nafusa was a daunting military challenge for any would-be occupier.[27] By the end of the 2011 uprising, Nafusi resistance not only emerged as a central element in the liberation of Tripoli, it had also done so without the kind of mass casualties experienced on the Misratan and eastern fronts.

This is not to suggest that the Nafusa got off lightly or that the Gaddafi regime did not use force in an attempt to suppress the uprising there. At the start of the uprising, there seemed to be factors working in the state's favor, particularly Zintan's tradition of loyalism to the regime. A more general factor working in the regime's favor was the diverse patchwork of communities along the Nafusa. Decades of social, political, and economic manipulation by the regime resulted in the Nafusa quickly being torn between rapidly polarizing communities – loyalist versus rebel – in February and March 2011. If anything, the Nafusa is widely known as the home of Libya's Amazigh (Berber) ethnic minority, most of them being Ibadi Muslims, whereas the vast majority of the country identify as Sunni Muslims of Arab ethnic origin. The towns of Yafran, Kabaw, Nalut, and Jadu are particularly known for Amazigh militancy. Zintan, however, is dominated by Sunni Arabs. The Gaddafi regime's suppression of the Amazigh identity was one factor that helped motivate support for the rebellion among some Amazigh communities in the Nafusa. Gaddafi's divide-and-rule approach to political management often saw Amazigh communities on the losing end of the strategy while the regime attempted to Arabize all aspects of the *Jamahiriyyah*, from personal names to education. The participation of Imazighen (Berbers) in the National Front for the Salvation of Libya, including its failed 1984 assassination plot, often led to collective punishment inflicted upon Nafusi communities. Persecution of Amazigh activists continued even during the years of piecemeal reform in the early 2000s, right up to the events of February 2011.[28]

During the early *Jamahiriyyah*, Zintan became an important regime outpost in the Nafusa. Longstanding tribal allegiances allowed the town to hold a privileged place in the system of inter-communal balancing that the Gaddafi regime used to construct and maintain order. Along the way, Zintan also developed a reputation for military acumen as its soldiers and officers climbed the ranks of the army. Though some Zintani officers participated in the failed 1993 military coup against Gaddafi, the town nonetheless continued to play an important role in the army and the social configurations underwriting the regime's hegemony in the years before the 2011 uprising. Indeed, the regime's most elite praetorian guard units stationed in and around the capital, drew recruits from Zintan as it did from other loyalist tribes like the Warfalla, Maqarha, Hasawna, Tarhouna, and, of course, Gaddafi's own Qadhadhfa.[29]

When the uprising began, Zintan's leadership was initially divided between its traditional allegiances and the popular desire for change manifesting all across Libya in mid-February 2011, including demonstrations in the streets of the town. In the Nafusa mountains, the regime attempted to recruit loyalist fighters and to intimidate otherwise noncompliant communities. Zintan's refusal to support these efforts emboldened other communities to join the rebellion, and soon alliances were built around the town's access to arms and military experience. Some communities, however, refused to join the rebellion; others claimed neutrality. The regime's allies, scattered across the Nafusa range, asserted themselves where they could. Soon the Nafusa was gridded by checkpoints and garrisons manned by loyalists and opposition fighters. As the 2011 uprising evolved, the politics of loyalism, resistance, and neutrality in the Nafusa revealed itself to be multidimensional and dynamic, drawing upon inter-regional rivalries rooted in long-established feuds, social identity, and access to resources that the *Jamahiriyyah* still controlled. Accordingly, the war in the Nafusa mountains was as much a war between Nafusi communities as it was a war between the regime and an uprising.[30]

Mirroring other sites of resistance across Libya, Zintan's forces were directed by a Military Council. This Council was headed by two key figures. One was Mohammed Al-Madani, a charismatic veteran of the Chadian war who had become a local religious figure in the years since. The other was Osama Juwaili, a former colonel in Gaddafi's army. Under their leadership and in close coordination with allied towns, the regime's efforts to reoccupy the Nafusa were halted. The result was a partial siege of the Nafusa in which the regime often engaged in indiscriminate bombardment from its positions below the mountains. Controlling the Tunisian frontier was a key priority for both the rebels and the regime, as evidenced by the fact that control over the Wazin border post changed hands several times. On March 2, the regime deployed an elite unit from the 32nd "Khamis" Brigade there. This move initially forced rebels to develop clandestine routes across Libya's frontiers as a stopgap measure. The fighting near the border even spilled into Tunisia during one battle in late April. Regime forces frequently lobbed artillery shells and fired rockets at rebel forces using Tunisia as a safe haven, though these indiscriminate attacks also put the Libyan refugee camps near Dehiba, Tunisia, at risk.[31] Zintani leaders also called upon longstanding connections with Saharan communities, notably allies from the Tuareg and Tebu ethnic minorities, to build support and supply systems. These networks were founded as much on traditional solidarities as they were on modern state institutions. Zintanis and their Saharan allies had all helped staff the regime's core security units in the final years of the *Jamahiriyyah*.[32]

From the air, NATO and the Arab League offered little direct support to Nafusi rebels until the middle of the summer. French weapons drops, however, helped the Zintani-led resistance to hold off the assaulting regime forces. On the ground, military aid and advising, along with humanitarian and other material assistance, flowed from the Gulf states of Qatar, the United Arab Emirates, and Oman via the Tunisian frontier, the latter of the three being motivated to support Libya's small community of fellow Ibadi Muslims. By May, military training camps were being established and a makeshift runway had been constructed; high-level visits from foreign advisors and even National Transitional Council executives followed in June.

The National Transitional Council's military leaders, notably Omar Al-Hariri, who visited the Nafusa in mid-July, attempted to bring Zintan under its control so as to create a unified military command and a coordinated strategy. These efforts bore mixed results because of the Nafusa's growing sense of independence and the widening divisions between the military leaders in each community, particularly between Nalut and Zintan. Divisions within the Nafusi resistance had already been exacerbated by the death of Mohammed Al-Madani on

May 1 and how Gulf patronage favored particular communities, leaders, and ideologies (i.e., Islamism). Inter-communal rivalry and clashes in the Nafusa continued in the months after Gaddafi's fall.[33] Zintan's leaders nonetheless successfully positioned themselves as the dominant political and military force in the region. Once viewed as marginal to the Libyan uprising, Nafusi resistance proved to be the decisive force that drove the Gaddafi regime out of Tripoli.[34]

From this point onward, Zintan's ambitions only increased, as did the number of revolutionaries joining its brigades. In the chaos of Tripoli's liberation, Zintani fighters were notorious for their looting activities. Everything from light arms to heavy construction equipment was seized and taken back home. Zintan's military connections in the former regime not only allowed it to target and confiscate key state assets, they also allowed it to obtain key responsibilities in the capital, such as serving as security for Mahmoud Jibril's office and controlling the main international airport. Zintan also gained control over the major oil fields in southwestern Libya, Elephant and Sharara. Manning all of these security commitments required building a force that extended well beyond the residents of Zintan or even the Nafusa. Zintan's military leadership built its coalition with those whom it trusted the most: former members of the Gaddafi regime's security services. Zintani power was also built upon traditional inter-communal alliances. Naturally, Zintan and its politico-military coalition were accused of being too close to the old regime, if not reconstituting it in a new form. For such critics, it was telling that the town's brigades did not participate in rebel assaults on the loyalist strongholds of Sirte and Bani Walid in September and October 2011. In early 2012, Bani Walid overthrew the local leadership that the National Transitional Council had imposed on it, a move that received Zintan's support. Latent loyalism, however, has been a weak predictor of Zintani behavior since the 2011 uprising. For example, Libyan ambassador Omar Brebesh, a Gaddafi loyalist, was detained, tortured, and murdered by Zintani militia members in Tripoli in January 2012.[35]

Zintan's greatest war prize and a key bargaining chip in the post-revolutionary environment was undoubtedly Saif Al-Islam, having found and captured him in November 2011 in the region of Ubari. Although Saif Al-Islam's prolonged detention in Zintan might have seemed contrary to the town's reputation for loyalism, it is likely that he would have suffered a far worse fate had he been captured by any other militia force or rendered to the International Criminal Court. Shortly after Saif Al-Islam's capture, Osama Juwaili was awarded the post of Minister of Defense in the new cabinet announced by the National Transitional Council that month. While the town's leaders refused to give up Saif Al-Islam to any other legal authority (domestic or international), they allowed him to be tried by a court in Tripoli in 2015, appearing via a video link from his Zintan prison. When a divisive national reconciliation and amnesty law was later passed by one of Libya's two contending governments, authorities in Zintan freed Saif Al-Islam and likely facilitated passage to a safe hiding place elsewhere in the country.

Saif Al-Islam's 2011 capture in the desert was also indicative of the new political economy that was driving Zintan's rise to power. The collapse of the Gaddafi regime precipitated conflicts among Nafusi communities over who would now control the flow of goods and people across Libya's western frontiers. Seizing the opportunity, Zintan quickly asserted itself as an important gatekeeper and facilitator of the various forms of trade – legal and otherwise – in the western Nafusa and the deserts of the Fezzan, particularly the lucrative international market in light arms looted from Gaddafi's arsenals. In addition to these active elements of Zintani power, there were passive elements as well. Saif Al-Islam was not the only hostage held to further Zintani interests. Major western oil pipelines and, more critically, pumping stations were also under Zintan control. These assets gave Zintan immense leverage as regional and national spoilers in the months and years to come.[36]

Fezzan and the Sahara

Like the Nafusa, Libya's vast Saharan interior – insofar as

it could be considered a single region – was viewed as an important zone of regime support when the uprising began in 2011. It was widely suspected that many non-Arab communities in Libya's Sahara would heed Gaddafi's call when he threatened to raise an army of African mercenaries to crush the February 17 movement. Gaddafi had long styled himself a man of Africa's great desert, and had frequently meddled in Saharan and Sahelian affairs. These episodes included the dispute over Western Sahara between Morocco and Sahrawi nationalists, the various Tuareg uprisings in Mali and Niger in the 1990s and early 2000s, the Darfur conflict between Khartoum and rebels in western Sudan, and – of course – his disastrous war in Chad in the 1970s and 1980s over the disputed Aouzou Strip. In reality, Gaddafi's allies in the Sahara did not rally to his cause *en masse*; many in fact joined the ranks of the rebellion or otherwise steered clear of the drama being played out along Libya's Mediterranean coast.[37] What actually occurred among Libya's Saharan populations was, again, not unlike the political dynamics witnessed in the Nafusa: the overlapping national struggles of the 2011 revolution intensified and transformed longstanding local conflicts that were often as deeply rooted in history as they were in the regime's four decades of social, economic, and political manipulations. Not only did these divisions play out between the major ethnic groups of the Libyan Sahara during the 2011 uprising, but there were also important divisions within each group. To brand any particular group as entirely "loyalist," one observer noted, "is a reductionist view that belies the complexities of their relationship with the Qadhafi regime."[38]

Of the three main populations in the Libyan Sahara (Arab, Tuareg, and Tebu), it was the Tebu of Libya's southeast who had been the most marginalized within the *Jamahiriyyah*. The Tebu people's traditional homeland was trisected by European colonialism into the modern states of Libya, Chad, and Niger, the latter two ranking among the world's poorest countries since gaining independence from France in 1960. The precariousness of life in the Sahara-Sahel, compounded by significant droughts in the mid-1970s and early 1980s, resulted in Tebu populations often seeking relief in oil-rich Libya. Despite Gaddafi's support for African liberation and his fondness for Saharan peoples, Tebu language and culture were constantly under assault by the *Jamahiriyyah*'s aggressive Arabization programs, as were the Amazigh cultures in the Nafusa mountains and the Tuareg of the southwest.[39] That Gaddafi's war against Chad over the Aouzou Strip (1978–87) was largely conducted on Tebu land further complicated political loyalties and socio-economic livelihoods, particularly when the Colonel sponsored one Tebu rebel leader, Goukouni Oueddei, against Chad's Tebu President, Hissene Habré. The ambivalence of the Gaddafi state toward the Tebu was likewise reflected in issues of citizenship and development, especially as Arab, Tuareg, and Tebu communities competed for resources in the expanding urban spaces of the Libyan Sahara, notably Ubari, Murzuq, Sebha, and Kufra. Tebu fighters joined the ranks of the internal security apparatuses the regime developed after the 1993 coup attempt, notably the Faris Brigade. Tebu responsibility for enforcing rule in central Sahara, however, was shared with the preeminently loyal Arabs from the Qadhadhfa, the Awlad Sulayman, and Sirte.[40] One of the most dramatic moves Gaddafi made against the Tebu was in 2007, when he revoked the citizenship of thousands. This provoked a major uprising the following year in Kufra, which the regime ruthlessly confronted with military force.[41]

For these and a number of other reasons, key Tebu opposition leaders, led by Issa Abdulmajid Mansour, were more than ready to revolt against the *Jamahiriyyah* in 2011, and largely did so with little aid from the National Transitional Council. Though the Council was eager to use the Tebu to demonstrate the widespread nature of the uprising, providing material support to the Saharan front was beyond the capacity of the Benghazi-based leadership. The Tebu, however, benefited from military support from Sudan, which had become acutely enraged by Gaddafi's recent meddling in the Darfur conflict.[42] Gaddafi's efforts to rally Tuareg against Tebu were preempted by traditional alliances that helped maintain peace between the communities. The

National Transitional Council also promised a powerful incentive to Saharan communities if they joined the rebellion: full citizenship. Securing their support for the rebellion, whether passive or active, would not only deny the regime fighters, it would also help guarantee that the February 17 revolution would not have to worry about its Saharan flank (e.g., Gaddafi's illusory battalions of African volunteer soliders). The regime's power was further eroded when Tebu militias helped occupy Libya's largest oil fields in the name of the revolution.[43]

These arrangements would carry into the post-revolutionary situation. Control over aspects of trans-Saharan commerce (legal and illicit) and protecting oil fields provided Tebu communities with significant political leverage, though these efforts to dominate the south in the name of the revolution would not go uncontested. Armed clashes between Tebu, Arab, and Tuareg communities – from Ubari in the west to Kufra in the east – continued to erupt well beyond the end of the *Jamahiriyyah*. Fighting in early 2012 claimed hundreds of lives before a ceasefire was enacted on April 1. Even the ostensibly neutral peacekeeping force sent from Benghazi to the Sahara, part of the Ministry of Defense's Libya Shield forces, was dragged into the Tebu–Arab fighting. Sebha witnessed deadly clashes between all three major communities, Arab, Tebu, and Tuareg alike, during the same period.[44] These conflicts were mainly over territory, resources, and trade routes. Tebu leaders strongly suspected that even the "nonaligned" Libya Shield forces were actually sent to Kufra to assert central government control over key Saharan resources and routes so that the benefits went north instead of south. Arab leaders in Kufra, however, alleged that the Tebu had used their affiliation with the National Transitional Council to wrest control over the flow of goods into and out of Libya's southeastern borders.[45] There were also allegations that significant numbers of Tebu were moving from Chad to Libya, taking advantage of the post-revolutionary chaos to claim residency if not citizenship. Tebu leaders, however, claimed that these were Libyans who had been stripped of their rights by the ousted regime.[46]

As much as claims to loyalism, resistance, and martyrdom were shaping the new Libyan polity, so too were opposing assertions over national identity. With so much at stake, debates over who was truly Libyan – and therefore who was not – gained an ominous power. Given the nature of the Libyan state since the 1960s, one in which an impressive welfare regime was built upon massive oil revenues, citizenship was an important tool of the Gaddafi regime. It was frequently used to entice loyalism among Saharan populations whose traditional homelands had been spatially disrupted by modern territorial boundaries. Libya's economic boom in the age of oil also drew many sub-Saharan Africans into the labor force to fill the need for informal, unskilled, or low-wage labor. When economic times were good, racism and xenophobia were minimalized; when times were bad, raising questions about citizenship in Libya was a thinly veiled attempt to delineate "native" and "white" Arab populations from "foreign" and "black" populations like the Tebu, the Tuareg, and the Tawerghans, as well as sub-Saharan Africans either seeking work in Libya or passing through on their way to Europe.

Among Libya's Arab populations in the north and the Imazighen of the Nafusa, there was often a feeling of resentment toward African populations because of the spending Gaddafi had lavished on his sub-Saharan allies while neglecting basic needs at home. After the fall of the regime in late 2011, citizenship debates among and about Libya's Saharan populations were already fraught given the socio-economic rights that citizenship had entailed in the *Jamahiriyyah* (i.e., housing, work, and other benefits). As the transitional authorities in Tripoli began the process of organizing elections in mid-2012, and as the nation began debating the shape of its future constitution, racialized discourses of nativism and citizenship affected Libya's Saharan populations most of all. Fezzani demands for greater regional autonomy, for example, were viewed suspiciously in the north either as a stepping-stone for Tebu and Tuareg independence or as an effort to gain control over vital Saharan resources like oil. These debates were rendered all the more ominous given rival assertions over who was allowed to protect the 2011 revolution, and protect it by force if need be.

One of the most powerful reverberations of the 2011 revolution in the Libyan Sahara was its effect upon neighboring Mali the following year. In January 2012, there was renewed fighting in the north of the country, a region that had seen decades of armed Tuareg resistance to authorities in Bamako. The rebel gains in northern Mali in 2012 led to a military coup in March over President Amadou Toumani Touré's handling of the conflict. With the Malian government destabilized and the military retreating from the north, the next two months saw several stunning victories by an uneasy coalition of Tuareg nationalists and trans-national Islamists based in the Sahara. Eventually the Islamists displaced the Tuareg nationalists as the ostensible leadership of the breakaway territory, a move that hastened calls for international intervention. The old vision of a secular Tuareg "Kurdistan" in the central Sahara, the republic of Azawad, disappeared under the tyrannical rule of Islamist puritans.[47] French military forces eventually intervened in early 2013 to push the Islamists out of the major population centers and back into their Saharan hideouts. For many observers, there were two factors that made the crisis in northern Mali possible. The first was the destruction of the *Jamahiriyyah,* which unleashed untold quantities of arms across Libya's ungovernable borders into the Sahel's trade networks. The second factor was one of Libya's main Saharan populations, the Tuareg, whose status in post-Gaddafi Libya was rendered as ambivalent as that of the Tebu.[48]

With the sudden end of the French empire in Northwest Africa in the 1960s, the Tuareg found their traditional Saharan homelands divided among the postcolonial states of Algeria, Burkina Faso, Libya, Mali, and Niger. For the Tuareg, a nomadic population known for maintaining some of the Sahara's longest and oldest trade routes, the imposition of new states and boundaries in the latter twentieth century created as many opportunities as it did difficulties. In Mali and Niger, longstanding Tuareg opposition to the governing authorities was rooted in their extreme geographical, political, and economic marginalization from the centers of power in the capital cities. Oil-rich Algeria and Libya, by contrast, were better able to project some of the benefits of their welfare states to their southern hinterlands. For Algiers and Tripoli, co-opting Tuareg populations – allowing their freedom of movement while focusing development efforts on their Saharan interiors – had an important national security element: the majority of North Africa's oil and gas fields lie somewhere in the Libyan and Algerian Sahara. Tuareg mobility across the central Sahara had been largely unimpeded prior to the rise of Islamist militancy following the civil conflict in Algeria in the 1990s, a development that was as concerning for states in the region as for the North Atlantic powers after 9/11. As the Saharan terrorism threat grew, it decimated crucial tourist revenues for Tuareg communities in Mali, Niger, and Algeria. More and more Tuareg youths were thus drawn to other modes of economic survival. Islamist activities in the Sahara soon began to intermingle with the various forms of Tuareg-dominated commerce running up and down the desert, everything from knock-off cigarettes to human trafficking. Catalyzed by the collapse of the Libyan state in 2011, the events in Mali in 2012, followed by a terrorist assault on a Saharan gas instal-lation in Algeria in 2013 by Al-Qaida, brought the question of trans-Saharan security to the attention of the international community, but these developments also had the effect of further constraining Tuareg livelihoods.

Prior to the 2011 revolution, Tuareg communities had played a key role in the trans-Saharan trade networks that had developed as a result of the economic systems in Libya and Algeria. The two countries' development strat-egies, which involved state subsidies on imported goods and oil, meant that these commodities could be sold for hefty profits in neighboring states. In exchange, things that could not be procured in Libya and Algeria, owing to the ineffi-ciencies in their state-dominated economic systems, would be smuggled back north. Indeed, one of the ways in which Libya eased the pain of international sanctions in the 1990s was through trans-Saharan smuggling. These lucrative flows were orchestrated at the highest levels of the regime, and so implicated Tuareg communities in its survival. The reputation of the Tuareg for loyalism to Gaddafi thus went beyond their formal role in the *Jamahiriyyah* as either recruits into the regime's various security forces (e.g., the Islamic Legion and the Maghawir Brigade) or government functionaries holding key posts in the southwest in districts such as Ghat, Ubari, and Ghadames. Tuareg loyalism was also a result of the ways in which Gaddafi positioned himself as a key intermediary in Tuareg disputes with Niamey and Bamako, as Libya's oil wealth was frequently used to help make the peace. Citizenship was also another way to entice Tuareg support, as when it was offered in 2005 to those willing to serve in elite regime security units such as the Maghawir Brigade.[49]

Thus Gaddafi called upon these key Saharan intermediaries to come to his aid when the uprising began in 2011. One of the most prominent regime allies was Amid Husain Al-Kuni, the Tuareg governor of Ghat, whose attempts to recruit mercenaries in 2011 landed him on the UN sanctions list. The Tuareg who answered Gaddafi's call in February and March 2011 were few in number, apart from those already serving in the security forces. Those that escaped the war alive faced the wrath of Libya's revolutionary brigades in the months and years that followed. In Ghadames, for example, supporters of the uprising drove many of the town's Tuareg away by destroying or seizing their homes and businesses.[50]

The most important role played by loyalist Tuareg in the uprising was helping key figures in the regime escape to Niger in 2011 and 2012. Beyond that, important Tuareg population centers like Ghat and Ubari fell to the revolution in late 2011 with little fighting. Nonetheless, many young Tuareg, dispossessed of their former jobs in Libya and otherwise persecuted in the wake of the February 17 revolution, were soon drawn to fight with their brethren in northern Mali. They brought with them troves of light weapons that Gaddafi had entrusted to his Saharan delegates.[51] Amid the chaos of late 2011, North Atlantic governments scrambled to secure Libyan weapons that could be used in international terrorist attacks (e.g., undeclared chemical and biological agents, along with highly portable surface-to-air missiles). These governments, however, were powerless to do anything about reports coming from Algeria, Egypt, Israel, Niger, and Tunisia that indicated that disturbing amounts of arms were flooding out of Libya, making their way to conflict zones in Africa and the Middle East.[52] Facilitating these flows along Libya's western corridors was an alliance of Zintani and Tuareg militias who began to dominate the circulation of arms, migrants, drugs, and other commodities from the Fezzan to the Nafusa to the Mediterranean coast.[53]

The East: Cyrenaica

For many Cyrenaicans, the 2011 uprising was as much a revolt against Tripolitanian hegemony as it was a revolt against the Gaddafi regime. Domestically and internationally, there was little surprise that the uprising began in Cyrenaica, and that Benghazi became the provisional capital of the revolutionary forces during the war against the regime. Among the various factors driving the initial February 2011 protests in Benghazi, there was Cyrenaicans' sense of having historically formed their own unique identity independent of Tripolitania, of having fiercely resisted the Italian occupation, and of having been the geographical, social, and political base of support for the first Libyan state. Brandishing the tricolor flag of the Sanusi monarchy in February 2011 not only resurrected a symbol strongly associated with Libya before Gaddafi, the flag visualized the tripartite regionalism – Tripolitania, Cyrenaica, and Fezzan – that the Gaddafi regime had tried so hard to efface. These symbolic gestures were, for many, rooted in sincere feelings that Cyrenaica had been disenfranchised within the *Jamahiriyyah* system despite the east's contributions to the modernization of the country from 1969 onward, particularly with respect to the region's oil wealth. Though Gaddafi's coup and the order he created would not have been possible without drawing upon traditional bases of social power in the east via military allies and tribal allegiances, Cyrenaica nonetheless represented a potential reservoir of opposition that had to be managed if not disabled over the course of four decades. This not only meant a process of extirpating Sanusi elements from the government and military, it also entailed a process of undermining the monarchy's sources of religious power (i.e., Sufi institutions) and its sources of social power (i.e., by redistributing land, crippling historically dominant families, and empowering subordinate ones). Benghazi, in particular, felt institutionally disenfranchised within the *Jamahiriyyah*; what efforts King Idris had made to establish the city as the shared capital of Libya were similarly undone after 1969.[54] There were a number of other features of the *Jamahiriyyah* that betrayed the regime's fundamental distrust of Cyrenaica. For example, the most elite regime security unit stationed in Benghazi in early 2011, the Fadil Brigade, was heavily staffed by recruits drawn from loyalist communities in Tripolitania.[55]

Cyrenaica's importance to the nation is nonetheless a brute fact. The region comprises half of Libya's landmass and over a third of its population. More importantly, it is home to Libya's largest and most productive oil fields, accounting for over three-quarters of the country's output. Cyrenaica was also the site of the first phase of the Great Man-Made River project.[56] Despite these contributions to the consolidation of the Gaddafi state, east–west tensions in Libya were a salient rift sitting below the surface of the *Jamahiriyyah*. Though narratives of Cyrenaican marginalization under Gaddafi were sometimes exaggerated, aspirations for autonomy, if not outright independence, remain deeply seeded among swaths of the region's population. That Cyrenaica even remained part of modern Libya after World War II was not a foregone conclusion at the time. There were considerable regional and international forces that could have easily pushed it toward independence. And since the 2011 revolution, some of the strongest voices for a federalist Libyan state have come from Cyrenaica, or, as it is called in classical Islamic geography, *Al-Barqah*.

Following the widespread and virtually simultaneous civil, military, and political mutiny across Cyrenaica in February 2011, the major cities of the eastern Libyan coast, from Benghazi to Tobruk, were largely untouched by the war between the regime and the revolutionaries. Coastal Tripolitania, by contrast, witnessed fierce battles and protracted sieges throughout the conflict, from the repression of the revolt in Zawiyya to the Gaddafis' last stand in Sirte. Owing to NATO's intervention, Benghazi was spared the worst of the regime's wrath after Gaddafi's forces broke through the rebel's frontlines in Ajdabiya in March.

Though revolutionaries in the west and the Sahara often viewed the National Transitional Council as a political body dominated by Cyrenaican interests, it in fact had little direct control and very limited influence over the various militia coalitions fighting the regime along Tripolitania's coast and in its highlands. To its credit, the Council resisted appeals for territorial compromise with the regime during the 2011 crisis, one that would have created a federal state but otherwise abandoned Tripolitania to Gaddafi's continued rule. Though this act of solidarity helped the revolution achieve its maximal aim of regime change, many in Cyrenaica felt betrayed as the capital quickly reemerged as the locus of power in post-Gaddafi Libya. The relative peacefulness of Cyrenaica in 2011 did not last, either. As the National Transitional Council decamped for Tripoli, various regional, national, and transnational interests would slowly drag Benghazi into a spiral of insecurity and violence. The September 11, 2012, attacks on US diplomatic and intelligence compounds in Benghazi, resulting in the death of the US Ambassador, only served to elucidate the intense divisions underlying the new Libyan polity that were erupting in Cyrenaica as much as elsewhere.

The historical development of Cyrenaican identity was a natural consequence of the country's geographical bifurcation, its development in the shadow of Egyptian might, and the strategies of rule deployed by Ottoman, Italian, and Anglo-American imperialists. In Cyrenaica, modern political life had been dominated by the *Sanusiyyah*, a Sufi brotherhood that had become a major social and economic force all across the region and into the Sahara and the Sahel by the late 1800s. The political character of modern Tripolitania, by contrast, was dominated by the relationship between two very different and contending forces: the traditional and localized bases of power outside the capital versus the urban elites of Tripoli, which included foreign rulers, their local deputies, and a nascent working class. The socio-economic dominance of the *Sanusiyyah* and its political transformation into a hereditary monarchy under British sponsorship allowed King Idris to present himself as the only coherent political force capable of governing an independent Libya in the mid-twentieth century. The 1969 military coup in Libya not only afforded the Gaddafi regime the opportunity to purge the government of all traces of the Sanusis, it was also an opportunity to subordinate the alliance of social forces in Cyrenaica that had underwritten and coordinated Sanusi power.

The durability of the *Sanusiyyah* in Cyrenaican political life, and its strong relationship to aspirations for regional equality, was embodied in National Transitional Council member Ahmad Zubair Al-Sanusi, descendent of the late, deposed king and champion of the eastern interests. Also leading the original National Transitional Council were two prominent figures whose powerful Cyrenaican families had historical ties to Sanusi power: Chair Mustafa Abdul Jalil and rebel military commander Abdelfatah Younis. The reemergence of old alliances was complemented by the flourishing of a long-repressed civil society across the east of the country.[57] Through its civic, political, and military coalition, Cyrenaica's traditional bases of power were well positioned to pursue their mutual interests and the interests of the region in post-revolutionary Libya. By early 2012, leaders favoring Cyrenaican autonomy were a vocal constituency within the regional transitional authority. A March 2012 conference of regional leaders and activists held in Benghazi, the Barqah Council, saw the vast majority of participants vote in support of a unilateral declaration of regional autonomy. These leaders likewise expressed discontent that the National Transitional Council had so quickly abandoned Benghazi after the fall of Gaddafi, and that it seemed to be continuing the process of relocating state institutions to Tripoli.[58]

Support for federalism in Libya has long been viewed suspiciously in the west of the country. There are concerns that such proposals have been about much more than an equitable distribution of state power and national wealth. Calls for federalism or Cyrenaican autonomy were often dismissed as attempts by traditional elites in the east – the old coalition of Sa'da tribes and the Sanusis – to reclaim and consolidate their lost national influence after the 1969 coup.[59] Opponents of regional devolution went beyond the Gaddafi regime; a range of groups and personalities within Libya, from the Grand Mufti, Al-Sadiq Al-Ghariani (Libya's highest religious authority), to the Muslim Brotherhood, have opposed federalism or eastern autonomy. Even within Cyrenaica, there were skeptics and opponents of federalism and autonomy. Though the federalists claimed to have the support of their own army, the *Jaysh Al-Barqah*, one of the region's largest militia coalitions actually opposed the March 2012 autonomy declaration.[60]

Between the cracks of the dominant coalitions in Cyrenaica emerged other political visions for the region and for the country as a whole. In the wake of the 2011 uprising, Cyrenaica's Islamist groups were as heavily armed as those militias claiming allegiance to national, regional, and local authorities. Three of the largest Cyrenaican brigades – Omar Mukhtar, February 17, and the Abu Salim Martyrs – were either led by, largely constituted by, or heavily influenced by Islamists of various tendencies, whether moderate reformists, conservative Salafis, or transnational jihadis.[61] As in Tripoli, the networks that formed the Libyan Islamic Fighting Group in the 1990s never really disappeared and easily reconstituted themselves during the revolt of 2011. In Cyrenaica, the Fighting Group and the Muslim Brotherhood had constructed particularly robust clandestine organizations over the decades, networks that the Gaddafi regime attempted to co-opt in the 2000s.

The struggle against Gaddafi and, more importantly, the struggle to influence the direction of the country afterward, saw new Islamist organizations enter the fray as well, ones that deployed networks of orthodox Salafi preachers and practitioners. Whereas the majority of the Salafi movement in Libya was apparently of the so-called "quietist" variety, more activist and even militant strands were empowered by the 2011 uprising. These Salafi fighters were often veterans of the war against the Soviet Union in Afghanistan and the Libyan Islamic Fighting Group or their descendants (both familial and ideological). Some also represented first-generation Al-Qaida fighters, former detainees from the US military prison in Guantanamo, Cuba, and even recent veterans of the insurgency against the US occupation of Iraq. Though some worked hand-in-hand with the mainstream of the revolution, other jihadi groups were openly hostile to the secular veneer of the National Transitional Council. For its part, the Council approached these Islamist groups and figures with extreme caution, recognizing their ability to taint international perceptions of the Libyan uprising. The isolated eastern city of Derna, in particular, gained a reputation for Islamist militancy, one dating back several decades. Indeed, there are indicators that the assassination of Younis was at the hands of Islamists from Derna who were seeking revenge against the former defense minister.[62] After the revolution, radical Islamists proved to be some of the most highly organized and motivated political coalitions not only in Derna, but in specific parts of Benghazi as well.[63]

From the National Transitional Council to the General National Congress

While the events of 2011 in Libya represented a period of sustained national unity, the civil war that emerged out of the February 17 uprising irreparably fractured the polity in ways that the National Transitional Council was incapable of admitting, much less managing. The original transitional plan developed by the Council in April 2011, largely by its leading political intellectuals, Mahmoud Jibril and Fathi Baja, envisioned an aggressive nine-month deadline for the creation and implementation of a new constitution, to be followed by the staging of a national vote for Libya's first democratically elected government. This process would be overseen by an enlarged transitional authority, a congress, with delegates drawn from almost every locality in Libya. Criticisms of the April 2011 roadmap often focused on its overly ambitious timetable, particularly the speed with which a constitution would receive popular ratification within such a remarkably short timeframe. After the fall of Tripoli in August 2011, there were also concerns that the now enlarged National Transitional Council was still dominated by technocratic expertise rather than democratically elected representatives from Libya's diverse regions and communities.[64] It soon became clear that, in the rush to war in early 2011 and in the effort to win it, Libya's transitional leaders had given as little thought to the "day after" issues of state-building and nationbuilding as had their North Atlantic supporters. Above all, no one, it seems, ever imagined the extent to which the revolutionary militias, rather than the old regime, would become the primary obstacle to post-conflict order and stability.

During the long summer of 2011, the National Transitional Council continued to work on what would become its Constitutional Declaration of August 3. The Declaration, which contained standard language regarding the rule of law and human rights, proposed that the democratically elected authorities would form an interim administration to keep the government running and write a new constitution. The Declaration also stipulated a formal starting date for the transition, which was the day the Council entered Tripoli and declared the civil war over. It was widely acknowledged that nine months was not enough time, and so the proposed transitional period was extended. Over the summer of 2011, other stakeholders also attempted to influence this process by proposing guiding documents and even rival constitutions for a new Libya. These stakeholders included everyone from individual Islamists and new militia coalitions to longstanding opposition groups, civil society activists, and regional interest blocs, notably Fezzani and Cyrenaican devolutionists, federalists, and autonomists. As a result of these divisive debates, the election of a new authority to replace the National Transitional Council was given priority. Though this body would still be transitional, it would at least be popularly legitimated rather than self-appointed.[65]

Once the Council entered Tripoli on October 23, the clock began ticking on the Declaration's timetable for elections and a new constitution. It gave Libya's transitional authorities until mid-2013 (i.e., twenty months or less) to complete two key steps. First, Libya would hold national elections – the first in Libya since the 1960s – in 2012 for a General National Congress. Out of these elections, a transitional government would be formed. Secondly, the interim government would engender a constitutional drafting body. Once a draft constitution was written, it would be subjected to a national consultation process and finally a country-wide referendum. Assuming its passage, Libyans would then complete the third step: the vote for Libya's first constitutional government as a republic.

In retrospect, the least realistic aspect of this proposed transition to constitutional governance was the time allotted to the process of drafting, revising, and ratifying the constitution: a mere three months (August to October 2012). What made this seem overly idealistic was the growing and formidable list of challenges and dilemmas facing Libya's new authorities. These included the need to reestablish national security while disarming the popular militias; empowering local governance while undoing the institutions of the *Jamahiriyyah*; providing basic services in the absence of legitimate authority and competent bureaucrats; asserting control over Libya's financial, infrastructural, military, and natural resource wealth, which had fallen into the hands of countless militias; upholding the rule of law without functional courts, prisons, and police; and, finally, initiating a process of national reconciliation in a situation where revolutionary fighters had committed as many horrendous crimes as those attributed to the Gaddafi regime and its loyalist allies.[66]

In late October, Jibril stepped aside to make way for a new Prime Minister, Abdurrahim El-Kib, an American-trained professor of engineering from a notable Tripolitanian family. A new twenty-eight-member executive body within the National Transitional Council, mandated to govern until elections in June 2012, was then announced in late November. The Council itself had nearly tripled in size, numbering eighty-eight. This Council was immediately confronted with the brewing militia crisis, a crisis that had led to sporadic clashes between rival groups and widespread demands from the *thuwar* for compensation, if not regular salaries. Libya's security crisis was exacerbated by the need to pay public workers to keep the country's basic services running. As the United Nations began unlocking Libya's financial assets (initially $20 billion out of some $150 billion under foreign control), more and more militias demanded remuneration for their service; in one instance, El-Kib was even held at gunpoint by a militia seeking compensation.

In an effort to get out in front of the militia problem, Libya's interim authorities appointed a new military chief of staff with strong ties to Misrata and Cyrenaica, Youssef Al-Mangoush, a retired officer from Gaddafi's special forces who had joined the rebellion in the east. The interim Interior Minister, Fawzi Abdel A'al, who would be in charge of folding many of the militias into the police forces, both local and national, also hailed from Misrata. Balancing them out was Osama Juwaili of Zintan, who held the defense portfolio in the new government. Though local frustration in Tripoli with the new occupiers often led to militias maintaining a lower profile, the National Transitional Council nonetheless accepted the presence of Zintani and Misratan *thuwar* as a necessary security measure for the time being and doled out high-level appointments accordingly.[67]

In some ways, the *thuwar*, having formed the Supreme National Council for Revolutionaries in early 2012, were more organized than Libya's civil authorities. This council, representing some 200 distinct brigades, not only acted as a kind of labor union for militias, it also assigned itself the role of being the revolution's ultimate guarantor.[68]

Technocracy or Islamism? The July 2012 Elections

As Libya headed toward its first national plebiscite since the days of King Idris, a number of basic electoral issues had to be decided by the National Transitional Council, all of which would become further points of contention between Libya's new centers of power. Registering voters, mapping districts, gender quotas, and candidate eligibility criteria all had to be established. Threats of electoral boycott, if not armed action, pushed the Council to make a number of controversial concessions. These concessions revealed the extent to which centralized governance was being held hostage to localized interests. Islamists, for example, succeeded in eliminating a 10 percent female quota in the General National Congress and restrictions on identity-based parties, whether ethnic or religious. Federalist sentiments, meanwhile, succeeded in having the sixty seats in the constitutional drafting body distributed equally between Tripolitania, Cyrenaica, and Fezzan, although seats in the transitional Congress ultimately did not reflect a proposed split of 100, 60, and 40, respectively. While some Fezzani leaders often suggested that federalism would be the only means to counterbalance the demographic hegemony of Tripolitania, opponents of federalism often alleged that the country's southern regions were being flooded by Tebu and Tuareg peoples from Libya's poorer neighbors, people who were seeking to affect the vote and take advantage of the country's robust welfare state. Critics of these post-revolutionary discourses of citizenship and "Libyanness" saw them as a perpetuation of the kind of racism that allowed "white" Libyan Arabs to maintain or reassert their socio-economic and political privileges over other minority populations like the Tawerghans, Tebu, and Tuareg. Waging their own identitarian struggle, Amazigh activists in the Nafusa, keen to see their language given official status, likewise pressed the interim authorities to make sure their voices would be heard when it came time to write the new constitution. Indeed, in a move that was viewed as a concession to the regional, communal, and personalized nature of political power in Libya, 120 of the 200 seats in the Congress would be awarded to individual candidates. The other eighty would go to the newly formed parties. And what role, if any, the Congress would play in the appointment of members to the constitutional drafting body proved to be one of the most toxic questions Libya's new government would face.[69]

Given the growing tensions in the post-revolutionary polity, it is easy to understand why there were concerns that the July 7, 2012, elections would become an occasion for violent disruption by potentially disenfranchised groups or radical Islamists. The vote in fact became an occasion for national celebration, with Libyans taking to the streets in displays of unbridled joy. Where there were protests against the vote, these occurred mainly in the east and proved largely inconsequential.[70]

All in all, over 2.5 million Libyans participated in the elections for the Congress, representing 80 percent of potential voters; over 1.61 million of these were women.[71] The outcome of the election similarly defied many expectations. Given the recent electoral success of the Muslim Brotherhood in Egypt and a similarly moderate Islamist party in Tunisia, *Ennahdha*, expectations were high that the Muslim Brotherhood, represented by Mohamed Sowan's Justice and Construction Party, along with Abdel Hakim Belhadj's *Watan* party, would deliver an Islamist-dominated parliament. Instead, the National Forces Alliance of Mahmoud Jibril – itself a coalition of nearly five dozen parties – won thirty-nine seats out of the seventy it contested, garnering nearly 50 percent of the vote. The only other party to obtain double-digit support was the Justice and Construction Party, which earned seventeen seats, winning less than 11 percent of the popular vote. Coming in third with just three seats was Mohamed El-Magariaf's National Front Party, which presented itself as the new face of the National Front for the Salvation of Libya. El-Magariaf was a native of Ajdabiya, and his eventual appointment as President of the Congress was seen as a gesture to address Cyrenaican unease with the unfolding transitional process.[72]

Of the nineteen other parties in contention, all but one gained between one and two seats in the Congress. The one that did not was Belhadj's *Watan*. Sometimes mocked by Libyans as the party of Qatar, *Watan* was one of the first to place glitzy billboards on the streets of Tripoli in the lead-up to the vote. They not only displayed unparalleled production values but often featured an unveiled female candidate, Lamya Abu Sidra, to stress the party's moderate Islamist views.[73] Libyans, however, proved wary of such obvious displays of foreign backing. Moreover, the proliferation of Islamist satellite television channels in Libya, whether supporting the Muslim Brotherhood or more orthodox Salafi viewpoints, was often viewed as evidence of meddling in Libya by Turkish or Gulf interests.[74]

The already conservative tendencies of Libyan society and concerns over foreign influence were said to have steered voters toward leadership that promised technocratic competence over ideology. These factors were particularly visible in terms of gender. The National Transitional Council, as noted, had set the quota for female representation in the General National Congress at a paltry 10 percent; after significant outcry, parties were mandated to alternate male and female candidates, though the 120 individual seats had no gender quota at all. Female candidates ultimately represented 45 percent of those vying for the eighty party seats, though only 3 percent of independent candidates were women and none filled any of the 120 seats allocated to individuals. The fact that Libyan women represented over 16 percent of the Congress membership was celebrated by some but raised concerns for others.[75] The relative success of the National Force Alliance rested in its broad coalition, which gave it the ability to have truly national reach. It successfully ran candidates in all thirteen districts. The other parties were more regionally and locally focused, fielding candidates in only one or two districts each.[76] Where moderate, conservative, and even Salafi Islamists had seemingly gained some lost ground was in the 120 seats set aside for individuals.[77] Overall, the result was not just ambiguous, it was one in which no candidate, party, or interest group could claim a mandate to lead.

In this context, the initial efforts to form an elected transitional government became a microcosm of the troubles Libya would face down the road. After the Council dissolved itself on August 8, 2012, the Congress set about electing its leadership.[78] The first attempts to create a government were led by Mustafa Abushagur, an American-trained engineer and a long-time activist with the National Front for the Salvation of Libya. Originally from Tripoli, Abushagur had a long career in US academia before becoming the National Transitional Council's Deputy Prime Minister in November 2011, a post he retained into the new congress. In the weeks that followed, Abushagur – having narrowly defeated Jibril for the opportunity to form a government – found his proposed cabinets subject to protests and threats of force by any constituency that felt marginalized or threatened by the unfolding process, whether inside or outside of the Congress. Unable to appease the Congress, Abushagur lost a vote of confidence in early October.

Concerns that Libya's transitional parliament would prove to be as ungovernable as the polity itself were initially quelled when the next candidate, Ali Zeidan, succeeded in forming a cabinet by the end of October 2012. A former Libyan diplomat, lawyer, and also an activist with the National Front for the Salvation of Libya based in Europe, Zeidan defeated a candidate from the Justice and Construction Party in his effort to seek the premiership despite several disadvantages: having been a long-term exile, hailing from the marginalized central-north region, and being his party's only elected representative. Though Zeidan succeeded in forming a government that seemed to strike a balance of interests, his sixteen-month tenure as Libya's first Prime Minister after the revolution was marked by the steady deterioration of the country's security.

The 2011 uprising and the immediate post-revolutionary situation had set in motion processes that no central authority could interrupt or tame. As political power further diffused from Libya's weak and divided central authorities in Tripoli, it further accumulated in the hands of the armed, aggrieved, and ambitious actors who had emerged elsewhere. What was left of the state was replete with systemic and multiplying vulnerabilities. These vulnerabilities allowed Libya's new centers of power to influence the direction of the transition, primarily through strategies of noncompliance, boycott, sabotage, and armed force.

4 | Hegemony or Anarchy? ———

While the growing militia menace in post-revolutionary Libya was cause for serious concern, there were other developments that occurred in the year following the collapse of the Gaddafi regime that were more encouraging. In addition to the elections of July 2012 and the formation of a government at the end of October, there was an explosion of civic organizations. Previously, nongovernmental organizations had been either suppressed by the regime or allowed to exist only insofar as they served its interests. While the *Jamahiriyyah* system originally saw no need for parallel organizations outside of its structures (i.e., a civil society), attempts to neoliberalize the economy in the first decade of the new century created a limited and controlled space for new associations and the press.[1] Not only did the 2011 revolution reveal a widespread yearning for independent civic organizations, but the years that followed saw them proliferate across the country. By 2014, as many as 4,000 new organizations were thought to be operating nation-wide.[2]

Libyan women led a number of these new independent organizations. The revolution and its aftermath were nonetheless a time of ambivalent feelings for many Libyan women. While there were hopes that the uprising would usher in a new age for women's advancement, the war itself witnessed widespread abuses against women, particularly the sensitive and contested issue of sexual violence committed by regime loyalists and revolutionary fighters. In communities struggling against the regime, women played a number of vital roles and even filled ones traditionally occupied by men who were off fighting the regime. One of Libya's upcoming female politicians, Wafa Bugaighis, noted, "Women in Libya played a frontline role in bringing down the entrenched dictatorship, and they are eager, and fully deserve, to reap the rewards of full political participation in the country they helped liberate." After all, she explained, Libyan women had "advocated for the revolution through media, smuggled weapons and ammunition between cities, tended wounded fighters, cooked meals for the frontline units, sold their jewellery to support the revolution, and sewed flags that were the symbol for this revolution [...]."[3] Despite the equal claim that Libyan women had on the 2011 revolution, there were violent actors who were determined to foreclose the possibility of them playing a more prominent role after the fall of Gaddafi. Bugaighis would tragically see her cousin Salwa Bugaighis, a founding member of the National Transitional Council and a vocal women's advocate, murdered in her own home in June 2014 as their country descended into a new civil war.

A Cancer on the New Polity: The Militias

The proliferation of armed organizations, their growing catalogue of abuses, and their influence on the transitional process (mainly as spoilers) were indeed of growing national and international concern. However, the legitimacy claimed by these militias made it difficult to confront them. The *thuwar* were equally empowered by the popular nature of the uprising, the despotic nature of the regime they fought, and the aura of international legitimacy that the NATO–Arab League intervention bestowed on them. What crimes the militias had committed in their crusade against the Gaddafi regime were largely brushed aside by the international community, even though the abuses of the *thuwar* often amounted to far more serious war crimes and crimes against humanity than the regime had perpetrated at the start of the uprising in early 2011.

The excesses of Libya's revolutionary militias started to come to light during the transitional period after the fall of Gaddafi. In their ongoing total war against the old regime, an archipelago of independently operated detention and torture centers was created by militias in various settings – from schools to abandoned apartments – to imprison and punish thousands of Gaddafi loyalists, real and suspected.[4] In some cases, the collective punishment of loyalism seemed as racially motivated as it was political, especially concerning the sustained ethnic cleansing and persecution of the town of Tawergha by Misratan militias.[5] Other communities perceived as loyalist, from residents of Sirte to the Tuareg of the southwest, faced threats, detention, abuse, displacement, and unlawful killing as well. Inter-communal strife between Zintani militias and members of the Mashashiya tribe, which initially flared up in the context of the uprising, continued to generate ongoing clashes, dozens of killings, and the significant internal displacement of Mashashiya communities.[6] The 2011 uprising also created a number of durable *intra*-communal disputes. Ongoing clashes between pro- and anti-revolution groups in Bani Walid throughout the 2011 uprising were exacerbated by post-conflict skirmishes with militias from Misrata and Suq Al-Juma'a seeking to capture regime figures and exact revenge for earlier killings. Clashes between loyalist and revolutionary factions in the Fezzan and the Sahara – from Ghadames to Sebha to Kufra – continued long after the fall of the Gaddafi regime.[7]

Many of Libya's new detention centers operated by militias in the west of the country were reportedly consolidated and legitimated as official prisons under the auspices of transitional authorities in Tripoli. A 2015 investigation, however, found that little had changed in terms of prohibitions on torture for nearly 2,000 detainees still waiting for their day in court.[8] The militias' growing record of abuses also encompassed summary executions and revenge killings (including the mass execution of dozens of loyalists in Sirte at the end of the uprising), looting, arson, and other forms of punitive action against former regime elements.[9] With the rapidly deteriorating security situation in Cyrenaica, reports of targeted and indiscriminate attacks against civilians began to accumulate throughout 2012 and 2013.[10]

Even nonviolent protests against the militias were met with harsh reprisals. On June 8, 2013, a militia operating under the sanction of the Ministry of Defense fired on a crowd of demonstrators in Benghazi, killing almost thirty. Five months later, on November 15, Misratan militias in the Gharghour neighborhood of Tripoli shot dead some forty people marching against their continued presence in the capital. Unsurprisingly, the scene quickly spiraled into sustained armed clashes between local residents and the occupiers.[11] Despite growing opposition to the rule of militias, however, there was little indication that they would retreat in the face of the popular outcry. "We decided that our goal is to keep the capital safe," explained Uthman Mlegta, commander of a Zintani brigade in Tripoli. "Once everything returns to normal we will give up our arms."[12]

To suggest that all militias were behaving as if they were above the law is to forget that, in many instances and locations, they effectively *were* the law. In the face of weak or absent central state structures, militias were often the closest thing to a functioning police force. The fact that foreign governments often contracted out their local security needs to Libyan militias – as the United States fatefully did in Benghazi – revealed the extent to which *thuwar* had become an essential component of the transitional period.[13] Policing, border patrols, inter-communal peacekeeping, oil facilities guards, national defense, and even election security for the July 2012 vote were all outsourced to militias that, in many cases, had already claimed those roles for themselves. As one expert on Libya concluded, "The strategy of trying to dismantle the regional militias while simultaneously making use of them as hired guns might be sowing the seeds for the country's descent into warlordism."[14]

Indeed, it was. Efforts under the administration of Ali Zeidan (November 2012–March 2014) to fold some militias into regular police and armed forces, while incentivizing others to disarm and disband, had little effect. The transitional administration's contradictory relationship with the *thuwar* – using militia power to subordinate militia power – could only be resolved domestically through a hegemonic coalition of political and military forces, yet none emerged in 2012 and 2013 to fill the vacuum left by the Gaddafi regime. Indeed, almost the opposite happened. It was, as one report noted, "a balance of weakness"[15] among Libya's main rivals – an anarchic equilibrium. None of the forces that finally went to war in the summer of 2014 could impose their will on the country. But they could at least deny hegemony to their rivals. By the time the North Atlantic community had recognized the depths of the militia crisis in Libya, pivoting from political assistance to security assistance came too late.

With so much at stake in post-revolutionary Libya, the intensity of political maneuvering only increased during the transitional period. In order to keep the peace, Libya's interim authorities had no other choice but to engage in a seemingly endless series of measures designed to placate their armed antagonists.[16] The sustainability of this governing strategy only worked as long as there were financial and other resources to throw at Libya's myriad challenges. Yet the country burned through its cash reserves and oil production began to decline in 2013 after a year of relatively stable output. Thus the capacity of leaders in Tripoli to incentivize cooperation became increasingly limited. To make matters worse, neither Libyans nor the United Nations gave serious consideration to the one option that might have stymied the bloodletting: an international stabilization force.[17] While it was clear that Libya was entering a period of growing political weakness and uncertainty in 2013, the international community largely retreated in the face of it. As the transition period became more fraught and violent, and with international attention largely focused elsewhere, the domestic need for any kind of security – militia or otherwise – only increased. One Misratan military official rightfully complained: "It's the politicians who are telling the revolutionaries to keep their guns – not the commanders!"[18]

International perceptions of the anti-Gaddafi militias finally began to sour once it was clear that the *thuwar* would not so quickly yield their newfound power to Libya's democratically elected authorities. Up until that point, the international community had obsessively fixated on the question of Islamist influence on the revolution and the role of Islamist fighters, arguably to the neglect of broader questions about the militarization of Libyan society and the fragmentation of state sovereignty.[19]

The Benghazi Crucible

Questions that should have been asked in March 2011 – questions about the potentially destabilizing forces being morally endorsed and militarily empowered in Libya – were only raised in a substantive way following the events of September 11, 2012, in Benghazi. That night, two US diplomats, including the Ambassador, J. Christopher Stevens, along with two US security contractors, were killed during an assault on State Department and CIA facilities.

In the weeks and months leading up to those events, Cyrenaica had already witnessed an increasing number of attacks by radical Islamists against US, British, UN, and other international targets like the Red Cross. Islamist militias had even displayed their military power in Benghazi by staging a parade in the city center amid the campaign for the upcoming elections for the General National Congress. Indeed, the level of radical Islamist activity in the east was an outcome of how the 2011 uprising emerged and proceeded. In Tripolitania, regime figures and apparatuses had been destroyed or dispersed after a long and bloody campaign, and often at the hands of Islamist militias. Cyrenaica, by contrast, had been spared a similar fate because of the large-scale defection of the core leaders and institutions in the first days of the uprising, which was then followed by the protective cover of the NATO–Arab League intervention. Whereas Islamists in the west – Tripoli in particular – faced a more fluid, dynamic, and open-ended situation, Islamists in the east confronted an entrenched, equipped, and organized elite that they opted to confront with terrorism.[20]

The September 11 attacks in Benghazi were initially thought to be the work of an enraged mob. Days beforehand, an inflammatory Internet video produced in the United States, one that denigrated tenets of the Islamic faith, started triggering protests throughout the Muslim world. This international unrest was undoubtedly part of the context in Benghazi, though others soon suggested that the attacks had been well planned and highly coordinated, possibly the work of a global terrorist organization like Al-Qaida. The reality was somewhere in between. The attack turned out to be the work of local jihadists. Their assault on the compound that night generated a degree of popular participation in the attack given the anti-American mood then percolating across the Islamic world.

Blame initially centered on *Ansar Al-Shari'ah*, one of several avowedly Islamist militias that had coalesced to fight the Gaddafi regime in 2011. Ahmed Abu Khattala, the ostensible leader of the attack, had been a secondary figure among Cyrenaican *thuwar* in 2011, though his notoriety grew after being implicated in the Younis assassination.[21] In the years that followed the Benghazi attacks, extensive partisan investigations in the United States were launched. Their almost exclusive, and often obsessive, focus was the role of then US Secretary of State Hillary Clinton in the affair. In the end, these investigations proved to be little more than partisan political theater designed to undermine her 2016 bid for the US presidency.

That the 2012 assault came as a surprise to anyone was difficult to understand given the obvious deterioration of security across Libya and the escalation of attacks on foreign targets in the east. The events in Benghazi should have instead raised serious questions regarding the clandestine work of the nearby CIA outpost and its twenty staff. Some reports have suggested that the US government presence in Cyrenaica was more invested in helping Libyan authorities funnel arms to anti-regime fighters in Syria than understanding the growing jihadi threat all around it.[22] This threat would finally come to full fruition in the wake of the 2014 civil war in Libya. Devotees of the Islamic State movement – the most radical and effective Islamist faction to emerge out of the Iraqi and Syrian civil wars – not only established a branch in Libya but also succeeded in claiming the city of Sirte as their primary base in North Africa.

Veterans of Jihad, Old and New

The elections of 2012 and 2014 brought increasing levels of attention to Libya's Islamists, as did the 2012 attack on US facilities in Benghazi. The descent into open civil war in 2014 then seemed to cement the view that Islamism was a critical factor in post-revolutionary Libya. Prior to 2011, it was no secret that some of the most ardent practitioners of international jihad had come from Libya, including founding members of Al-Qaida. Disaffected youth and Islamist activists gladly escaped the *Jamahiriyyah* to fight the Soviet occupation of Afghanistan in the 1980s. There, in Pakistan and Afghanistan, many of the so-called "Arab Mujahidin" gained military skills, built transnational networks, and planned to bring the jihad to their home countries.

As with the insurgencies in neighboring Algeria and Egypt in the 1990s, Libya's own Islamist guerrillas, the Libyan Islamic Fighting Group, attempted to apply lessons learned in Afghanistan to their war against the Gaddafi regime. In all three cases (Algeria, Egypt, and Libya), these insurgencies neither rallied popular support for their armed campaigns nor significantly destabilized the governments in question. Instead, they desperately turned to terrorism. In Egypt, *Al-Jama'ah al-Islamiyyah* infamously resorted to killing foreign tourists in 1997. Even more infamously, radical elements of the Algerian Islamist insurgency resorted to the mass slaughter of civilians – many its former supporters – around the same time. In Libya, the Fighting Group's militarily inept and socially isolated guerrilla campaign quickly led to its defeat at the hands of Gaddafi's forces in Cyrenaica in the late 1990s. Even the regime's mass murder of hundreds of imprisoned Islamists during in the 1996 Abu Salim prison uprising did little to precipitate widespread Libyan support for the Fighting Group's campaign.[23]

At the time of the 2011 uprising, Libya's most militant and high-profile Islamists were well known to foreign governments and experts. Critics of NATO's intervention even pointed out that Western governments might have unwittingly or indifferently contributed their airpower to a rebellion significantly constituted by Islamist activists, if not members of Al-Qaida. Chief among Libya's infamous militant Islamists was Abdelhakim Belhadj, a man who fit the classic profile of the first-generation international jihadi: a highly educated veteran of the Arab volunteers who fought against the Soviet Union during its occupation of Afghanistan in the 1980s. In the 1990s, Belhadj returned to Libya to use his knowledge and experiences to oust the Gaddafi regime as a commander in the Fighting Group. Following the suppression of the insurgency by Libyan security forces, he reportedly regrouped with Al-Qaida in Pakistan and Afghanistan in the late 1990s, then under Taliban rule. There he reconnected with other militant activists who were regrouping after similar failures in Algeria, Bosnia, Chechnya, and Egypt.

The US invasion of Afghanistan after September 11, 2001, scattered Al-Qaida. Belhadj and his wife Fatima were on the run for a time, only to be captured in 2004 following a joint US–British intelligence effort to find them. At this point, Belhadj and Fatima entered the dark world of "black sites," the CIA's secret global detention system, where they experienced "enhanced interrogation." Soon thereafter, they were rendered to Libya to be tortured by the Gaddafi regime as well.[24] Belhadj's death sentence was eventually commuted as a part of an amnesty program, spearheaded by Saif Al-Islam, for Libyan Islamists who renounced violence. Belhadj nonetheless became a leading figure in the anti-Gaddafi resistance in Tripoli once the 2011 uprising got underway. As the post-Gaddafi polity began to take shape, Belhadj and others like him were more or less a known quantity in Libyan politics. Questions nonetheless remained as to the commitment of other former and active jihadists to the kind of post-revolutionary order endorsed by the National Transitional Council and its North Atlantic patrons. With the widespread diffusion of arms within the society, those actors with more radical agendas were in a far better position to pursue truly revolutionary change. What that might look like was another open question, though a leading voice within the Libyan Islamic Fighting Group, Sami Al-Saadi, had once articulated the organization's philosophy in the 1990s as being in opposition to both the Gaddafi regime and the Westernization of international order known as globalization.[25]

As a result of Libya's decades of externally and internally imposed isolation, there was little foreign understanding of the mainstream of Libya's Islamist movement in 2011 and 2012. This isolation was compounded by the fact that, like all other elements of domestic opposition to Gaddafi's regime, Islamists were forced to operate largely in secret – and for good reason. Since coming to power in 1969, Gaddafi's repression of organizations like the Libyan Muslim Brotherhood had been relentless. For the regime, this repression was as ideologically motivated as it was political. In theory and reality, the *Jamahiriyyah* sought to monopolize all aspects of associative life so as to negate the need for political parties and civil society, including independent religious activity. Gaddafi's vision of the perfect society – heavily influenced by his particular and eccentric reading of Islam – also attempted to subsume religious life within the all-encompassing nature of the *Jamahiriyyah* state.[26]

Libya's Muslim Brotherhood was thus never allowed to develop into a robust mass organization like the Egyptian counterpart that influenced it. Whereas the pseudo-democratic Egyptian regimes of Presidents Anwar Sadat (r. 1970–81) and Hosni Mubarak (r. 1981–2011) cleverly manipulated the Egyptian Muslim Brotherhood so as to divide both the Islamist movement and the rest of the political opposition, there was no space within the totalitarian *Jamahiriyyah* for any form of associational life that was not articulated within Gaddafi's vision, at least until the reforms of the early 2000s. There were two important effects of this historical intolerance toward opposition. One was the highly extra-territorial nature of Libya's opposition figures on the eve of the revolution, whether leftist, liberal, or Islamist, including the Muslim Brotherhood. The other effect was the way in which Libya's repressive institutions inadvertently created oppositional networks. The infamous Abu Salim prison in Tripoli, which ironically functioned as an incubator for radical and moderate Islamists, was one of those key sites. There Islamists forged networks of solidarity and plans for a post-Gaddafi future. Though the Islamist movement in Libya had been somewhat co-opted by Saif Al-Islam's efforts to reform the state in the 2000s, key Islamist leaders refused to heed the regime's calls to denounce the protests in February 2011, often resulting in their imprisonment during the revolution.[27]

A significant contingent of Libya's Islamists came together in 2011 not only to oppose the Gaddafi regime, as many had for decades, but also to offer a vision of Libya in opposition to the neoliberal, technocratic, and accommodationist tendencies within a rebel leadership that seemed too quick to make alliances with eleventh-hour regime defectors.[28] For example, the National Transitional Council plan to seize and secure Tripoli – a plan drawn up in response to Western demands for one – was entirely dependent on last-minute defections of high-level regime officials. Given the decades of persecution, imprisonment, and torture that Libya's militant Islamists had suffered, particularly members of the Fighting Group, there was an understandable reticence among them to make compromises with former regime officials, particularly those from the security establishment.

At the same time, feelings of mistrust appeared to be mutual. In March 2011, the National Transitional Council issued a perfunctory statement denouncing both "extremist ideas" in the revolution and "allegations aiming to associate Al Qaeda with the revolutionists in Libya."[29] North Atlantic support for the Libyan uprising created a strong incentive for the Council to downplay the role of radical transnationalist Islamists in the revolutionary militias. The same, however, could be said of Western European and North American leaders, whose strategic aim in Libya – regime change – required turning a blind eye to the new and veteran jihadist elements being tacitly endorsed and materially empowered by their intervention in the 2011 Libyan civil war.

At the same time, the terms "jihadist" and "Islamist" could often be misleading in a context like Libya where levels of religious conservatism were relatively high and where motivations for joining militias were more economic than ideological. Describing the formation of so-called "Islamist" militias in Cyrenaica (e.g., the February 17 Revolutionary Martyrs Brigade, the Martyr Omar Mukhtar Brigade, and the Abu Salim Martyrs Brigade), Frederic Wehrey found that they were in fact constituted by "restless young men of the east [...], drawn by the promise of an ethical code, camaraderie, adventure, and income." He added, "Battling loyalist forces, these young men found a new purpose. And when Qaddafi fell, they found it hard to go back to what they were before."[30]

The exigency of the 2011 rebellion blurred or eliminated distinctions between nationalist, Islamist, and transnational jihadist militias fighting the Gaddafi regime. Indeed, veterans of the Fighting Group often found themselves fighting side-by-side in 2011 with defectors from the same elite counterterrorism units that had brutally repressed their insurgency in the 1990s.[31] After the capture of Tripoli, it would take several months for the dust to settle and for those distinctions to finally become clear to the outside world. As the Islamic State movement had yet to form into a coherent threat in either the Middle East or North Africa, foreign concerns fixated on the presence of Al-Qaida in Libya. However, the often-bitter domestic and international experiences of Libya's veteran jihadists seemed to insulate the 2011 uprising from such influences. Al-Qaida's North African branch nonetheless made use of the post-revolution chaos in Libya, funneling its plundered armories to their operations in other countries, notably in the central Sahara.[32]

In 2011, the experiences and organizational capacity of veteran Libyan jihadists were channeled into the nationalist struggle of the revolution. Indeed, when the time came for the clandestine revolutionary cells in Tripoli to oust the dictatorship in August 2011, it was Islamist groups who had laid much of the groundwork for the sudden and overwhelming urban uprising that purged the remnants of the regime from the capital. Prominent figures like Ali Al-Sallabi, an exiled Islamic scholar living in Doha, and Arif Ali Nayid, a Sufi scholar and an entrepreneur, used their international religious connections to gain Qatari and Turkish political support for the Libyan uprising. More importantly, they gained material support for the Islamist plan to liberate Tripoli with or without the help of the internally riven National Transitional Council in Benghazi. The arms being delivered to Libyan rebels by France, Qatar, and eventually the United Arab Emirates – though a clear violation of the UN embargo – further exacerbated divisions within the revolution by empowering Islamists and undermining the Council's ostensible civilian oversight of the military campaign in Tripolitania. In the end, the dominant impression was that rebel groups in the capital, joined by Misratan and Nafusi militias, were the ones who had won the war.[33]

Dawn of the Islamists: From Bullets to Ballots

As is often the case in revolutions, those who claim to represent the rebellion and those who did the actual fighting in Libya were often two very distinct groups, united only in their opposition to the regime itself. When it came time to govern the post-Gaddafi polity, these divisions were exacerbated. Official power rested in the hands of an increasingly divided and unaccountable National Transitional Council, of which upward of half were nominally Islamist to one degree or another. Concerns about the Muslim Brotherhood's influence on the Council often led to tense confrontations. Such tensions had marked the early days of the revolution as well. A secret April 2011 meeting of Libyan Islamists in Turkey, organized by Ali Al-Sallabi and with alleged Qatari support, was viewed as an effort to form an Islamist front to take control of the revolution.[34] Equally concerning for members of the Council was the superior military organizational capacity often displayed by Islamist-led or -dominated militias in both the east and the capital.[35] The possibility of Islamist unity, however, was undermined by longstanding regionalist attitudes, such as the dominance of Cyrenaicans on the early Council,[36] and the geography of the 2011 uprising, notably the relative international isolation of Tripoli and Misrata during the war.

After the fall of the regime, Tripoli's militant Islamists were certainly not alone in feeling betrayed by the National Transitional Council. Their contributions to the uprising, like many others, did not necessarily translate into representation in later iterations of the expanded Council.[37] Belhadj, for example, had reportedly expected a cabinet-level appointment for his military leadership but did not receive one. At the same time, the putative coherence, efficacy, and sacrifices of the Islamist militias were arguably overstated in many instances, particularly by the Islamists themselves and their international sponsors.[38] Misratan and Zintani militias were much more emblematic of the real sources of political power taking shape in post-Gaddafi Libya. These dominant militias primarily drew their strength from a strong sense of traditional communal identity, along with collective sacrifice and suffering during the 2011 uprising. They also quickly set about seizing state and economic assets across Tripolitania and Fezzan to bolster their position vis-à-vis each other, other militias, and the National Transitional Council.

In this context, it made sense for Libya's Islamist movement to seek power through different channels. One approach was to emulate the successes of Islamist parties at the ballot box in countries like Morocco, Tunisia, Turkey, and post-Mubarak Egypt. There were other reasons to pursue this tack as well. The National Transitional Council's constitutional declaration set out a transitional process in which the interim elected government would have input into the drafting process, an area of struggle that Islamists were keen to influence.[39] Pursuing an electoral strategy made additional sense for the mainstream of the Libyan Islamist movement so as to counter domestic and international perceptions of Islamists as overly prone to armed militancy. The Brotherhood also had to overcome years of anti-Islamist propaganda from the Gaddafi regime, as well as suspicions that it, like the Libyan Islamic Fighting Group, had been too quick to participate in Saif Al-Islam's national reconciliation efforts prior to 2011.[40] However, the Muslim Brotherhood soon staked out a position within the post-revolutionary polity that put it in opposition to the conciliatory politics of its more secular and liberal opponents, dominated as they were by exiled technocratic elites and former regime officials.[41]

To these ends, Libya's Muslim Brotherhood formally reconstituted itself in November 2011 in Benghazi, naming Bashir Abdelsalam Al-Katbi as its leader. In and of itself, this meeting was momentous: it was the first public meeting of the Muslim Brotherhood in Libya for several decades. The Brotherhood's primary electoral vehicle, the Justice and Construction Party, which would work in coalition with other Islamist groups and leaders,[42] was unveiled in March 2012 with Mohamed Sowan of Misrata – also a former Abu Salim prisoner – as its leader. The growing connection between the Brotherhood's political power and Misrata's economic and military power was facilitated in part by the latter's connection to Qatar, a state that had long sponsored the Brotherhood internationally, and the former's connections to Turkey, a country with which Misrata has traditionally maintained longstanding economic relations and whose current government under Prime Minister Recep Tayyip Erdoğan was increasingly dominated by a party, the Turkish Justice and Development Party, that shared many affinities with the Muslim Brotherhood.

With the help of Ali Al-Sallabi, some Islamists in Tripoli were able to forge an alliance with their Misratan occupiers on both ideological and political grounds. In the lead-up to the 2012 elections, the Libyan Brotherhood was thus able to hit the ground running because of its relatively robust domestic networks and its connections to international sources of support. The latter included likeminded organizations, parties, and figures across the Muslim world, as well as the largess of the Qatari state. With this support, the Brotherhood quickly established its own media outlets and charitable organizations.[43] Despite these clear advantages, however, the Justice and Construction Party's performance in the July 2012 elections was widely considered lackluster.

Broadly speaking, the results of the 2012 vote suggested that Libya lacked a truly national political party that could successfully subsume the country's diverse interests and stakeholders under one organizational apparatus. More specifically, the vote also revealed the patchwork of divisions emerging across the ideological spectrum of Libya's Islamist movement. In early 2012, the Brotherhood had refused to join a grand Islamist coalition proposed by Ali Al-Sallabi. And in its efforts to obtain international legitimacy, the Brotherhood had often shunned some veterans of the Libyan Islamic Fighting Group and radical Salafi-jihadi types, thus creating room for other Islamist political organizations.[44] Attempting to outflank the Brotherhood's moderate wing, Sallabi and Belhadj formed the *Watan* party (often translated as the Homeland Party). Aiming for the more conservative end of the spectrum, Sami Al-Saadi created the Centrist National Gathering.[45] At the same time, almost all of Libya's newfound leaders and parties adopted Islamist rhetoric to one extent or another, which often rendered Islamist and non-Islamist parties a distinction without a difference in post-Gaddafi Libya.[46] For example, there was almost near universal consensus among Libyan leaders and parties that classical Islamic legal principles (so called *shari'ah* law) should inform the post-revolutionary constitution.[47]

To the limited extent that orthodox Salafis were even interested in standing for election in a Western-style parliamentary system, their strength was similarly divided along a number of axes. Their prior relationship to the Gaddafi regime before the revolution weighed heavily on their electoral prospects. Not unlike veterans of the Fighting Group and some Muslim Brothers, elements of the Salafi movement in Libya had been co-opted by the Gaddafi regime late in its tenure, and some had initially spoken out against the uprising.[48] Internal doctrinal splits within Libya's Salafis likewise played a role in limiting their electoral participation. Whereas the "quietist" Salafi distaste for formal politics and their deference to legitimate leaders extended from the pre-revolutionary era to the post-revolutionary era,[49] the more "activist" Salafis channeled their frustrations with the transitional period into more militant forms of action, whether at home in Cyrenaica (notably in Benghazi and Derna) or abroad (the new battle-fields of Syria and Mali). As noted above, eastern Libya, for reasons relating to the 2011 civil war, had become a much more active zone for Islamist militancy in 2012. According to one estimate, Cyrenaican Islamist militias soon claimed over 10,000 members, including groups like *Ansar Al-Shari'ah*, the Omar Mukhtar Brigade, the Abu Salim Martyrs Brigade, the February 17 Martyrs Brigade, and the Shura Council of Islamic Youth.[50]

Control over Libya's religious institutions and leadership was one area where Salafi Islamists were clearly making headway. The new head of the country's religious estab-lishment, Shaykh Al-Sadiq Al-Ghariani, frequently expressed support for some of Libya's most conservative religious groups and agendas,[51] to the extent that he would be viewed as a partisan actor in the coming civil war. Not only were Salafi activists and militants busy asserting control over mosques as the *Jamahiriyyah* collapsed, some Salafis openly antagonized and attacked Sufi and Christian institutions, in one instance, in August 2012, going so far as to raze one of Tripoli's most venerated Sufi shrines in plain view of the central authorities, local security forces, and the international community.[52]

Cleaning House: Accommodation or De-Gaddafization?

A number of issues were at the top of the General National Congress's already lengthy agenda when it took power in August of 2012. Chief among them were ongoing debates about the process by which Libya would draft and ratify its post-Gaddafi constitution. Shortly before the 2012 elections, the National Transitional Council passed a controversial law that capitulated to regional politics. Instead of a commission of experts appointed by the Congress, the proposed constitutional assembly would now be directly elected by the Libyan public based upon equal representation from Tripolitania, Fezzan, and Cyrenaica (i.e., twenty representatives each). Though this new approach had been a concession to concerns emanating from Fezzan and Cyrenaica in the lead-up to the 2012 vote, it served its purpose by securing those regional constituencies' participation in the July 2012 vote. The law was then reaffirmed by the Congress in 2013, a move that suggested the extent to which Libya's interim authorities were more comfortable with a politics mediated by regional interests and personal connections than a politics of mass parties and intellectual-technocratic expertise.[53]

An even more controversial set of laws proposed limiting the participation of former regime officials in the new Libyan state. Though the National Transitional Council's leadership had been heavily populated with high-level regime defectors, this had enhanced the legitimacy of the revolution. However, the Council passed a rule that none of its members could stand for election in 2012. For some Libyans, this was not enough. A piece of legislation passed by the Congress in May 2013, known as the Political Isolation Law, went even further. It had the effect of barring upward of half a million Libyans from serving at any level of government. To get the law passed, revolutionary militias besieged the Congress, literally holding them at gunpoint. Though some Libyan leaders had recognized the dangers of mimicking the haphazard "de-Baathification" programs that had plunged Iraq into an ethno-sectarian civil war after 2003, there was a sizable constituency in Libya that was demanding the reconstruction of Libyan state institutions as if from a *tabula rasa*.[54]

In protest, Mohammed El-Magariaf resigned from his post as President of the Congress (i.e., as Libya's interim head of state). El-Magariaf was a respected personality who had led the National Front for the Salvation of Libya since its founding in the early 1980s, often at great personal risk. Yet his government service in the 1970s disqualified him from holding office under the Political Isolation Law. The ranks of the National Forces Alliance, the largest party in the Congress, were reportedly devastated as well by the law's passage.[55] The Political Isolation Law was undoubtedly drafted in response to demands from various constituencies for truth, justice, and accountability for the crimes and abuses of the Gaddafi regime. At the same time, it politically disenfranchised some of Libya's most competent and experienced officials during a transitional period in which their knowledge and talents were desperately needed. The law thus risked exacerbating one of the most salient divisions growing within the polity: those seeking accommodation with former elements of the regime and those seeking a more thoroughgoing revolution. For many of Libya's Islamists, the Political Isolation Law was also good politics. It not only fulfilled a pledge made during the revolution, it also destabilized the centrist technocrats leading the Congress. The ascendancy to the head of the Congress of Nouri Abusahmain, although an independent Amazigh candidate from Zuwara, was widely viewed as a move that consolidated the Muslim Brotherhood's grip on the interim government.

Though the effects of the Political Isolation Law would continue to reverberate for months and years to come, the larger question was to what extent viable state institutions could even be harvested from the problematic, distrusted, and now war-torn frameworks of the *Jamahiriyyah*.[56] To make matters worse, the revolution had generated even more antipathy toward the remnants of the old regime: that is, its agents and institutions. The events of 2011 had effectively accelerated the fragmentation of a deliberately fractured polity. The radical privatization and localization of governance and security that occurred during the uprising, fueled by the seizure and looting of state and military assets, created archipelagos of armed communities that were often in conflict with each other over historical, recent, and emerging grievances. Though militias ostensibly held all of the power in Libya, most were relatively weak unless they joined larger coalitions. Their capacity to influence the fate of post-Gaddafi Libya rested in their ability to manipulate, largely through passive noncooperation or active sabotage, the manifold social, political, and infrastructural vulnerabilities in the emerging order. A few militias were even entirely reactionary, having formed to protect their community from the *thuwar* and other armed criminal networks, notably in Bani Walid, Tarhuna, and western Tripolitania.[57]

In a climate where the old security institutions were viewed as key enablers of the Gaddafi regime, simply reviving the established police and military was also rejected by revolutionary elements. The first Interior Minister under the Zeidan administration, Ashur Shwayl, had himself been a former police officer, a fact that likely hindered his efforts to subordinate the militias to central authority.[58] Not only were many revolutionary factions opposed to utilizing old institutions and actors, but the rank and file of Libya's security forces had often been dissuaded from returning to work by the fervor of the revolutionaries. In other cases, police and military units had either been decimated in the uprising or their numbers had been dispersed among the millions of Libyan refugees and asylum seekers in Tunisia, Egypt, and elsewhere. To a certain extent, similar structural and labor issues enfeebled the state bureaucracy as well.[59]

Libya's judicial system was particularly dependent upon officials with ties to the old regime. Many courts attempted to return to their normal functions in early 2012, though they were often caught between accusations of loyalism to the old regime and the militias running the formal and informal prison systems.[60] While structural and personnel changes were quickly instituted by the National Transitional Council at the highest judicial levels in late 2011 through the Supreme Judicial Council, justice at the local level was much more varied. From the Jabal Al-Akhdar in the northeast to the central desert region, prosecutors, judges, and courthouses were subjected to constant threats and intimidation in their efforts to establish judicial regularity in the new Libya.[61] The Judicial Police, ostensibly in charge of prisons, were unable to gain control over Libya's various and proliferating detention facilities, much less consolidate them. Elite units like the Ministry of Foreign Affair's Diplomatic Police and the

Ministry of the Interior's Anticrime Unit would both prove to be spectacular failures as well. The 2013 Political Isolation Law then became a tool used by some revolutionaries to purge the police and judicial system.[62] The power vacuum at the national level in post-revolutionary Libya meant that the privatization of policing went hand in hand with the privatization of justice and reconciliation. As one report on the situation noted, "This has all the hallmarks of a vicious cycle: impatience with the pace of justice and overall mistrust embolden armed groups; their increased activism undermines the state's ability to function, including on matters of law and order; and this in turn vindicates the armed groups' claim that it is their duty to fill the vacuum."[63] As much as the international community was powerless to force Zintani militias to hand over Saif Al-Islam to the International Criminal Court, domestic authorities were powerless to address the ongoing persecution of ethnic minorities such as the Tebu and the Tawerghans.[64] By mid-2016, the International Commission of Jurists noted that Libya's successive interim authorities had not only failed to create an independent and accountable judiciary, but Libya's courts also remained effectively constituted and governed under Gaddafi-era laws.[65]

Who Governs Whom? Taming the Militias

Reconstituting the security sector proved to be a Sisyphean task for Libya's interim authorities. As one regional expert argued, "[Libya's] attempt at wholesale reconstruction of the security sector went far beyond anything attempted in the other Arab Spring countries, but this ultimately ended in a resounding failure that has left the country with two warring governments, each with its own, dysfunctional security structure."[66] Security sector reform under the National Transitional Council and General National Congress proved to be ineffective and often contradictory. In the absence of functional central institutions, localities received funds to form their own Military Councils, if they did not already have them, which would begin the process of registering fighters and coordinating their regulation with central authorities. Minister of Defense Osama Juwaili even offered cash payments, between $1,800 and $3,000, just to get militia members to register their names with his ministry, though he notably avoided having them register their weapons as well.[67]

Indeed, one of the most significant failures of Libya's transitional authorities was their failure to institute effective mechanisms to disarm the militias in the first place. The Council's Warriors Affairs Commission, later rebranded the Program for Reintegration and Development, was given an $8 billion budget in early 2012 to address the militia issue through demobilization and employment programs, though it appears that the line between social assistance and political patronage was as nonexistent in that program as it was in others.[68] Putting a positive spin on these developments, the head of the UN Mission in Libya, Special Representative Ian Martin, provided an audience in Benghazi with this optimistic assessment in April 2012: "[T]here is little indication that [the *thuwar*] wish to perpetuate the existence of brigades outside state authority. Moreover, we are seeing some appreciable progress in the development of state capacity and state authority over brigades in the provision of security, under the direction of the Ministry of the Interior and of the Libyan Army."[69] The truth of the matter would prove to be quite the opposite.

There was a fundamental flaw with almost all of the programs aiming at militia demobilization or formalization in post-revolutionary Libya: they simply incentivized more militia membership, not less. Estimates suggest that upward of three-quarters of the active militia members in 2013 had in fact played no role in the fighting in 2011.[70] As Libyan analyst Karim Mezran noted, being a revolutionary militia member was not just about social prestige, it was, "in the absence of professional opportunities, a permanent job."[71] With the institution of monthly stipends for militias operating under both the Ministry of Defense and the Ministry of the Interior, Libya was soon inundated with a new class of militias: the post-revolution revolutionary.[72]

Militia membership had effectively become a state employment program for young males in a country where the majority of the population was forty years of age or younger. Moreover, broad segments of the Libyan population had been conditioned by Gaddafi's welfare state for over four decades to expect as much from their government (i.e., employment and subsidies), though these militia compensation and remuneration schemes created palpable tensions between "real" revolutionaries (i.e., combat veterans of the 2011 uprising) and the militias who had emerged in their wake.[73] Training programs offered for Libyan recruits in Jordan, Turkey, and Britain were widely assessed as failures owing in large part to the recalcitrance of the trainees to be subjected to professional military life. A foreign military training effort in Zintan was upended when an adversarial group attacked the facilities, making off with weapons and other supplies.[74] An even thornier issue was the thousands of armed actors, upward of 7,500, who refused to be registered by the state because of their engagement in organized crime or their pursuit of extremist political agendas.[75]

Militias that received or leveraged state backing often used their official status to pursue their own economic and political agendas. A telling case was the Libya Shield forces. Eschewing offers to join the regular army under the leadership of Chief of Staff Youssef Al-Mangoush, Libya Shield units formed independently as regional "bottom-up" peacekeeping initiatives in Tripolitania, Fezzan, and Cyrenaica, though they eventually received Ministry of Defense backing.[76] Their membership was ostensibly constituted by mixed and rotating units from several communities, which would theoretically allow Shield forces, in the name of the revolution and the central government, to insert themselves as a nonpartisan force between warring communities, as they had along the Tunisian border and in the deep south (Kufra and Sebha).

Questions were also raised as to whether or not efforts to secure Libya's increasingly destabilized border regions were in fact efforts to control – not to eliminate – clandestine trade networks through which humans, arms, drugs, and other commodities easily flowed in and out.[77] Indeed, as much as militias benefited financially from receiving government recognition and compensation, both official state forces and unofficial armed groups actively sought and procured independent sources of funding that afforded them a degree of autonomy from Libya's weak and vacillating central authorities. For example, militias from Zuwara established a border guard that was later approved by the Ministry of Defense in March 2012. These militias then used that authority to assert control over the local smuggling trade and to antagonize communities perceived as anti-revolutionary. Likewise, former fighters with the Libyan Islamic Fighting Group claimed to have formed a National Guard to protect borders and essential infrastructures.[78]

For many Libyans, the putative neutrality of all these "official" forces was always in question. The dominance of Misratan and Zintani militias among the ranks of Libya Shield forces was one such source of concern. Accusations of partisanship were specifically leveled at Defense Minister Juwaili for promoting Zintani interests through ministry programs. At the same time, Misrata used the mantle of Libya Shield to continue its campaign of persecution against the stronghold of Gaddafi loyalists in Bani Walid. Others voiced concerns that the Libya Shield forces would become a backdoor for elements of the old regime to insinuate themselves into the new military.[79] Indeed, the central government appeared to be losing control over these forces, as more and more divisions emerged to claim membership, and thus salaries for their soldiers.[80] Both the Ministry of the Interior and Zintan's Sawa'iq Brigade benefited from illegal arms sales from the United Arab Emirates in the form of armored personnel carriers, assault rifles, and uniforms.[81]

In fostering the Shield militias, Libya's interim authorities had allowed these forces to overstep the army's traditional role of defending the country's sovereignty against external threats in order to assert a central role in the maintenance of its internal security. Though this was problematic on its own, it also created tensions with the country's established military and police forces, as well as with the new security units being created by the Ministry of the Interior. Moreover, some 56,000 police officers, nearly two-thirds of the *Jamahiriyyah*'s civil security force, had been disqualified from serving by early 2012.[82] In order to fill this vacuum, Minister of the Interior Abdel A'al from Misrata created the Supreme Security Committee in October 2011, which deputized militias under the ministry's authority. With advising and training assistance from the United Nations and Jordan, Supreme Security Committee units attempted to function as a kind of national police force or gendarmerie. Shortly before the 2012 election, these units would claim – on paper, at least – over 80,000 personnel.[83] In reality, most were no more than *thuwar* in crisp new uniforms with salaries reportedly 50 percent higher than the old police force.[84]

What thus appeared to be overlapping jurisdictions and competencies between the Ministry of the Interior and the Ministry of Defense were just as much spheres of contestation between factions vying to control the state after the revolution. Libya's reconstituted intelligence and counterintelligence agencies were likewise accused of serving special interests rather than national ones. In the east of the country, there were reports of entire Salafi militias being deputized as Supreme Security Committee forces, such as the Abu Salim Martyrs Brigade in Derna.[85] Authorities even deputized *Ansar Al-Shari'ah* units in Benghazi in early 2013 for counternarcotics and other security work.[86] As late as 2015, a UN investigation found that the Libyan Central Bank appeared to be issuing checks on behalf of the Ministry of Defense to the militant Islamists of the Benghazi Revolutionaries Shura Council for millions of dinars.[87] Subsequent initiatives to fold units of the Supreme Security Committee into a national police force and units of Libya Shield into a National Guard or the regular army were slow and painstaking. To make matters worse, some Supreme Security Committee and Libya Shield units often resisted these efforts, leading to new grievances between central authorities and revolutionary militias.[88]

While Gaddafi-era institutions like the established military and police were understandably viewed with suspicion, Libya's new security institutions were quickly proving ineffective, self-serving, corrupt, and partisan in their own right. Units within the Supreme Security Committee and Libya Shield infamously blockaded the parliament, demanding passage of the Political Isolation Law in mid-2013.[89] Efforts to police Libya's new police, for obvious reasons, ran the risk of incurring their wrath. Officials who investigated and attempted to punish corruption within the new security forces faced constant threats and intimidation. "[I]t would be impossible for me to give the order to arrest a militia member," insisted a high-level commander in Cyrenaica, "Impossible."[90] Despite their power, these official state forces nonetheless came under intense criticism for partisanship and dereliction of duty.

Given the extent to which Libya Shield and Supreme Security Committee forces had quickly discredited themselves over the course of 2012, Islamists and Misratans found their way into the ranks of a new coalition, the Libyan Revolutionaries Operating Room, born out of the Supreme Revolutionaries Council. This organizational framework soon became the leading military coalition of anti-accomodationist tendencies backing the Political Isolation Law, and even received orders from the President of the Congress, Abu Sahmain, in mid-2013.[91] The fragmentation of official state security bodies was witnessed elsewhere as well. The Petroleum Facilities Guard, a Gaddafi-era institution whose commander, Ali Ahrash, had defected to the revolution, soon became a vehicle for regionalist, ethnic, tribal, and communal ambitions, depending on which field, pipeline, refinery, or port any particular unit happened to have assigned itself the task of defending.[92] In Cyrenaica, where pre existing state structures were less affected by the revolution, almost none of the new security institutions developed in Tripoli took root. Former units of Gaddafi's military, including the Special Forces, maintained order and security under the leadership of General Khalifa Haftar, particularly against the growing threat of violent Islamist extremism.[93]

The shortcomings of security sector reform in Libya were vividly illustrated by the October 10, 2013, kidnapping of Prime Minister Ali Zeidan, allegedly at the hands of an Islamist militia. Islamist sentiments in the country had indeed been enflamed the previous week when a US Special Forces raid snatched a longtime Al-Qaida operative, Anas Al-Libi, from his home in Tripoli, taking him back to the United States to face trial. Some Libyans faulted Zeidan for failing to confront this gross violation of Libyan sovereignty; others were convinced that Zeidan had actually approved the US operation. Whether or not Zeidan's kidnapping was actually a botched coup by Islamists, it had become common practice for militias to threaten lawmakers – individually or the Congress as a whole – in order to steer the government's agenda.[94] Few were even surprised by the abduction. Zeidan and his troubled administration had made little progress toward their key agenda items: a new constitution, the rehabilitation of core state institutions, and the taming of the *thuwar*. In the end, Zeidan's opponents in the Congress finally succeeded in ousting him in March 2014. This time the pretext was more convincing: his administration had failed to stop a rogue Cyrenaican militia at the port of Sidra from loading a foreign tanker with crude oil. A US special forces team eventually seized the tanker near Cyprus and returned it to Zawiya. By the time the tanker was back in Libya, Zeidan's leadership had been terminated in a vote of no confidence. Citing concerns for his personal safety, he fled the country, but did so illegally, under a cloud of suspicion and allegations of corruption. His replacement, Abdullah Al-Thani, the Defense Minister, would fare no better in his efforts to steer Libya away from catastrophe.

Fingers in the Dam: Political and Economic Crises Converge

When the North Atlantic powers opted to support the 2011 Libyan uprising with their military might, it was widely assumed that the country's advanced levels of development, its natural resources, and its financial assets would facilitate a smooth transition to a post-Gaddafi order. Libya indeed boasted world-class infrastructures in many parts of the country, and was ahead of its North African neighbors according to various developmental indices. There was also a highly educated elite, at home and abroad, eager to reengage with their country. Initial estimates spoke of over $100 million in foreign cash reserves and opportunities for hundreds of billions of dollars in potential foreign direct investment. Libya itself held some $120 billion in foreign investments, from the global financial sector to development projects in Africa. There were also hundreds of millions of dollars in Gaddafi family assets and properties across the world that could be seized as state property by Libya's new authorities.[95]

And of course there was Libya's neglected energy sector. Officials with the country's National Oil Corporation boasted that it would be easy to bring production back up to speed, as hydrocarbon-related infrastructure had surprisingly suffered only minor damage during the 2011 uprising. Some even suggested that Libya could return to its pre-revolutionary output of at least 1.3 million barrels per day in just over a year's time.[96] Since the early 1990s, Libya's production had hovered around the mark of 1.5 million barrels per day, a target that was almost reached in late 2012. With global oil prices often rising above $100 per barrel in 2012, the country's domestic economic activity, spurred by state subsidies and a large public sector, appeared to recover rapidly as well.[97]

Such assessments proved naïve. They overestimated the capacity of the international community to help as much as they underestimated the capacity of various constituencies within Libya to derail the transitional process. At the end of the revolution in 2011, the full scope of the country's needs in terms of international assistance was still unclear. All the major international institutions that would play a role in Libya's rehabilitation – the United Nations Support Mission in Libya, the European Union, the World Bank, and a multitude of other inter- and non-governmental organizations – were still getting their bearings in the summer of 2012. At the time, it was assumed that the country's substantial financial and natural endowments would underwrite a rapid and effective peacebuilding effort, though this assumption was made without giving due consideration to other demands on those funds, ones that would emerge as a result of the 2011 war. The National Transitional Council claimed that there was $170 billion in Libyan frozen assets it should have access to, though the international Libyan contact group and other agencies patronizingly sought to make sure that those funds would be transferred and used in a way that benefited Libyans and not any specific interest group. Needless to say, the neocolonial overtones of this approach did not sit well with Libya's new leaders, who felt that they were being punished for Gaddafi's sins and hamstrung by these policies.

The task of governing Libya was made all the more difficult by the precipitous decline in state revenues as oil production faltered and the transitional authorities burned through the country's cash reserves to keep the peace. Not only were militias being constantly placated, but so was the general population. With nearly five-sixths of the working-age population serving in the public sector, and with absentee rates over 50 percent in the bureaucracy and the official security sector, salaries were as much a welfare scheme as a source for rampant corruption for employers.[98] A December 2012 survey of Supreme Security Committee units found that nearly 40 percent of the 162,000 members on its payroll were not actually serving; a year later, only 12 percent of this total had passed the required training to become police officers.[99] Direct subsidies to all Libyan citizens instituted in early 2012 only put further pressure on the central bank. Hafed Al-Ghwell, a Libyan with the World Bank, described these payouts to militias and other citizens as simply "the biggest robbery in the history of humanity."[100]

Adding insult to injury, global oil prices declined over the course of two years, going from over $100 per barrel in mid-2014 to as low as $40 in early 2016. This came as a surprise to many; ongoing political turbulence across the world's primary oil-producing regions in Latin America, the Middle East, and Africa (Libya included) suggested prices would remain above $100 per barrel. The problem appeared to be a significant glut of excess oil on the inter-national market, despite the marginal loss of Libya's normal contribution of around 1 to 1.5 million barrels per day. The exceptionally high prices of the previous years had ironically undermined the oil industry. High prices had incentivized the development of previously unprofitable sources of oil and gas using new and more expensive techniques of extraction on land and out at sea. These new sources of oil began to overwhelm markets, driving prices down.

The drop in global oil prices also came at a time when Libya was struggling to restore its capacity to extract, refine, and export oil and gas. Though the country's oil could theoretically remain profitable at extremely low prices, global oversupply often meant even Libya could not turn a profit. Meanwhile, the political imperative to maintain government salaries for civil servants and local authorities, as well as food imports, only increased as the country's future became increasingly uncertain. For the first time since the early 1980s, Libya's central bank entered a phase of deficit spending from 2014 onward, though at rates unparalleled in the country's history as an oil exporter.[101]

While most of OPEC's member states would soon face the imperative to impose production cuts, Libya's National Oil Corporation struggled just to restore and maintain production. With so many disparate stakeholders across the country's three historical regions, each controlled different aspects of the hydrocarbon infrastructure: from extraction sites and refineries to pipelines, storage tanks, and export terminals. Coordinating all of these different groups, each of which could singlehandedly disable oil production or export, often proved impossible. As various actors and infra-structural vulnerabilities began to undermine oil production throughout 2013, they drove export levels down to numbers not witnessed since the 2011 uprising.[102] By late 2014, Cyrenaican federalists had succeeded in blockading most oil exports from eastern terminals, denying Libya some $40 billion in revenues.[103]

In an effort to recuperate their lost legitimacy in the face of growing security and economic crises, Libya's transitional authorities – having extended their lapsed mandate – set about organizing a series of votes in the first half of 2014.

Unfortunately, the cumulative effect of these votes was to deepen the political crisis. Interim Prime Minister Abdullah Al-Thani managed to hold on to power despite challenges to his leadership, mainly from the Islamist bloc of the Congress. The election of the sixty-member constitutional drafting body was finally held in February 2014, though voter registration and turnout rates were 50 percent below their 2012 equivalents. In some voting districts, ongoing violence reduced participation as well. And while the composition of the Assembly was designed to appease Cyrenaican and Fezzani interests by dividing the representation equally among Libya's three historical regions, the Assembly's weak quota for women and ethnic minorities was subject to heavy criticism and a near total boycott by Amazigh communities. Working from Al-Bayda in the increasingly insecure east, the subsequent efforts of the Assembly, like that of the Congress, were subject to threats and attacks that delayed and interrupted its work, often for months at a time.[104]

If it seemed that the transitional process outlined in the 2011 declaration was starting to get back on track with the creation of the Constitutional Assembly, such hopes were short lived. The crisis between those seeking a radical break with the past and those seeking accommodation with actors and institutions from the old regime continued to deepen. Not only did the Political Isolation Law threaten to disenfranchise a large number of Libyans, the Congress also passed a law that immunized all revolutionary militias from prosecution for crimes they committed during the 2011 uprising. Additionally, any attempts to criticize the revolution and its agents would be subject to punishment. While the Political Isolation Law made national reconciliation incredibly difficult, the latter two measures made it effectively impossible, as the legitimate grievances of those on the losing side of the 2011 war were invalidated. Yet the contentiousness of the laws being enacted only served to squander what limited political capital Libya's central authorities had gained in the 2012 elections.

The increasingly dysfunctional and unpopular Congress finally opted to abandon its work and reconstitute Libya's interim government in the form of two elected institutions: a House of Representatives and a presidential executive. To further assuage eastern concerns about Tripolitanian dominance, the Congress declared its intent to relocate the new legislature to Benghazi. Whether the President would be popularly elected or appointed by parliament was a divisive question the Congress simply deferred to the House, whose primary task was to oversee the final stages of the transitional process once the Constitutional Assembly finished its work.

As with the vote for the Constitutional Assembly earlier in the year, the June 25 vote for the House of Representatives saw voter registration and turnout rates less than half of what had been generated in the 2012 election for the Congress. First-past-the-post electoral rules for a portion of the seats further weakened the House's tenuous mandate. In heavily contested districts, the winning candidates often carried the vote based on a few hundred supporters. Insecurity in some districts led to twelve seats going unfilled. Analyses of the vote suggested that Islamists had lost ground while traditional and technocratic elites had made some gains, albeit in the context of very poor turnout and an Amazigh boycott.[105] It was thus unclear whether or not Libyan society had actually rebuked Islamist politics or just the extreme anti-Gaddafi agenda; the main effect of the vote was to obfuscate, rather than clarify, the will of the governed. In the confusion that followed, a group of politicians unilaterally reinstated the Congress on August 23, 2014, with a new Prime Minister, Omar Al-Hassi. This occurred a little over two weeks after the first meeting of the House of Representatives under Al-Thani.[106] From then onward, Libya had two competing governments.

The Revolution's Unfinished Business: Toward Civil War, Again

There were many reasons for the lack of popular enthusiasm for the June 2014 elections, chief among them was the fact that, for all intents and purposes, Libya was in a state of open civil war. Libya's second civil war arguably began over a month before the June 2014 elections. In the east of the country, radical Islamist groups and armed gangs were waging a campaign of terror and extortion, especially in Benghazi. Bombings and assassinations, often by anonymous perpetrators, were becoming increasingly common. Assailants also targeted those with ties to the former regime, such as members of the elite Al-Saiqa Brigade, one of the *Jamahiriyyah*'s special forces units that had defected to the revolution.[107] The growth of kidnapping rackets, which saw hundreds of Libyans abducted for ransom in 2014, was acutely felt in Benghazi.[108]

In an effort to confront this metastasizing insecurity in Cyrenaica, General Haftar, then in his early seventies, launched Operation Dignity on May 16, though without sanction from Libya's transitional authorities. Haftar's forces opened with attacks against *Ansar Al-Shari'ah*, leading to more clashes and terrorism. Assassinations of politicians, lawyers, journalists, and other civil society activists – killings most often placed at the feet of radical Islamists – continued throughout the summer of 2014 in Cyrenaica, further adding to the climate of fear and anarchy that Operation Dignity sought to end.[109]

The coalition that formed Operation Dignity was initially composed of Haftar's own loyalist forces. Most of these troops had joined Haftar, a formerly exiled general, when he returned to help lead the 2011 military campaign against the Gaddafi regime. Drawing strength from some of Cyrenaica's dominant tribal confederations, the network of Dignity affiliates was later extended to include allied militias from the oil crescent and the wider Sirtica plain. Operation Dignity also gained support from allies in the Kufra region, coastal Tripolitania, the Nafusa, and the Fezzan. Political endorsements were issued from the National Forces Alliance and figures like Mustafa Abd Al-Jalil. Questions were nonetheless raised as to whether or not Operation Dignity was merely a limited counterterrorism effort or something more ambitious. Haftar himself stated that he saw no difference between the terrorists destabilizing Benghazi and the moderate Islamists seeking to hold on to power in the Congress, including the Muslim Brotherhood.[110] And given that some of the militias fighting Haftar in Cyrenaica were politically, or at least ideologically, aligned with the Islamist-backed coalitions then controlling parts of coastal Tripolitania and the Congress, it was easy enough for Haftar's opponents to claim that Operation Dignity had in fact declared war on the central government.[111] That said, Haftar's campaign would soon learn that its foes in Cyrenaica would not yield so easily. Three years would pass before Operation Dignity could claim to have definitively secured Benghazi, and even then its hold was violently contested.

Nonetheless, what Haftar appeared to be constructing was much more than a security force capable of taking on extremists in Cyrenaica. Operation Dignity would eventually constitute one of the most coherent politico-military forces in post-Gaddafi Libya. Much of its strength and legitimacy would be rooted in actors and communities that had been increasingly marginalized within the post-revolutionary order. Indeed, the initial grievance at the heart of Haftar's "dignity" campaign was the extent to which those Libyans with real military experience, training, and leadership abilities found themselves being treated with less respect, and often with outright suspicion, during the 2011 war and the months afterward. Haftar, despite having opposed Gaddafi since the late 1980s, found that his ties to the old regime continued to work against him as he sought a place for himself and his allies in the new Libya. As the agenda of Libya's revolutionaries grew more and more antagonistic toward former regime figures, a backlash was bound to occur. The Political Isolation Law was only the last affront in a series of maneuvers against accommodationists that contributed to the rise of Operation Dignity.

In the months and years to come, Operation Dignity would thus be cast by its opponents as a counter-revolutionary effort by old regime stalwarts. Domestic and international critics of Haftar likewise voiced concerns about the all too cozy relationships between former high-level officials in the *Jamahiriyyah*, whether civil or military leaders, found in Operation Dignity. A constant fear shared by many Libyans was whether or not the country's veteran technocratic elites were seeking to reconstitute the social alliances and security institutions of something that might be called Gaddafism, perhaps even in partnership with leading members of the Gaddafi family. Saif Al-Islam, after all, was being held by militias allied to Operation Dignity in Zintan.

Haftar's personal ambitions were also questioned, as he was frequently depicted as a potential military dictator. Operation Dignity's commitment to a democratic transition was undoubtedly put into question when Zintani militias launched a failed attempt to unseat the Congress in mid-May 2014, well ahead of the vote for the House. Not only were Haftar's suspected ambitions a motivating factor behind the resistance to Operation Dignity, the conduct of the ostensibly professional forces of his Libyan National Army likewise raised concerns. As the struggle for the east degenerated into bitter urban warfare in 2014, Dignity's militias proved as capable of committing egregious violations of human rights and humanitarian norms as the Islamist militias they were combating.[112]

Claiming that the remnants of the old regime had finally shown their true colors, Libya's revolutionaries began to consolidate their gains more aggressively. With the passage of the Political Isolation Law and the blessing of Congress President Abu Sahmain, Libya's hardline revolutionaries launched their own military campaign against their accommodationist foes.[113] This campaign, branded Operation Libya Dawn, would largely entail the ejection of Zintani militias – the main representatives of Dignity's military coalition in Tripolitania – from the capital. July 2014 saw several battles led by the Libyan Revolutionaries Operation Room against Zintani forces for control over key locations and infrastructure. The fighting resulted in the near total destruction of Tripoli's international civilian airport, though Zintani forces had finally been routed. The pyrrhic victory of the Misratan–Islamist alliance over Zintani forces, which at least denied Haftar the possibility of bringing troops to the capital via Egyptian or Emirati airlift,[114] nonetheless saw billions of dollars in damage to aircraft, terminals, and other buildings, rendering the entire facility inoperable for years. The battle for the airport also convinced the international community that Libya was no longer a safe place for foreigners. In short order, Tripoli witnessed the rapid exodus of foreign journalists, agencies, businesses, and governments; large numbers of diplomatic staff withdrew, while many embassies were temporarily shuttered. An August 2014 video of Dawn fighters from Misrata joyfully playing in the pool of a US diplomatic facility in Tripoli evoked raw memories of the events in Benghazi two years beforehand. It also seemed to suggest, perhaps unfairly, an affinity between those who had taken control of the capital in the summer of 2014 and those who had infamously killed the US Ambassador in 2012.

Further developments also allowed Libya's new rival governments to claim legitimacy. With the capital and surrounding areas under the control of Congress-allied forces, the House of Representatives fled to the far east of the country where Haftar's army was concentrated. Convening in a ferry docked at the port of Tobruk, Libya's twelfth largest city and just 100 miles short of the Egyptian border, the House insisted that it was now the true representative of the Libyan people. In November, the Libyan Supreme Court nullified the March 2014 amendment to the interim constitution that had paved the way for the June vote for the House of Representatives, a ruling that provided the resuscitated – though technically lapsed – Congress with legal standing.[115] The United Nations and the major North Atlantic powers nonetheless opted to continue to recognize the July 2014 elections as legitimate as they had at the time of the vote. The House thus became Libya's legitimate central authority in the eyes of much of the international community. Yet almost 50 percent of the House's seats either went unfilled at the time of the original vote or were empty because of boycotts from a growing anti-Haftar bloc.

While legitimacy was one thing, governing was another. Two essential and symbiotic state institutions, the National Oil Corporation and the Central Bank, both based in Tripoli, attempted to continue their work – paying government salaries and financing vital imports – regardless of the country's fractured sovereignty.[116] Control over Libya's core infrastructures – water, electricity, and oil – varied from locality to loyalty, having been divided among the country's various factions in the war of 2011. A failed Misratan effort to take control of the oil crescent in late 2014 from forces nominally allied to Haftar's Libyan National Army established battle-lines in the center of the country that would remain more or less unchanged over the course of 2015.

The Dignity–House coalition and the Dawn–Congress coalition received other forms of international support that only served to exacerbate the new civil war. While Libya ostensibly remained under an international arms embargo monitored and maintained by the UN Security Council, Haftar's forces benefited from Egyptian, Saudi, and Emirati support. Prominent international supporters of the Muslim Brotherhood – notably Turkey, Sudan, and Qatar – backed the nominally Islamist Dawn coalition. Critics of the Dawn coalition, both domestic and foreign, alleged cooperation between its forces and Libya's radical Islamist militias, notably those operating in Cyrenaica and those that would eventually join with the Islamic State movement. Foreign and domestic support for these radical Islamist groups was less overt than the conspicuous assistance rendered to the Dignity campaign.

Libya's second civil war would also witness sporadic acts of foreign military intervention, though there was none of the humanitarian pretension that surrounded the UN-authorized intervention in 2011. Brute geopolitical interests would come to define foreign meddling in the Dawn–Dignity war. Planes from Egypt and the United Arab Emirates engaged in bombing raids on Tripoli against forces allied to the Congress shortly after the victory of Libya Dawn in the battle with Zintan for the capital. There were also allegations that Haftar was coordinating with Sudanese rebel groups for the purposes of recruitment and control over Libya's southeastern corner. While Saudi and Emirati support for Haftar's initiative could be chalked up to diverging interests between most of the Gulf Cooperation Council states and Qatar, Cairo's military intervention seemed equally motivated by the desire to deny the Egyptian Muslim Brotherhood a safe haven to the west. Indeed, the military regime in Egypt had only come back to power in July 2013 under General Abdel Fattah el-Sisi, who had suspended the constitution and removed the country's democratically elected President, Mohammed Morsi of the Muslim Brotherhood. As the Egyptian regime set about dismantling the Brotherhood at home, it increasingly collaborated with Haftar and other allies in Libya. And soon all sides in Libya's civil war would receive military and intelligence assistance from the United States and other North Atlantic powers in the fight against the Islamic State.

5 | Libya on the Brink ————————

The dissipation of central authority and human security in Libya from 2011 onward created a context in which radical Islamist groups had significant leeway to pursue a strategy of social purification and political destabilization. As had been witnessed in other jihadi movements in recent memory, notably Algeria in the 1990s and Iraq in the 2000s, terroristic violence had proven an effective means to wage asymmetric warfare, from selective targeting of civil society activists to mass indiscriminate attacks in crowded public spaces. In their efforts to provoke the state into over-reacting through horrific violence, jihadists in various armed conflicts had used terrorism to achieve two key ends: first, to prove their bona fide commitment to the cause and, second, to control the Islamist opposition by polarizing it. Such violent techniques had allowed radical flanks to dominate insurgencies despite being a minority within the broader armed resistance. However, what putative success these strategies achieved in the short term often proved to be unsustainable in the long run when it came to military victory and seizing state power.

The case of Libya and the Islamic State proved to be no different. During and after the revolution, Islamist militias were accused of murdering several hundred former regime officials. In the post-revolutionary phase, secular intellectuals, journalists, politicians, and activists, particularly those pushing for gender equality, found themselves subject to threats and acts of physical violence. Perhaps the most infamous was the June 2014 assassination of Salwa Bugaighis, a human rights lawyer and former National Transitional Council member. By then, Prime Minister Al-Thani had already classified several of these groups as terrorist organizations, though it was a case of too little, too late.[1] Also common were efforts by radicals to destroy religious establishments and buildings associated with other Islamic sects and doctrines. During this campaign, which saw over 100 such sites damaged, razed, or bombed, it appeared that some elected officials and security agencies tacitly condoned these attacks through their inaction.[2]

The violent cleaving of Libya's interim government in mid-2014 was eclipsed on the international stage by the stunning military victories of the Islamic State organization in Syria and Iraq. Three years into the brutal civil war in Syria, the organization had managed to subsume a significant portion of the anti-regime insurgency under its control and, in so doing, seized large portions of Syrian territory. It did so with the aid of veterans of the anti-US insurgency in Iraq, the very conflict in which the Islamic State's founders had also cut their teeth. The Islamic State organization then triumphantly returned to Iraq, taking its third largest city, Mosul, as its provisional capital in June. It thus appeared to accomplish what none of its predecessors – from the Muslim Brotherhood to Al-Qaida – had come close to achieving: substantive military control over territories in the Islamic heartlands.[3]

Modern Islamist and contemporary jihadi movements had long articulated their goals in terms of establishing an Islamic state (*al-dawlah al-islamiyyah*), either in their countries of origin or through a federation of territories across the Middle East, if not into northwest Africa and central Asia. What therefore made the Islamic State's June 2014 declaration of independence noteworthy was the extent to which its claim of *de facto* sovereignty over swaths of Syria and Iraq seemed credible. A similar declaration of independence in northern Mali in 2012, though receiving far less international attention, was even more directly connected to the ongoing collapse of the Libyan state. Both Libyan arms and fighters had contributed to the formation of a nascent Islamic state around Timbuktu before UN-backed forces, led by French troops, reestablished central government control in 2013. Libyans had also gone to Syria in significant numbers to continue the fight against tyranny after the success of the 2011 uprising against Gaddafi. Some of these Libyans returned with new ideas about how to wage jihad and for what reason.

Seeking to capitalize on the apparent geopolitical momentum the Islamic State had generated in the Syrian civil war, several personalities and organizations within Libya's radical Islamist movement began reframing their social action, political objectives, and armed resistance in likeminded ways in 2014. Before then, Libya's nationalist and transnationalist jihadi militias had coalesced into several *shura* councils, notably in Benghazi and Derna. Opposition to Haftar's Dignity campaign helped unite several of Cyrenaica's Islamist councils and militias, including *Ansar Al-Shari'ah*, into a loose coalition of forces that contested the Libyan National Army's dominion over the east, locking Haftar's forces into a long, cruel fight over Benghazi.

Clear indications of a connection between the Islamic State movement in southwest Asia and Libya finally emerged in late 2014. In November, Derna-based Islamists declared fealty to Abu Bakr Al-Baghdadi, the head of the global Islamic State movement and self-declared *Khalifah* (leader) of the Islamic world.[4] From then onwards, Libya's Islamic State affiliates deployed tactics adapted from their colleagues in Syria and Iraq, notably the highly choreographed use of intense acts of violence, neatly edited for dissemination on the Internet. Mimicking such videos, Islamic State activists in Libya published a recording in February 2015 in which twenty-one Coptic Christians from Egypt were executed by beheading a few weeks after their abduction in Sirte.[5] Though this video succeeded in announcing to the world the Islamic State's new province in Libya, it soon precipitated airstrikes from Egypt and galvanized much of the Libyan opposition – Islamist and otherwise – against the Islamic State's puritanical vision.

The most startling achievement of the Islamic State in Libya was its conquest of Sirte in mid-2015, driving out the occupying Misratan forces. Sirte then became the organization's main Libyan base of operations and its most sizable foothold outside of the Levant and Mesopotamia. In other locations across Cyrenaica and Tripolitania, the Islamic State failed to achieve similar levels of control, though there were indications that the organization was attempting to make good use of Libya's Saharan interior for logistical, financial, and recruitment purposes, just as jihadi fighters had done throughout the first decade of the twenty-first century in the central-western part of the Sahara–Sahel region. More often than not, it was other Islamist militias that prevented the Islamic State from establishing an organizational presence in key locations like Tripoli. A January 2015 suicide attack on the Corinthia, a major international hotel in Tripoli, home to both foreigners and government officials, proved to be the organization's only major action in the capital. In the east, Cyrenaican federalists guarding the oil crescent were a bulwark again the Islamic State's advance toward key hydrocarbon infrastructures on the coast. The Libyan National Army's campaign in Benghazi, coupled with infighting between jihadi militias, denied the Islamic State significant purchase in Cyrenaica outside of Derna. There, similar internecine fighting among nationalist and transnationalist jihadi groups likewise blunted the Islamic State's efforts to implant itself.[6] Indeed, the consolidation of the Islamic State's grip on Sirte developed in response to the resistance it faced in Derna, which the organization eventually abandoned in 2016.[7]

The successful ensconcement of the Islamic State in Sirte held interesting parallels with the organization's rise out of the chaos of the Syrian civil war that began in 2011 and, more tellingly, its subsequent incursion into Iraq in 2014. In Iraq, active and passive support for the Islamic State primarily came from Sunni Arab communities who faced increasing marginalization after the 2003 Anglo-American invasion, largely at the hands of the now Shia-dominated governments in Baghdad and the security forces created by the United States after the fall of the Saddam Hussein regime. Outright international favoritism shown to Kurdish regional authorities and military forces was another source of ire. The withdrawal of US forces in 2011 left Sunni Arabs, notably those who had collaborated with the American counterinsurgency effort, exposed to the state terror of the Shia regime in Baghdad. The Islamic State's successful invasion of Iraq partially benefited from the support of Sunnis, especially those with extensive military experience under Saddam's regime and those who had violently resisted both the US occupation and the security forces of the Shia government.[8]

In Libya, the Islamic State would similarly make inroads among a population that had been dispossessed of their political power by civil war and foreign intervention. That the organization would find support among the inhabitants of Sirte, a city previously known for its loyalism to the staunchly anti-Islamist regime of Gaddafi, seemed counterintuitive at first. These developments began to make more sense when one considered the ways in which Libya's revolutionaries had punished Sirte in 2011 and marginalized it in the years that followed. Like the Sunni Arabs of Iraq, loyalists to the Gaddafi regime appeared to embrace the extremism of the Islamic State in the face of interim authorities that were demonstrably hostile to their interests. With the aid of knowledgeable and battle-hardened veterans of other transnationalist jihadi campaigns, as well as an influx of new foreign volunteers, nationalist Islamist militants joined forces with politically and economically dispossessed communities to forge an alliance to reimagine the modern nation-state and then violently create it, starting in Sirte.

The Tragedy of Sirte

Though there were some salient parallels between the rise of the Islamic State in Libya and southwest Asia, their differences – and the specifics of the Libyan context – were far more revealing. The Islamic State undoubtedly took advantage of the fact that Sirte had been on the losing side of the 2011 war. As it was Gaddafi's adopted hometown, its fortunes grew exponentially during his four decades of rule. Serving as a blank slate upon which the modern infrastructural glories of the *Jamahiriyyah* and, later, pan-Africanism could be physically constructed, Sirte was transformed from a small seaside village into one of Libya's largest cities, serving as an important administrative center. It thus came as little surprise that Gaddafi opted to make his last stand in Sirte in 2011 after the fall of Tripoli. Not only was the fury of the revolutionaries inflicted upon the people and buildings of Sirte during Gaddafi's final desperate days, the city also witnessed significant looting and other acts of collective punishment by the *thuwar* in the immediate aftermath. At the time of the first elections in 2012, residents not only complained about the lack of effort from the interim authorities to address the unparalleled levels of destruction reaped upon the city by the *thuwar* in 2011, they also complained about the general sense that the entire city was still being made to suffer for the crimes of the Gaddafi regime, both past and recent. During the early transitional period, Sirte's authorities had been kept on a short leash by their revolutionary occupiers. They were prohibited from forming local defense forces lest Sirte form the kind of counter-revolutionary militias that had allowed places like Bani Walid to defy and successfully challenge the *thuwar* in numerous armed confrontations.

The seizure of Sirte, however, was not the result of military acumen on the part of the Islamic State in Libya. Unlike the organization's stunning conventional military campaign in western Iraq in 2014, its presence in Sirte was established gradually, building on initial contacts made in 2013.[9] This infiltration was enabled by the increasing focus placed on Tripoli and Benghazi before the fracturing of Libya's sovereignty in mid-2014. Emerging from the interstices of the failed transitional period, the Islamic State took full advantage of Sirte's political alienation and its relative geographical isolation, being almost equal in distance from the primary urban battlefields in the east and west. As long as the eastern oil facilities remained under the control of the Petroleum Facilities Guard, the management of Sirte by

Libya Shield forces, mainly Misratan militias, was of little importance to officials in Tripoli compared to the country's other problems.

It was thus Sirte's marginalization within the post-revolutionary order that allowed the Islamic State to insinuate itself into the city and take control. An important aspect of this marginalization was the political disenfranchisement of the social forces that had helped underwrite Gaddafi's power in Sirte and beyond. A UN report from early 2016 describes the rise of the Islamic State in Sirte as initially premised on cohabitation between the movement's activists and the city's most important political actors at the time: first, the regionally dominant and loyalist tribes of the Qadhadhafa and the Magharba; second, former security officials from the Gaddafi regime; and, third, *Ansar Al-Shari'ah*. *Ansar Al-Shari'ah* in Sirte had been dominated by Misratan Salafi activists, and so was thought to be working in the interests of the broader Libya Dawn coalition in Tripoli and Misrata. Instead, *Ansar Al-Shari'ah*'s extremist views allowed it to become an important ideological and organizational precursor of the Libyan branch of the Islamic State.[10]

As the prestige of the Islamic State's brand grew internationally in 2014 and as foreign jihadi fighters found their way into Libya, young men in Sirte also began to join or defect to the organization, as did many other Libyans. Questions were thus raised as to whether or not the Islamic State in Libya might be able to ground its political project and military power in the social alliances that had underwritten Gaddafi's rule. A coalition of this nature would theoretically allow the Islamic State to project its campaign to the west (via Bani Walid and Zintan) and to the south and east (via the central oases to Sebha, and then from Kufra to Cyrenaica).[11] This proved not to be the case. The unique confluence of events that had allowed the Islamic State to metastasize in Sirte only existed there. And as foreign fighters from North Africa, the Middle East, and even central Africa augmented its ranks, the Islamic State in Libya began to take on its own character, eschewing the indigenous social relations that had incubated it. As an anonymous tribal *shaykh* from Sirte insisted to Human Rights Watch, "[T]he power is in the hands of the foreigners."[12]

What compensation the Islamic State in Sirte was able to provide to its fighters often came from a combination of foreign donations, taxation of local citizens, and dispossessed or abandoned property, whether in the form of food, durable goods, or housing. There were even efforts to sell Libyan antiquities on the international black market. Above all, the Islamic State in Sirte benefited from a one-time cash injection of over $2 million taken from the city's branch of the Central Bank. None of this, however, allowed the organization to establish an effective economy or to enact competent governance.[13] As health and other services grew increasingly scarce, residents found themselves unable to access resources being monopolized in support of the Islamic State's fighters. With more and more of Sirte's citizens fleeing the city, economic accumulation through expropriation proved to be an unsustainable strategy for the Islamic State to create and maintain order in Sirte.

In the face of declining financial resources, the Islamic State – its ranks having increased to several thousand – began to fall back on violence and terror to galvanize its supporters, to subordinate its allies, to punish its opponents, and to impose its puritanical vision.[14] Following the organization's model in Iraq and Syria, brigades of morality police terrorized the citizenry in their efforts to enforce a thirteen-point charter based on their understanding of Islamic law. Forced gender segregation, compelled female veiling for women older than ten years of age, coerced Islamic education, summary punishments, arbitrary detentions, and show trials were the new norm. Infractions, ranging from public smoking to "witchcraft" (i.e., traditional cultural or Sufi practices), could result in fines, lashings, imprisonment, or death. Public executions in the city center and nearby locations, including decapitation by sword, soon became commonplace throughout 2015 and into 2016. Bodies were frequently left on scaffolding to rot.[15] An August 2015 massacre of several dozen members of the Furjan and Warfalla tribes, members of which had revolted against the Islamic State, seemed to silence all future dissent.

But quelling this uprising also put a limit on the capacity of the organization to build a broader socio-political alliance so as to achieve any subsequent military gains. Even more telling about the rise and rule of the Islamic State in Sirte was the fact that it precipitated the flight of over four-fifths of the city's population to other areas of Libya.[16]

With the outbreak of a new civil war in mid-2014, both the Dawn and Dignity coalitions were initially focused on consolidating their respective grips on Tripoli and Benghazi. And with Cyrenaica's main jihadi organizations – the various *shura* councils and *Ansari Al-Shari'ah* – locked in combat with Haftar's army, the Islamic State was able to co-opt and coerce its way to power in Sirte. By June 2015, it had not only secured control over most of the city center but had also driven the Misratan fighters from their base at the civil–military airport. In so doing, the Islamic State created a significant territorial buffer around Sirte, the provisional capital of the Caliphate's new North African province.

Though the Islamic State's military accomplishments in Libya would always pale in comparison to those in Iraq and Syria, its presence was enough to disrupt most foreign perceptions of the Libyan conflict. What was going on in Libya could no longer be dismissed as another intractable civil war in the Arab world. The conflict was in fact far more serious, complicated, internationalized, and pressing than had previously been assumed. After all, unforeseen social and political dynamics had somehow allowed a militia of possibly no more than 500 domestic and foreign jihadi fighters, armed and equipped with the typical suite of light weapons and modified pickup trucks, to secure one of Libya's largest cities.[17] With Sirte as its base, only 200 kilometers of coastal desert separated the Islamic State from Libya's most important oil storage and export facilities. And in the weeks to come, the organization's fighters would work hard to close the gap. The lackadaisical attitude of the UN Security Council and North Atlantic powers toward Libya's deteriorating security was no longer a luxury either could afford.

Dawn versus Dignity: The Structures of War and Peace in the New Libya

In the aftermath of the new civil war that erupted in summer of 2014, the United Nations mission in Libya essentially reverted from peacebuilding to peacemaking. As discussed in the previous chapters, international peacebuilding in Libya after the 2011 uprising had been a case of too little, too late. And if nation- and statebuilding assistance to Libya had been woefully insufficient following the collapse of the Gaddafi regime in late 2011, such assistance was tempered by extreme reluctance and incapacity from mid-2014 onward. In 2012 and 2013, international assistance to Libya's transitional authorities had centered on political advising, pushing for elections to establish legitimate authority and to improve the capacity of the central government. While this approach was understandable, it underestimated the dire economic situation and the more insidious problem of the militias.

With the onset of a new civil war, international initiatives to help Libya from mid-2014 onward faced a difficult dilemma: work with either side – Dawn or Dignity – and be accused of partisanship; work with neither side and helplessly watch Libya implode.[18] Apart from ostensibly neutral yet highly competent institutions like the National Oil Corporation and the Central Bank, foreign governments, organizations, and businesses were caught between two claims of legitimacy. In many cases, firms and agencies opted to work with local governments instead, where there was often effective and popular leadership, as well as more or less reliable security.[19]

The local was indeed an often ignored or misunderstood element of Libyan society, whether in the context of the Gaddafi regime, the failed transition, or the ongoing civil war. Contrary to prevailing understandings of Libya's post-revolutionary conflict as either religious or tribal in nature, there is evidence to suggest that the civil war erupted despite – not because of – the interests and actions of most tribal leaders and religious authorities.[20] More often than not, the Dawn–Dignity civil war was interpreted as a war between

Islamists and secular liberals, with the Congress–Dawn coalition representing the former and the House–Dignity coalition representing the latter. What truth there was to this thesis was undermined by the various ways in which this bifurcation – Islamists versus secular liberals – was just as often complicated and contradicted.

On the one hand, framing the second Libyan civil war in terms of Islamists and liberals failed to recognize the centrality of Islam to almost all major actors in the civil war. On the other hand, forces like Haftar's Libyan National Army and Zintan's militias were often described as secular by simple virtue of the fact that they were fighting self-identified Islamists. As much as religion was a relevant factor in the Libyan civil war, it was always a question of *how* Islam should inform political life, not a question of *if*, for almost all constituencies in Libya.[21] In the months and years to come, Libya would witness significant escalation in the levels of violence between various kinds of Islamist militias. In 2016, Misratan forces, aligned with the pro-Muslim Brotherhood administration in Tripoli, would wage a fierce battle against the Islamic State in the streets and alleyways of Sirte with US military support. Such apparent Islamist-on-Islamist fighting was not limited to the campaign against the Islamic State, either. In the east, where Operation Dignity mainly confronted Islamist militias in Benghazi and Derna, there appeared to be signs of increasing Salafi influence on Haftar's forces, as well as the regional political structures allied to him, in the form of the Madkhali school of orthodox practice associated with Saudi Arabia's "quietist" state-sponsored Islam.

Efforts to frame Libya's civil war as an inter-tribal conflict were similarly misconstrued or misleading. Manifestations of "tribal conflict" in post-revolutionary Libya were in fact often rooted in economic motivations. The Gaddafi regime's property and housing policies, for example, were often contradictory, if not politically manipulative, thus laying the groundwork for conflicting claims.[22] And as noted in previous chapters, ethnic and tribal framings of Libyan violence tend to obfuscate the *intra*-tribal and *intra*-ethnic nature of conflict in some areas and communities. Narratives of tribal and ethnic violence also obfuscated the role of tribal leaders as forces of reconciliation who opposed the alliances and armed actions of their members. The extent to which pro-Gaddafi tribes allied themselves – and were later subjugated to – the Islamic State in Sirte should be understood in relation to the fact that tribal leaders were often unable to control the actions of their young male constituents. Having been marginalized by the revolutionary regime, these young men were then seduced by the grand historical narratives and material promises of the Islamic State.

More importantly, exclusively religious or tribal under-standings of the conflict failed to take into account the extent to which some of Libya's most important peace-makers were tribal and religious figures.[23] The security and judicial vacuum that developed from 2011 onward led many communities to employ their own mechanisms for dispute mediation and resolution within and between communities, from efforts to calm Misratan–Bani Walidi tensions after the 2011 revolution to the aftermath of the 2014 civil war.[24]

In fact, popular attitudes in Libya tended to look negatively upon outspoken militant Islamists, particularly those who invoked religion to justify violence or to defend the alleged aims of the 2011 revolution. By 2016, figures like Belhadj, Sallabi, and Grand Mufti Ghariani were viewed by 90 percent of the population as impediments to peace. Given the partisanship displayed by national-level religious figures and institutions, survey data suggested that there was nonetheless strong support for local religious authority as a mechanism to resolve conflict between communities.[25] Ghariani, in particular, was the subject of ridicule in political cartoons and on social media for his tone-deaf statements, which often seemed wildly out of step with the society at large.[26] These popular opinions echoed survey data from over a decade before that suggested similar levels of confidence in local representatives above national-level ones.[27] The ample social resources available for inter-communal recon-ciliation at the local level was thus suggestive of the growing disconnect between the quotidian realities faced by most

Libyans and the hardening positions of elite political figures at the national level.[28]

Despite this growing disconnect and structural tensions between the local and the national in post-revolutionary Libya, there were good reasons to think that the civil war could be resolved through internationally facilitated mediation. An important point of consensus shared by almost all Libyans, one upon which a peace process could be grounded, was a shared commitment to Libya as an independent state and as a unified nation. Unlike the civil wars in Lebanon (1975–90) and Syria (2011), to which Libya increasingly drew unfair comparisons, Libyan national identity was not marked by the kinds of ethnic and sectarian rifts that so often seemed to make other civil wars terribly intractable. Though there were important social cleavages in the country regarding ethnic and religious identity, particularly the status of minorities (e.g., Imazighen, Tawerghans, Tuareg, Tebu, and Ibadi Muslims), these divisions largely manifested in terms of local-level conflicts. The main driver of the civil war at the national level was nonetheless political in nature: who would be allowed to define and lead the post-revolutionary state in Libya?

The absence of any viable secessionist movement was also an added benefit to the peace process. Just as the Islamic State's radical transnationalism failed to resonate with most Libyans, the same held for separatist rhetoric coming from marginal actors in the east, the Sahara, or the Nafusa mountains. Even the idea of devolved regionalism, ad hoc autonomy schemes, or a tripartite federalism, which had vocal support in Cyrenaica and Fezzan, never found widespread appeal among most Libyans. If anything, the 2011 uprising was fiercely nationalist in character, as was the civil war that followed three years later. Depending on how one looked at the situation, the incomplete transitional process was perhaps a blessing in disguise. Though the country was drifting perilously close to total collapse and mass violence, few were wedded to Libya's transitional institutions per se. The House and the Congress were just means to different ends. What actually mattered was what the rupture of 2014 had made abundantly clear: as much as revolutionaries insisted that there would be no return to Gaddafist rule, accommodationists had made it clear that they would no longer be sidelined or subordinated. Lastly, there was also a sense in which the levels of violence in Libya had not yet reached a point of no return. In the five years since the 2011 uprising, the number of deaths associated with Libya's various armed conflicts amounted to 3,617 violent fatalities by the end of 2014. Syria, by contrast, had suffered over 178,000 fatalities from its civil war during the same period.[29]

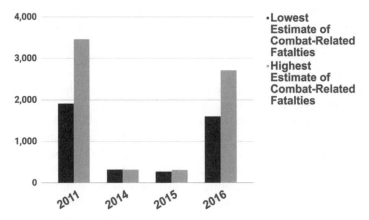

Figure 5.1. Estimates of deaths in Libya related to armed violent conflict, 2011–16.

Source: Uppsala Conflict Data Program and Allansson et al., "Organized Violence, 1989–2016."

Bridging the Gap: Toward a Unity Government

These parameters – a strong sense of national identity, universal commitment to Libya's territorial integrity, the *tabula rasa* state, the legitimacy of local authority, and the relatively low rates of violence – helped set the stage for a multilateral dialogue process initiated by the UN envoy to Libya, Bernardino León, in January 2015. Choosing Geneva as a safe and neutral meeting place, León engaged a broad array of Libyan stakeholders throughout the negotiations. In addition to inviting representatives from the House and Congress, he brought in local councils, militia leaders, traditional notables, and civil society activists. Deputies from the two parliaments were invited to attend as representatives of particular constituencies and not as delegates from rival bodies. These UN talks would eventually lead to the Libyan Political Agreement at year's end.

Not everyone in Libya was supportive of León's approach to peacemaking (i.e., multi-track diplomacy) or the UN initiative itself. The most vocal opponents were elements within the Congress, who attempted to block their colleagues from participating. Those critical of the Geneva process often alleged that the talks amounted to foreign meddling in Libyan affairs. Given the salience of anti-interventionary sentiments within Libyan political culture, critics of the process, from accommodationists in the east to Islamists in the capital, marshaled such rhetoric in order to attack the negotiations and the agreement that eventually resulted. Any UN engagement with unelected leaders was thus bound to raise concerns and protests that, once again, Libya's politicians were being circumvented by outside actors.[30] At the same time, the Congress's political legitimacy at the international level was tenuous at best, maintained only by the fact that it controlled the capital and had strong militias supporting it. Any process that treated the House as a co-equal belligerent implicitly challenged the Congress's narrative that the government in Tobruk and the Libyan National Army were counter-revolutionary renegades, if not simply criminals. Voices within the House, however, were equally skeptical for almost the same reason. There was nothing to negotiate, according to officials in Tobruk, except for the disbanding of the political and military forces controlling the capital.

The deterioration of security, the rise of the Islamic State, and the precipitous decline in state revenues, owing in large part to disrupted oil production and depressed global prices, nonetheless added urgency to the task of political reconciliation for domestic and international actors. And while the United Nations could not force anyone to participate in the talks, North Atlantic powers could at least determine who would benefit from oil sales, security cooperation, and exceptions to the arms embargo. This incentive structure helped impel the peace process, dubbed the Libyan Political Dialogue, throughout 2015.

The Libyan Political Agreement, reached at the end of the year during a final round of negotiations in Skhirat, Morocco, proposed a quasi-bicameral Government of National Accord with a new executive body. The Agreement maintained the House of Representatives in Tobruk as the country's main legislative body but gave the rump General National Congress in Tripoli a consultative role as the High Council of State. Executive authority would pass to a new body, the Presidential Council. Once empowered by votes of confidence in the House and the Congress, the Presidency Council would have a one-year mandate (with the possibility of renewal) to bring political and economic security to the country so that the transitional process would end with the creation of a constitutional democratic republic. In the meantime, the presidency would have the ability to appoint the heads of the military, security, and intelligence agencies. The Agreement also empowered the presidency to create interim security bodies to carry out its orders and to disarm and disband militias, or otherwise fold them into official state forces. The man chosen to head the new government as Prime Minister and Chair of the Presidency Council, Fayez Al-Serraj, a moderate technocrat from Tripoli serving in the House of Representatives, was selected largely because he was an unknown quantity in Libyan politics.[31]

A number of flaws nonetheless worked to undermine the Skhirat Agreement over the course of its implementation in 2016. One of the key issues – considered a deal breaker for either side – was the status and powers of the head of the armed forces in relation to the interim executive. In principle, the issue was about establishing proper civilian leadership over the military; in reality, it was a question about Haftar's role in the transition, which the House demanded and the Congress rejected. For this reason among others, the Agreement notably had little to no backing from key figures such as Nouri Abusahmain, head of the Congress, and Aguila Saleh, head of the House, as well as important militias. As critics inside and outside of Libya noted, the final stages and outcome documents of the Skhirat Agreement had been largely negotiated and signed by second-tier political figures.

Though there was noteworthy domestic support for the Agreement in Libya, particularly in Tripolitania, its strongest supporters were international.[32] First and foremost was the new UN envoy, German diplomat Martin Kobler (appointed in November 2015), and the Agreement's primary backers on the UN Security Council, which were France, Britain, and the United States. Indeed, the Security Council in its Resolution 2259 welcomed the Agreement and endorsed the proposed Presidency Council on December 23, less than a week after the signing in Skhirat. Kobler had pushed the Agreement through with the Security Council's backing by insisting, first, that the negotiations were near collapse and, second, that any agreement was better than nothing, particularly in the face of the Islamic State threat and the escalating migration crisis in the Mediterranean. In the international media, the Libyan Political Agreement was often characterized as a comprehensive peace agreement, a solution to all of Libya's challenges. In reality, it was, at best, a roadmap to a roadmap – a way to get the transition back on track. The far more difficult process of negotiating the final outcome of Libya's transitional process – the Libyan state itself – would have to come later, once a recognized, competent, and effective authority was in place to stop the fighting and guide the transition. It should also be kept in mind that, all the while, the Constitutional Assembly was ostensibly working on a draft document in the eastern city of Bayda.

International backers of the Agreement cited the need to create momentum and facts on the ground in support of an internationally endorsed transitional authority. Detractors, however, suggested that pushing ahead without any actual agreement among the principal leaders of the major factions would unnecessarily complicate and escalate an already convoluted and volatile situation. Meanwhile, the UN initiative seemed largely dismissive of a parallel process featuring members of the House and the Congress, the Libyan–Libyan dialogue, which had in fact made some headway in late 2015 as well. The agreement in Skhirat was also reached under a cloud of controversy: former UN envoy León reportedly negotiated a high-profile job in the United Arab Emirates while he was still attempting to mediate Libya's conflict.[33] Given the Emirate's role in supporting Haftar and other Dignity-aligned forces, this potential conflict of interest convinced many opponents of the Libyan Political Agreement that its principal architect had been bought by Gulf money. The Security Council and the European Union were likewise criticized for prioritizing their own interests in counterterrorism and migration above the interests of the Libyan people.[34] What thus began as an effort to reconcile the House and the Congress under a transitional unity government ended with the international community largely anointing a third major authority in Libya in early 2016, one that could legitimately authorize foreign military and humanitarian interventions.

The Mediterranean Refugee and Migration Crisis

Terrorism and migration were indeed front and center when it came to the US and European agenda for Libya in 2015 and 2016. Both issues were related to the fact that there was no longer a single authority in Libya capable of governing the country's 3,750 miles of land and sea borders. Across those frontiers, the flow of refugees and migrants increased as Libya's central state capacity decreased. Since the events of 2011, the number of arrivals in Europe from Libya, Egypt, Tunisia, and eastern Algeria had increased from just over 15,000 in 2012 to over 181,000 in 2016, with departures from Libya constituting the vast majority. Stricter controls on eastern Mediterranean migration routes through Turkey after 2015 saw departures from Libya outpacing all other routes into Europe for the first time in 2016.[35] By early 2016, the International Organization on Migration was reporting figures that suggested upward of one million migrants and refugees were in Libya. While some foreigners had been living and working in the country for years, if not decades, a significant percentage of recent arrivals to Libya were thought to be taking advantage of the country's anarchy in order to attempt Mediterranean crossings. Among them were economic migrants and conflict refugees, many of whom were victims of voluntary and involuntary human trafficking.

The largest clusters of these new communities of migrants and refugees in Libya had amassed in western Tripolitania, which offered the closest beaches to the shores of European islands. That said, even the shortest distance between Libya and the first Italian islands was harrowing. Compared to the Aegean Sea or the mere ten miles separating Morocco and Spain, nearly 180 miles of ocean stands between the major launching point of Zuwara in western Libya and the Italian island of Lampedusa. It was thus a sign of the sheer desperation of these migrants and refugees that they risked the crossing, often in overcrowded boats and ships of questionable seaworthiness. The frequency with which these vessels became stranded, capsized, or sank, leading to dozens, if not hundreds, of deaths at a time, further underscored the urgency of the situation. During the first three months of 2016 alone, nearly 30,000 migrants reached Europe from Libya, while nearly 1,000 died during the transit. On May 29, 2016, for example, over 600 migrants died when three boats all capsized en route to Europe. That same week, Italy also reported rescuing 13,000 migrants.[36] The causes of this migration and refugee crisis went well beyond the collapse of central authority in Libya in 2014, as well as the various economic conditions and armed conflicts driving humans from their homes to risk the journey through the Sahara to Libya's shores. Facilitating international migration had in fact become big business in Libya. A 2016 Italian report suggested that international human trafficking in Libya was generating annual revenues of over $380 million in each of the country's main migration hubs.[37]

The growth of international human trafficking in Libya developed in parallel with another insidious form of rent collection supporting the livelihoods of militias and other criminal networks: kidnapping. While accurate statistics were difficult to collect, Libya's Red Crescent Society received over 600 reports of missing or kidnapped persons between early 2014 and mid-2015; 80 percent of those were registered in Benghazi alone. While several hundreds of these simply amounted to political assassination by "disappearance," other victims were used as hostages in the ongoing Dawn–Dignity conflict. Indeed, Amnesty International implicated militias allied to both the Tripoli and Tobruk governments in the practice of kidnapping. Victims reported being tortured and held in horrific conditions. Foreigners were also targets for political and financial reasons.[38] International migrants faced arbitrary detention or forced labor until their alleged debts were paid off to smugglers. Female migrants, both adults and minors, were often sold into sex slavery all along the smuggling route, from the first major stop in Sebha all the way up to coastal Tripolitania.[39] A late 2016 study conducted by the UN Refugee Agency, the UNHCR, found that a significant percentage of migrants had actually traveled to Libya to find work there, only to be driven onward to Europe because of the horrible conditions and treatment they faced at the hands of Libyans.[40] The situation was made all the worse by the historical weakness of state institutions in Libya's vast and remote Saharan regions of the Fezzan and Kufra.[41]

While European Union member states were able to operate in international waters to address the burgeoning migration crisis, operations in Libya's territorial waters closer to shore were hamstrung in 2014 and 2015 by the absence of a legitimate central authority to approve such operations. Working with one side, the other, or both Dawn and Dignity simultaneously could delegitimize the EU's efforts and leave its ships vulnerable to attack either by the militias calling themselves the Coast Guard or by smugglers protecting their trade. The Libyan Political Agreement, reached in December 2015, theoretically allowed a more coherent anti-migration strategy to materialize, though the Agreement's structural weaknesses and political opponents would end up hampering these efforts. Similar to counterterrorism cooperation in the fight against the Islamic State (see below), European attempts to stymie the flow of migrants would lead to accusations of partisan involvement in Libya's civil war.

Beyond partisan interference in Libya's civil war, a more substantial problem with these anti-immigration initiatives was the prioritization of abating symptoms over addressing causes. The roots of the Libyan migration crisis were not simply the collapse of the transitional process and the outbreak of open civil war in 2014. A bigger issue was how state failure and armed conflict had created an environment in which local actors could freely pursue their own financial and security interests, whether out of collective necessity or out of a desire for commercial gain. Simply put, human trafficking in Libya had become an important source of employment, generating over one billion dollars annually for communities up and down the smuggling routes. For Saharan border communities, entry-level positions in human trafficking easily outpaid government salaries. That these communities represented some of Libya's most marginalized, dispossessed, and impoverished suggested the extent to which there were strong financial incentives in place to guarantee the delivery of migrants to the Mediterranean coast.[42]

The Economics of Chaos

Domestic and international human trafficking and kidnapping were just two of the activities that contributed to the political economy of chaos sustaining Libya's civil war.[43] A major source of revenue for armed groups on both sides of the Dawn–Dignity divide, as well as jihadi organizations and even UN-designated terrorist groups, continued to be the Libyan state itself. Both the Tripoli- and Tobruk-based governments used what cash they had on hand to continue the system of subsidizing militias, whether to maintain loyalties or to placate restless constituents struggling to make ends meet.[44] When asked why Libyan authorities were continuing to pay salaries for some 140,000 militia members, the British Ambassador, Peter Millett, described it as a jobs program for the country's vast reservoir of unemployed males: "Bored young men can join a militia, then they have a salary and something to do."[45]

Libya's leaders likewise remained committed to maintaining the salaries, as best they could, for the vast state bureaucracy as a form of social welfare, though the burden – $14.5 billion annually – easily drained what little revenue was generated through increasingly meager foreign oil sales.[46] Complicating matters was an ever-increasing cash crisis. As the Libyan dinar lost value against global currencies, Libyans were having more and more trouble accessing sufficient amounts of cash once banks implemented daily borrowing limits. Since the start of the 2014 civil war, the Libyan dinar had depreciated 60 percent by early 2016. The Libyan economy as a whole was expected to be the world's fastest shrinking over the course of the year that followed.[47] By October, the World Bank deemed it "near collapse."[48]

Government subsidies on basic goods, though aiming to support the society, often supported black market activities instead. Such goods could be easily sold in neighboring countries for a profit. For example, subsidies on medical supplies, which were becoming increasingly scarce in Libya, were in fact being diverted from hospitals to international black markets.[49] Government-supported import/export businesses facilitated other forms of corruption as well, whether laundering money or simply moving it out of the country by paying for goods that never arrived. State-subsidized imports were also a cover for the importation of illicit goods using falsified documents.[50] None of these activities, however, were new or a result of the increasing disorder that emerged after 2011. Libyan communities had been engaging in these forms of trade for decades in order to survive the economic failure of the *Jamahiriyyah* and the international isolation of the 1980s and 1990s. What was new was the extent to which these activities were helping underwrite civil war and terrorism.

Oil was a particularly lucrative commodity for smuggling given the extent to which the Libyan authorities subsidized diesel and gasoline for their citizens. Petrol station owners reportedly diverted entire tanker trucks delivering oil from storage tanks to smugglers heading for Egypt, Sudan, Chad, Niger, or Tunisia.[51] Diesel that cost ten cents per liter at the refinery was reportedly sold for over ten times as much in Tunisia. Even in small quantities, profits could be substantial. Enterprising smugglers, for example, added secret gas tanks to cars so as to evade suspicion at the borders.[52] On the high seas, oil smugglers using small boats carrying a few hundred barrels at a time reportedly collaborated with European criminal networks in Italy and Malta, as well as the Libyan Coast Guard. Estimates suggested that Libya lost $360 million in potential revenue in 2016 owing to these activities.[53] Even larger ships, however, still attempted to make off with Libyan oil with the complicity of port officials and the militias guarding them. In February 2016, for example, a Sierra Leonean tanker attempted to sneak away with 10,000 barrels of gasoline before the Libyan navy intercepted it.[54] By 2017, petrol smuggling had become such a huge problem that ordinary Libyans were finding it difficult to fill their own cars. In response, some militias took it upon themselves to stop this trade. At the same time, other militias offered business protection from thievery and smuggling, though such practices often amounted to simple extortion or rent-seeking.[55]

While the Mediterranean migration crisis and the Islamic State grabbed all the international headlines, the continuing circulations of arms both into Libya and out of it – despite the enhancement of the UN arms embargo by the Security Council in mid-2014 – presented an enormous security challenge for nearby states in the region. As the short-lived Islamic state in northern Mali had made clear in 2012, the plundering of Gaddafi's armories in 2011 would reap unimagined and disastrous effects across Africa and the Middle East. Controlling and profiting from these arms flows had become a lucrative concern in post-revolutionary Libya, one that implicated the major participants in the conflict – Dawn and Dignity forces – as much as geographically peripheral communities and politically marginalized actors. In March 2016, the official UN body charged with monitoring the security situation in Libya noted the following: "[A]rms and ammunition are continuing to be transferred to various parties in Libya, with the involvement of [UN] Member States and complex networks of brokering companies that do not appear to be deterred by the arms embargo."[56] As the report goes on to explain, the beneficiaries of these transfers included military forces allied to the Tobruk- and Tripoli-based governments. While Egyptian and Emirati transfers of helicopters, jets, and armored vehicles to Haftar's Dignity forces in the east and west were barely concealed, most of the large militia coalitions were primarily interested in the procurement of light weapons and ammunition, the kinds of arms necessary for urban combat and irregular warfare. One of those suppliers was the government of Turkey, whose President, Recep Tayyip Erdoğan, had aligned his country's foreign policy toward Libya in support of the Muslim Brotherhood and its Misratan allies. Sudan, as well, provided arms to these same factions, including Russian- and Chinese-produced ammunition. Investigators from the United Nations also discovered that combat aircraft flown out of Operation Dawn's base in Misrata were being piloted and maintained by a private network of actors involving citizens of Jordan, Moldova, Ukraine, the United States, and Ecuador.[57] How Libya's major armed factions paid for these significant military outlays was as opaque as the supply chains that delivered and supported them.

Equally opaque, and just as problematic, were the clandestine networks smuggling weapons out of Libya. Two attacks on Western tourists in Tunisia in 2015 brought some much needed attention to the ease with which weapons were hemorrhaging out of Libya. Second to oil smuggling, the selling and transporting of arms was one of the most lucrative activities for Libyan border communities in the face of their country's economic disarray and political collapse. Given the ongoing conflicts in and around Algeria, Chad, Egypt, Niger, Sudan, and Tunisia, all were either destination markets or transit points for the small arms trade. These flows easily piggybacked on top of the region's robust smuggling networks that traded in goods and humans. Weapons in Syria and Israel, in addition to Mali and Nigeria, would eventually be traced back to Libya.

The wider networks now circulating commodities, illicit goods, weapons, and people had largely developed over the course of several decades, emerging in response to the economic opportunities created by, first, the failures of socialism and liberalization in the states of North Africa and, second, the desperate poverty of the Sahel. Decades of war in West, Central, and Northern Africa in places like Western Sahara, Liberia, Sierra Leone, Chad, Algeria, and Darfur had also facilitated informal trade networks specializing in arms and other goods. While migration and human smuggling across the Sahara and into the Mediterranean had long been a major European concern, the rise of arms and drug smuggling in the 2000s began to draw increasing attention, particularly when Al-Qaida-aligned jihadi groups from the Algerian civil war began operating their own kidnapping, smuggling, and protection/extortion rackets in the central Sahara at the same time. With the weakening and eventual collapse of the interim national authorities in Libya after the 2011 revolution, local actors along its borders, particularly those among Tuareg, Tebu, and Arab communities in the deep south, engaged these trade networks for various, though often interconnected, reasons, whether personal gain, political opportunism, or economic survival.

Counterterrorism First, Peace Later: Defeating the Islamic State

The Skhirat Agreement initially did little to disrupt the dynamics sustaining the ongoing civil war in Libya. Concerns that the Agreement would actually worsen the situation were not without warrant. But for the North Atlantic powers backing the Agreement, Libya's multiplicity of grassroots conflicts and the unresolved divide between revolutionaries and accommodationists were of secondary importance. The primary concern was to have a legitimate national authority in place that could authorize nonpartisan international assistance to address the migration crisis and, more importantly, to confront the Islamic State.[58] All other considerations were deemed secondary. The North Atlantic community essentially reasoned that the rehabilitation of the Libyan body politic could not go forward until the cancer of the Islamic State was eliminated. Yet as Libya entered its fifth year of turmoil in 2016, Western Europe and the United States were not the only foreign interests playing a role in Libya's fate.

For obvious reasons, the new UN strategy for addressing the Libyan conflict – counterterrorism first, peace later – was being driven by broader considerations that went beyond Libya. As the Islamic State seized territory across the Arab world, the North Atlantic powers increasingly viewed the crisis as geopolitical in scale. The Syria–Iraq crisis had not only generated the worst refugee flows since World War II, it also seemed capable of threatening the existence of several states in the Middle East. The need to drive the Islamic State from Iraq and Syria moreover seemed capable of drawing NATO, Russia, and the Gulf into direct confrontation as proxy warfare gave way to direct intervention in 2014 by the United States and in 2015 by Russia.

In the context of the Libyan civil war, the Islamic State crisis simultaneously exposed the weaknesses of the Dawn and Dignity coalitions while offering both sides opportunities to advance their political and military campaigns. That neither the Dawn nor the Dignity coalition had been in a position to do more than contain the Islamic State threat throughout most of 2015 spoke volumes about Libya a year on from the events of mid-2014. The Libyan National Army's ongoing quagmire in Benghazi and the Islamic State's defeat of the once-feared 166 Brigade of Misrata in May 2015 revealed the extent to which neither of Libya's competing interim authorities was in a position to mount an expeditionary campaign. Misrata, in particular, needed time to prepare before its brigades could engage in the kind of punishing urban warfare necessary to retake Sirte.

In telling ways, however, the Islamic State crisis in Libya inadvertently played into the hands of authorities in Tripoli and Tobruk. Sirte's agony certainly fit into Haftar's narrative that Libya could not afford the luxury of violent extremism, though it would actually fall on the shoulders of his rivals in Tripoli and Misrata to take on the Islamic State. And while the coalition between Dawn forces and the Congress was accused by its opponents of being ideologically sympathetic to the Islamic State's agenda, the crisis in Sirte allowed Misrata's militias to position themselves as the only viable military force capable of mounting and sustaining a siege in Sirte. Taking the fight to the Islamic State in Sirte had clear benefits for the Dawn–Congress coalition as well. It would allow Dawn-allied forces and their political backers to draw a sharp line between their brand of conservative political Islam and the puritanical extremism of the Islamic State. A Misratan-led campaign against the Islamic State would also help repair their international reputation after having unseated Libya's internationally recognized authorities in the summer of 2014 and having driven most of the international community out of Tripoli.

Before the campaign against the Islamic State could begin in earnest, Libya first needed one government, not two. The December 2015 Libyan Political Agreement ostensibly created just that – a unified interim authority incorporating both the Tobruk-based House as the lawmaking body and the Tripoli-based Congress as a consultative body. Under the direction of a Presidency Council chaired by Fayez Al-Serraj, the international community now felt confident that Libya's interim authorities could legitimately request and coordinate foreign support in the campaign against the Islamic State. Before this could happen, however, Serraj, the Presidency Council, and the broader cabinet had to be approved by the House and actually be present in the capital before its work could begin. Since the signing of the Agreement in Morocco, it was unclear whether or not any of the forces controlling the country's borders would allow the Council to take up residency in Tripoli or elsewhere in Libya. Not only was the House leadership refusing to approve Serraj's proposed national unity government, the Congress and allied militias were also making open threats against the Council's proposed membership and even UN envoy Martin Kobler.[59] Grand Mufti Ghariani threatened to "open the door of jihad" on this new Government of National Accord should it be imposed.[60] In response to these threats and obstructions, Serraj's foreign backers began the process of placing sanctions on leaders in the House and Congress for holding up implementation of the Libyan Political Agreement. There were even accusations that humanitarian aid was being withheld to put pressure on reluctant authorities.[61]

Months of anticipation finally came to a head when Serraj and members of his cabinet arrived unceremoniously in the capital on board a Libyan naval vessel from Sfax, Tunisia, at the end of March. While protected at the Abu Sitta naval base, Serraj began receiving envoys and delegates from local councils, militias, ministries, and other stakeholders. Serraj's international backing meant that his government could legitimately use Libya's major financial assets, including $85 billion in cash reserves.[62] Pledges of loyalty from the Petroleum Facilities Guard and control over the National Oil Company likewise added to his influence and made it clear that his rivals in Tripoli were losing their grip on core state assets. International economic, diplomatic, and military support likewise sought to drive home the impression that the Government of National Accord was "the only game in town," as one former US Ambassador to Libya put it.[63] That message appeared to be getting through. The support of Misratan political leaders and militia brigades not only allowed the Presidency Council to move into the capital, it also allowed Libya's new authorities, in concert with Western allies, to begin the process of confronting the Islamic State head-on.[64]

This is not to say that foreign military interventions against the Islamic State in Libya had been entirely on hold. Airstrikes, surveillance, and on-the-ground counterterrorism assistance with select Dawn- and Dignity-aligned militias had already been taking place since mid-2015, notably US air raids on Islamic State units in Derna in November and Sabratha in February 2016. The latter attack had targeted a hub for Tunisian fighters associated with terrorist assaults on foreigners in Tunis and Sousse in 2015. In the Sahara, already-existing French deployments of 3,500 troops aimed to restrict the circulation of jihadi groups across the vast borders of

Mauritania, Mali, Niger, and Chad.[65] These deployments, which followed the French campaign against Al-Qaida-allied forces in northern Mali, sought to prevent Libya's Islamic State from using the desert as a fallback position, just as Algerian jihadi groups had succeeded in doing at the turn of the millennium. That said, the growth of the Islamic State in Libya led increasingly to speculative accounts of its reach within the region. For example, one report – based entirely on US officials citing second-hand information – alleged strong connections between the Islamic State in Libya and the Boko Haram insurgency in northern Nigeria.[66]

With Serraj's Presidency Council established in Tripoli, international security assistance was rendered more directly – and less covertly – to forces supporting the Government of National Accord. Misratan militias, some of whom helped secure the Presidency Council's permanent presence in Tripoli, would lead the ground campaign against the Islamic State. Fighting between Misrata, the Islamic State, and other forces had in fact been ceaseless and often vicious. To the east of Sirte, the Petroleum Facilities Guard held off the Islamic State, preventing its seizure of Libya's most important downstream oil infrastructures, though battles near Ras Lanuf and Es Sider in January 2016 saw the Islamic State cause significant damage to storage tanks and other installations. To the south and west, Misratan militias had limited the Islamic State's push into Tripolitania and the central oases.

The Misratan effort to retake Sirte was coordinated through a new operational structure, ostensibly under Serraj's ultimate command, known as *Al-Bunyan Al-Marsus* (frequently translated as Solid Structure or Solid Foundation). The 2016 summer campaign, which would last through the fasting month of Ramadan, saw the Islamic State's outer defenses rapidly collapse by the end of May. The Petroleum Facilities Guard went on the offensive as well, taking the towns of Ben Jawad and Nawfiliyah from the Islamic State. Though aligned with the House, the Petroleum Facilities Guard, led by an outspoken Cyrenaican proponent of federalism, Ibrahim Jadhran, would more or less collaborate with the Misratan forces to encircle the Islamic State. The immediate and sizable gains made by the Misratans and Jadhran's fighters seemed to suggest that assessments of the Islamic State's capacity in Libya, like those offered by the US Africa Command, had greatly overestimated, if not exaggerated, the organization's military strength.[67]

Though the Islamic State fared poorly on the open terrain of Libya's coasts and deserts, the urban environment of Sirte was more well suited to its brand of terroristic guerrilla warfare. The Misratans' efforts to liberate Sirte slowed and then ground to a halt once the Islamic State had been reduced to a few hundred fighters by July and were entirely contained in the city center.[68] At this point in the campaign, and backed with an appeal from Serraj for assistance, international forces officially joined the fight in early August 2016, going beyond the covert assistance that had been rendered by special forces and intelligence agencies since the start of the year.[69] Despite this political backing from the Presidency Council and foreign military collaboration, Misratan forces, like all other militias in Libya, nonetheless had to make do with very little in terms of arms and other supplies given the UN arms embargo. Weapons for the fight were often purchased off the black market using donations collected from wealthy Misratans. Even basic things like meals for the troops had to be organized through grassroots support networks in Misrata and ferried to the frontline soldiers.[70] While the Sirte campaign once again demonstrated Misrata's unparalleled *esprit de corps*, the months-long war of attrition was highly indicative of the steep material constraints faced by armed groups in Libya.

Just off the coast of Libya, a small US aircraft carrier dispatched fighter jets and bombers to drive Islamic State fighters out of their hideouts. Attack helicopters provided close air support to the Misratan-led forces on the ground fighting house-to-house battles against snipers and suicide bombers. This highly coordinated offensive paved the way for the eventual collapse of the Islamic State in Sirte under the relentless pounding of bombs, missiles, and artillery. By year's end, *Al-Bunyan Al-Marsus* declared the liberation of the final district under Islamic State control. For the foreign powers who had aided in the campaign, the battle for Sirte became an important template for hybrid domestic–international counterterrorism operations against the Islamic State, one that would be replicated in the liberation of the even larger stronghold of Mosul, Iraq, in 2017.

The Misratan forces had paid a steep price in blood during the seven-month campaign of fighting street-by-street. Over 700 were reportedly killed and some 3,200 had been wounded. As with the 2011 revolution, the Misratans vowed that these deaths had not been in vain. "The blood of the martyrs was not for nothing," Misratan fighters reportedly chanted after the fighting was over.[71] Indeed, it was unlikely that the Misratans would make the same mistakes they had made during their previous occupation of Sirte from late 2011 to 2015. Beyond the need to prevent the reemergence of the scattered and diminished Islamic State, there were other reasons for *Al-Bunyan Al-Marsus* to maintain a robust security presence in Sirte. While the Islamic State had quickly outworn its welcome in Sirte, the citizenry's gratitude toward their Misratan liberators was tempered.[72] These reasons included memories of Sirte's treatment by revolutionary forces during the 2011 war, as well as the ongoing marginalization of loyalists to the old regime, a marginalization effort often championed by the Misratan forces and the factions within the administration in Tripoli supporting them. Central Libya, long a bastion of support for Gaddafi, could easily fall to Haftar's forces given the cause of political accommodation they were defending. The occupation of Sirte and control over the central oases was now a strategic imperative for *Al-Bunyan Al-Marsus*. Sitting between Dawn and Dignity's forces was one of the greatest material prizes in Libya, the oil crescent, dutifully occupied by the Cyrenaican federalists of Ibrahim Jadhran's Petroleum Facilities Guard.

If the defeat of the Islamic State had set the stage for a resumption of direct hostilities between Dignity and Dawn forces, then the question was when, not if, it would happen. "[T]he great fear is what comes next," noted one of the top experts on Libyan affairs.[73] For the head of the Misratan military council, Ibrahim Baitulmal, the answer was simple:

war with Haftar. "Sometimes war is imposed on us," he told Reuters. "[W]hen the enemy approaches, you have to defend yourself."[74]

Internationalizing the War to Come

For the North Atlantic community and the UN Secretariat, the victory in Sirte proved that the Libyan Political Agreement and the Government of National Accord had been a wise investment. There were, however, many other foreign powers attempting to steer Libya's fate. While Egyptian, Saudi, and Emirati support for Haftar – both direct military intervention and indirect forms of aid – continued unabated, reports of French involvement with the counterterrorism campaign in Benghazi, including the loss of three French soldiers in a July 2016 helicopter incident, drew strong reactions from authorities in Tripoli and the wider Islamist community in Libya. As Haftar's forces made no distinction between Islamic State fighters and other militant Islamist groups, French counterterrorism support effectively contributed to a military campaign that was targeting Cyrenaican allies of the Dawn coalition. With the Islamic State scattered and attempting to regroup in the country's vast interior, Haftar's major opponents in Cyrenaica were mainly the Derna Mujahidin Shura Council and the Benghazi Defense Brigades, the latter being an amalgamation of Islamist groups and anti-Haftar fighters that formed in mid-2016. Two years into the Dignity campaign, the militias constituting Haftar's so-called "Libyan National Army" continued to face stiff resistance in both Benghazi and Derna, even as the Islamist resistance found itself increasingly boxed into smaller and smaller areas. What foreign support was rendered to Haftar's fighters was still nothing like the close military cooperation given to *Al-Bunyan Al-Marsus* in Sirte by the US Marine Corps, a force with unparalleled recent experience in urban counterinsurgency warfare.

If it seemed that international political and military support was shifting toward the Dawn coalition given its support for Serraj's administration and the Misratan victory in Sirte, a new actor entered the conflict in 2016 that seemingly rebalanced the equation. After several years on the sidelines, Russia began taking a more active interest in the Libyan civil war in 2016. In the immediate aftermath of the 2011 revolution, it was difficult for Russia to play a constructive role in Libya, as many Libyans viewed Russia as a key enabler of Gaddafi's rule. Moscow had been the regime's major arms supplier for decades, and at the time of the uprising in 2011, Russia had some $10 billion in various agreements with the Gaddafi regime.[75] Unsurprisingly, Russia abstained from the UN resolution to authorize military intervention in March 2011. In retrospect, this abstention began to seem increasingly justified in the context of Libya's failed transition, the deterioration of security, and the emergence of a civil war in 2014. Moscow's abstention also fit a more general pattern of Russian skepticism toward NATO's role in global affairs after the Cold War, particularly the treaty organization's overzealous use of military power in the name of humanitarianism, from the wars in Yugoslavia in the 1990s to Afghanistan after 9/11 and finally Libya in 2011.

Renewed Russian interest in Libya also came about as a result of the geopolitical vacuum created by the Obama administration's policies toward the Middle East. In naïvely supporting armed rebellions in Libya and Syria, the United States had helped empower the very social, political, and economic forces that led to the Islamic State. And while Russia's stake in the Gaddafi regime had been largely economic, Moscow's support for the regime of Bashar Al-Assad was a strategic priority, given the unfettered access to the Mediterranean Sea that Russia's naval base in Syria provides. Responding to a request for military assistance from President Assad in July 2015, Russian forces began launching strikes against "terrorists" – the Islamic State and other armed opposition groups in Syria – a few months later. The downing of a Russian civilian flight over the Sinai Peninsula on October 31, 2015, claimed by the Islamic State and killing all 224 on board, provided Russia with even more motivation to participate in the global campaign against the Islamic State that the United States had launched in September 2014. In the months that followed, the Russian military would engage in thousands of strikes against Assad's opponents, helping the Syrian regime and its Shi'ah allies – Iran and Hezbollah – to turn the tide of war slowly and brutally.

Russia's involvement in the Libyan civil war would exhibit nowhere near the same level of engagement, though its actions would seem just as overtly partisan. By 2015, it had been well established that Moscow was more in geopolitical alignment with the international allies supporting the Tobruk government and Haftar's army (i.e., Saudi Arabia, the Emirates, and Egypt) than with the pro-Muslim Brotherhood bloc supporting the Congress–Dawn coalition in Tripoli (i.e., Sudan, Qatar, and Turkey). As with all parties in Libya's civil war, most were eager to see the international arms embargo lifted, and Haftar's forces were particularly keen to lay claim to Russian arms transfers that had been suspended in 2011. Working through Egypt, whose older Russian armaments could be easily adapted for use by Dignity forces, the Libyan National Army made it clear in early 2015 that it saw Russian military aid as key to its success in Cyrenaica, if not ultimate victory in the long run.[76] More overt Russian gestures of political support for Haftar began in the middle of 2016, just as North Atlantic counterterrorism assistance was ramping up in Libya. On June 27 and November 29, Haftar made high-profile visits to Moscow, where he was received by high-level officials, including Minister of Defense Nikolai Patrushev and Foreign Minister Sergei Lavrov.

Between these two meetings in Moscow, Haftar-aligned forces made a sudden, unexpected, and successful advance into the oil crescent region southwest of Benghazi in September. With Misratan forces locked into combat with the Islamic State in Sirte, elements of the Libyan National Army launched a surprise attack on Jadhran's unsuspecting Petroleum Facilities Guard forces on September 11, coinciding with the eve of Eid Al-Adha, the most important holiday in Islam. Even more surprising was the fact that few shots had been fired. Whereas the Petroleum Facilities Guard had survived prolonged engagements with Misratan forces at the end of 2014 and against the Islamic State in early 2016, Jadhran had been outmaneuvered by Haftar at the social level: Cyrenaican tribal leaders, notably the Magharba, allowed Haftar to convince the rank and file of the Petroleum Facilities Guard not to put up a fight.[77]

Though the move was instantaneously denounced by the UN envoy and the North Atlantic powers backing Serraj, Haftar and the National Oil Corporation just as quickly reached a deal, which allowed the oil to flow less than a week later. For good reason, the Libyan National Oil Corporation was happy to see Jadhran go, as he had made a short career out of holding a significant percentage of the country's oil exports hostage for his militia's financial gain.[78] In early 2016, for example, Mustafa Sanalla, chair of the National Oil Corporation, accused Jadhran of denying Libya over $50 billion in oil revenues by holding up exports.[79]

With the eastern oil fields and pipelines already under the control of militias aligned with the Libyan National Army, the seizure of the oil crescent gave Haftar direct control over most of Libya's production capacity.[80] Moreover, two of Haftar's allies in the west, Zintani and Tuareg militias, gave the Dignity coalition control over important oil infrastructures on the other side of the country. In the months that followed, Libyan production began trending toward pre-2011 levels and international investment in the oil sector began to increase. Though the revenues would continue to be controlled by the Government of National Accord, Haftar was widely credited with helping save the Libyan economy from collapse. The repercussions of the Libyan National Army's surprise advance into the oil crescent thus seemed to suggest that the balance of power in Libya was not necessarily shifting in the favor of the Government of National Accord as its North Atlantic backers had assumed it would.[81]

The extent to which Russian support for Haftar had reinvigorated the Dignity campaign, after months of grinding warfare in the streets of Benghazi, remained an open question at the end of 2016. One fact, however, seemed clear: Russia was squarely in Haftar's corner. On January 11, 2017, Haftar was again received by the Russian Ministry of Defense, this time on an aircraft carrier that had docked in Tobruk. Though Moscow was not yet willing to violate the UN arms embargo openly, covert forms of Russian military involvement in Libya's civil war – material aid and intelligence assistance via special forces, private contractors, and Egyptian and Emirati proxies – began to parallel the kind of shadowy counterterrorism assistance being rendered by France, Britain, Italy, and the United States in the fight against the Islamic State.[82] Indeed, beyond the desire to recover a dependable and lucrative market for its arms industry, Russia's interest in supporting the House of Representatives and the Libyan National Army, not unlike its support for Assad in Syria, was seemingly about sending a geopolitical message to the United States: two can play at that game.

A response of sorts came a week after the Russian navy visited Haftar in Tobruk. On January 19, 2017, in his final act as commander in chief of the US military, President Obama ordered a coordinated airstrike on a suspected Islamic State camp south of Sirte, deploying drones from Italy and B-2 stealth bombers from Missouri. The purported death toll, upward of ninety militants, was a devastating blow against the remnants of the Islamic State in Libya. Whether or not Moscow was one of the intended audiences of the strike, it was a stunning display of the immense and unrivaled global reach of the US military.[83]

Toward an Endgame?

Three key developments in 2016 set the stage for a new phase in the Libyan civil war: the Libyan National Army's seizure of the oil crescent, the scattering of the Islamic State, and the reoccupation of Sirte by Misratan forces. The resumption of direct confrontation between Dawn- and Dignity-allied forces thus seemed imminent. The ability of the Presidency Council to prevent the civil war from escalating was limited as much by its inability to enact meaningful national governance as by its strong association with – if not total reliance upon – the political and military opponents of Haftar and the

House. While Serraj's appointments to government and military posts made some effort to achieve national unity, the Presidency Council shared the capital city with the new High State Council, essentially a reformulated General National Congress led by an important Misratan figure, Abderrahman Swehli.

Beyond the issue of partisanship, the failings of the Libyan Political Agreement were also rooted in the rushed diplomatic process that brought the Government of National Accord about, the haphazard way the Presidency Council was installed in Tripoli, the refusal of leaders in Tobruk to cooperate, and, as always, the conflicting agendas of the international community. In brief, what the December 2015 Skhirat document envisioned and what was the reality a year later were two completely different things. The greatest impediment toward the actualization of the Agreement was undoubtedly the refusal of Aguila Saleh, President of the House of Representatives, to allow the required vote on the Libyan Political Agreement, never mind the House's role in the approval of Serraj's proposed cabinet appointments. Even with EU and other unilateral sanctions imposed upon him, Saleh and his allies in the House used a number of parliamentary tricks to prevent or stall debate, often by simply denying a quorum through boycotts. Undeterred, the new authorities in Tripoli, the Presidency Council and the High State Council, pressed ahead; both began acting as the Government of National Accord despite having no parliamentary mandate to do so.[84] Indeed, Swehli would go so far as to declare the House void in September 2016, claiming that his body, the High State Council, was now the country's parliament.

For the most part, it was the political and security alliance between Misratan factions and the Presidency Council that allowed Serraj's transitional administration to function at all, though the Council itself was marked by intense internal debates and frequent boycotts by its members that further debilitated its efforts. Another mark against the Government of National Accord was its inability to guarantee security in Tripoli. Not unlike the National Transitional Council and the first General National Congress, the Government of National Accord found itself at the mercy of the various armed groups and criminal networks operating in the capital.

The Government of National Accord also continued to share the capital with a rival, the Government of National Salvation, a coalition of militias and political figures claiming to be the true representatives of the 2014 General National Congress.[85] Led by Khalifa Ghwell, who had also been sanctioned by the international community for obstructing the UN peace process, the Salvation government rejected the Skhirat Agreement and continued to claim electoral, judicial, and constitutional legitimacy. Ghwell even led an attempt in October 2016 to seize a number of important facilities in the capital, which some media reports described as a failed coup against Serraj. What followed were a series of militia clashes across the capital for several days. For Tripoli's residents, these periodic outbursts of violent confrontations between militias had become a feature of daily life in the capital.[86]

Another factor working against support for Serraj's administration was the extent to which its seating in Tripoli inadvertently perpetuated Cyrenaica's second-class status within Libyan politics. As the region was the birthplace of the 2011 revolution, its leaders and interest groups had attempted to use their newfound political power to restore Benghazi's pride of place as Libya's shared capital, as had been the case under the Sanusi monarchy. The fact that the Cyrenaican agenda was increasingly marginalized during the transition became one of the factors leading to the rupture of 2014, with accommodationists, federalists, and other regional interest groups in the east making common cause with House leaders and Haftar's Dignity campaign. Similar to the National Transitional Council and both iterations of the Congress (before and after 2014), the Libyan Political Agreement mistakenly continued to privilege Tripoli as the locus of power.

By late 2016, it was clear that the Skhirat Agreement had not so much engendered a single national transitional administration as it had simply added a veneer of international legitimacy to the same Misratan- and Islamist-dominated political–military coalitions that had purged the newly elected House from Tripoli in 2014. Islamist leaders in Tripolitania also continued to voice moral support for those groups still resisting the Libyan National Army, whether the Benghazi and Derna *shura* councils or the newly formed Benghazi Defense Brigades, despite these groups' association with terrorism and transnational jihadists. Once in power, Serraj's government also tried to counter Haftar's influence by appointing Cyrenaican rivals to the Presidency Council, such as Mahdi Al-Barghathi to the post of Defense Minister. The Libyan National Army's largely nonviolent seizure of the oil crescent in September 2016, however, proved that Haftar's base of social support was actually growing in the east.[87]

Controversy nonetheless continued to follow Haftar as the Libyan National Army solidified its grip on Cyrenaica while simultaneously pushing, albeit slowly, into Fezzan and Tripolitania. Of the many accusations leveled against Haftar, one of the most frequent was his alleged authoritarian tendencies, if not a desire to establish himself as a military dictator along the lines of his main international ally, President el-Sisi of Egypt. Haftar's support for those seeking political accommodation with former regime officials likewise engendered concerns that he was seeking to revive aspects of the *Jamahiriyyah* or to institute a kind of Gaddafism without Gaddafi. Both concerns were not without warrant. Not only did the House offer amnesty to former regime officials for actions taken against the 2011 uprising, Saleh helped bring martial law to parts of Cyrenaica by declaring a state of emergency in June 2016. This allowed the Libyan National Army to take control of local civilian municipal councils by installing military governors and committees.[88] Moreover, contacts between Haftar and former high-level officials in the Gaddafi regime, including Saif Al-Islam from his "prison" in Zintan, were hardly discreet.[89] Videos of overtly pro-Gaddafi units within the Libyan National Army, brandishing the green flag of the *Jamahiriyyah*, frequently found their way onto Libyan social media networks.

In addition to constructing a social and political basis for the Dignity campaign, Haftar reportedly worked to create a religious base of support as well through alliances with Salafi religious leaders and their armed followers. Many of these appeared to be associated with the Madkhali school of Sunni thought, which has its roots in Saudi Arabia's state-sponsored brand of Islamic orthodoxy. This so-called "quietist" Salafism advocates respect for established authority and opposes political agitation, whether of the populist variety (e.g., the Muslim Brotherhood) or the armed kind (e.g., Al-Qaida and the Islamic State). Madkhalism had in fact taken root in Libya during the late Gaddafi period in the early 2000s. Saif Al-Islam's efforts to co-opt both moderate and radical Islamists, in order to renew the regime's social foundations, had welcomed this brand of Salafism for obvious reasons. As Madkhalism is religiously orthodox yet deferential to established political authority, its appeal to dictatorial leaders is no mystery. Not only did a growing alliance with Madkhali figures and groups help Haftar's Operation Dignity establish its religious bona fides, it also suggested a constellation of allies possibly connecting the Libyan National Army to one of Tripoli's most powerful militias, Abdelraouf Kara's Special Deterrence Force, a nominally Salafi opponent of both the Islamic State and the Islamist militias allied to Belhadj, Ghariani, and the Salvation government.[90]

One of the most serious accusations leveled against the Libyan National Army – an accusation that actually applied to almost all armed factions in Libya[91] – was the extent to which its forces were continuing to engage in human rights violations, war crimes, and crimes against humanity, particularly as the battle for Benghazi seemed to enter its final phase in 2017. In the long-running siege of Benghazi's Ganfouda neighborhood and nearby districts, which represented the last pockets of resistance to Haftar's forces, international human rights organizations documented crimes committed by the Libyan National Army such as summary executions of prisoners of war, willful killing of civilians, indiscriminate bombing from the air, and the desecration of corpses, eventually leading to an International Criminal Court investigation against some of Haftar's forces.[92] Similar accusations would be leveled against the Libyan National

Army in its fight to take Derna, particularly the use of aerial bombardment in civilian areas.[93] That said, the Libyan National Army and the people of Benghazi also continued to be menaced by car bombs, assassinations, kidnappings, and other forms of terrorism regularly attributed to Haftar's foes.

All across Libya, the human toll of the conflict was readily visible, particularly the high levels of forced displacement. Nearly two years into the Dawn–Dignity conflict and five years after the start of the uprising, the UN High Commissioner for Human Rights, Zeid Ra'ad Al-Hussein, issued a report detailing the continued use of indiscriminate warfare in civilian areas, torture, unlawful detention, disappearances, kidnapping, child soldiers, assassinations, and gender-based violence, as well as the exploitation of migrants and other vulnerable populations.[94] Those populations included over 400,000 Libyans who had been internally displaced during the 2011 uprising, the transition, or from 2014 onward.[95] By late 2015, nearly two and a half million Libyans, including a quarter of a million refugees and migrants, were eligible for international humanitarian assistance owing to their displacement amid the ongoing fighting and political turmoil.[96] On top of that, millions of Libyans had taken up residency in neighboring countries, mainly Tunisia and Egypt.[97] Among the country's internally displaced populations, upward of 90,000 residents of Benghazi had been forced to flee the city since mid-2014.[98]

Though concerns about the social, political, and military forces backing Haftar were as warranted as criticisms of his methods on the battlefield, it was nonetheless obvious in early 2017 that the more gains the Dignity coalition made, the more support it earned across Libya. Quick to capitalize on its success in the oil crescent in September 2016, the Libyan National Army began pressing into the center of the country. Around this time, airstrikes attributed to both sides or their foreign proxies began marking the region between Jufra and Sebha as the next front in the civil war. There Haftar's forces soon confronted the Third Force militias from Misrata and regrouped elements of the Benghazi Defense Brigades.

Deploying large numbers of Tebu fighters from Libya as well as others with ties to Chad and Sudan's Darfur region in March 2017, the Libyan National Army made its move.[99] In the weeks that followed, a series of back-and-forth battles for control over military installations and towns ensued. Toward the end of May, a massacre of dozens of Libyan National Army fighters suggested the levels of desperation facing the Islamist–Misratan forces seeking to maintain their grip, which collapsed soon thereafter. The Libyan National Army had thus succeeded in nearly linking its Cyrenaican base of support to its main Fezzani and Tripolitanian allies. This feat gave Haftar's forces direct and indirect control over a significant amount of the country's oil infrastructures in the west, adding to the Libyan National Army's hold on oil production in the east.

At the same time, Tripoli continued to be wracked by sporadic clashes between militias, some backing the Government of National Accord and others opposing it, though such flare-ups were just as often related to the kind of inter-communal disputes that had flourished in the absence of national security and state authority. Turmoil on the outskirts and in the streets of Tripoli, the continued decline of the economy, and interminable political paralysis all played into Haftar's narrative that order and security needed to be brought to the capital. Though media reports at the time suggested that Dawn's forces would quickly push from the central oases to the loyalist region of Bani Walid and then into the capital region, the Libyan National Army's next move was anyone's guess.[100] The battle-lines drawn in mid-2017 more or less held for the rest of the year. Meetings between Serraj and Haftar in the United Arab Emirates in May and France in June did little for the cause of peace in Libya. In fact, the second meeting, convened by recently elected French President Emmanuel Macron, was as much an implicit recognition of the Skhirat Agreement's failures as it was an explicit recognition of Haftar's power and the constituents he represented. As the second anniversary of the Libyan Political Agreement approached with little to show for it, the new UN envoy to Libya, Ghassan Salamé of Lebanon, was also unable to bring the House on board to modify the agreement. Salamé's proposal to break the impasse was to hold elections for a new interim President by the end of 2018, even in the absence of a finalized constitution. Though such elections would usher in Libya's fifth transitional administration since 2011, Salamé's proposal was surprisingly met with enthusiasm from most core stakeholders as voter registration quickly got underway.

International policy toward Libya, dominated as it was by the North Atlantic powers, had to face several uncomfortable facts as the country's civil war approached its fourth year in 2018. The trends since the fall of Gaddafi easily suggested that the conflict could persist, as it had for several years, in a state of anarchic equilibrium, irrespective of Libya's nominal leaders. As with its predecessors, whether the National Transitional Council or the General National Congress, the Government of National Accord never became the unifying and commanding force that its foreign supporters had hoped it would become. Indeed, quite the opposite was the case. The fate of Serraj's administration fit the general pattern since 2011: as national-level governance proved increasingly unable to deliver security and prosperity, Libyans used other means to meet those ends, ones that were more geographically immediate. In turn, these quotidian survival strategies, particularly the radical privatization and decentralization of security unleashed in the 2011 uprising, undermined the social and political foundations of already weak central state structures.[101] The tragedy of the Government of National Accord, as Serraj readily admitted near the end of his first year in office, was not so much that his administration fell into the same trap as its predecessors. It was that he was pushed into it by those seeking a quick fix to the twin crises of the Islamic State and Mediterranean migration.[102]

Conclusion

The fifth anniversary of the Arab Spring was a time of somber reflection across the region. Despite holding national elections that led to brief periods of Islamist rule, Tunisia and Egypt both witnessed a resurgence of what came to be called the deep state: networks of entrenched public and private actors who appeared to hold, and wield, real power in those countries. While these oscillations of power unfolded with little violence in Tunisia, Egypt saw increasing levels of protest and repression facilitate the return of military rule at the behest of business elites and elements of the old regime. In both cases, Tunisia and Egypt, large segments of the society in fact seemed to be demanding a return to the dependable technocratic security regimes of old.

The Moroccan monarchy, which had weathered the shock-waves of the Arab Spring through political and economic concessions to popular demands, had embarked upon a strategy of regime survival but with diminishing returns. The need for security and order, moreover, continued to rationalize persecution of Western Saharans who had risen up in late 2010 against Morocco's occupation of their lands. Algerians, ever wary of the security state lurking behind the façade of the entrenched political classes helming their government, continued to accept their status quo, knowing full well what electoral unpredictability had unleashed on their country in the 1990s.

In the Gulf, Bahrain remained under the firm grip of Saudi Arabia and the monarchy it helped to support in Manama. Meanwhile, Bahraini civil society activists faced harsh sentences and treatment for protesting against their leaders in 2011. Growing divisions between Gulf leaders and their contrasting geopolitical visions furthermore served to exacerbate the disintegration of the Yemeni state, leading to the region's second largest humanitarian crisis behind the ongoing civil war in Syria. The Syrian uprising was indeed the greatest catastrophe of the Arab Spring, if not the early twenty-first century, having given birth to the most violent civil conflict since the massacres in Rwanda in 1994 and the largest refugee crisis since the end of World War II.[1]

Formed in the crucible of the recent war in neighboring Iraq, the Islamic State organization, an offshoot of Al-Qaida, had taken advantage of the Syrian civil war to enhance its institutional and military structures, eventually seizing large portions of territory across Syria and Iraq in 2014. By 2016, the Islamic State found itself under a multipronged assault from a variety of local, regional, and international actors, including the United States and Russia, in both Syria and Iraq. The threat posed by the Islamic State had afforded Washington and Moscow golden opportunities to augment their military support for opposing sides in the Syrian civil war, the ultimate effect of which was to intensify and prolong the bloodshed. As the walls began to close in, the Islamic State resorted to a desperate campaign of encouraging and legitimating acts of petty terrorism across Europe and elsewhere. Having lost its strongholds in the Levant, Mesopotamia, and North Africa by 2017, its dreams of restoring the Caliphate had run up against the cold realities of geopolitics.

Taking Stock

Libya's place among this tragic constellation has been largely documented in the preceding pages. To be clear, the 2011 uprising and the broader Arab Spring were not the sole cause of Libya's tragedy. As Chapter 1 demonstrated, the violent and disordering forces that were unleashed within the Libyan polity in early 2011 had been coiling up inside and outside of the country for years, if not decades. But neither the causes nor the consequences of the 2011 Libyan uprising were evenly distributed across the country, as Chapters 2 and 3 respectively make clear. The reasons for the revolution in Libya, much like its outcomes, were as multiple and as contradictory as the drivers of change in Tunisia, Egypt, and Yemen, though often altogether different as well.

Behind the heterogeneity of triggers and outcomes in the Libyan revolution were the ways in which the political economy of the *Jamahiriyyah* – its successes and failures, strengths and vulnerabilities – had contributed to both the fury of February 2011 and the possibility of its social organization. Contrary to the view that Libyan society has been, and always will be, intensely local in its political predisposition, this study has argued something different. The seemingly decentralized nature of Libyan politics is as much a result of three factors: how the country was governed by its colonial and postcolonial rulers; how the country's economic development was managed, whether through settler plantations, central planning, or the neoliberal marketplace; and how the various constituent elements of Libyan society responded to these through localized strategies of survival. Ultimately, the interrelated nature of the causes of the 2011 revolution, the means by which Libyans organized against the Gaddafi regime, and the conflicts that emerged afterward are suggestive of the modern roots of Libya's anarchic state. As Chapters 4 and 5 attempt to make abundantly clear, the civil conflicts that took shape after the collapse of the Gaddafi regime were as much determined by the ways in which modern forms of state power were enacted upon Libyan society from within and without as they were by the ways in which the 2011 revolution unfolded.

After all, today's Libya would be unrecognizable were it not for the blessing and the curse of oil. The country's vast natural wealth, which continues to be squandered even amidst the ongoing civil war in 2018, has become a curse in the economic sense and in a geopolitical sense. Oil not only brought about rapid socio-economic dislocation, it radically repositioned Libya's standing in world politics in the 1960s. It then enabled the Gaddafi regime's quixotic efforts to challenge the dominance of the North Atlantic powers at the height of the Cold War. These political, economic, and military misadventures eventually led to the country's international isolation and eventual containment under a rigid scheme of sanctions and embargos. What this meant for Libyan society in the 1990s, whose economy was still reeling from the 1986 oil price collapse, was the intensification of local survival strategies that manipulated the state when necessary and circumvented it when possible. This social evasion of the state was matched by the regime's own evasion of politics in the 2000s. Its rule became more technocratic, market-oriented, and antagonistic to the very ideals of the *Jamahiriyyah*. If anything, the 2011 uprising in Libya was a clash between social forces that had grown distrustful of central authority and a central authority that had grown increasingly indifferent to the society it governed.

Though the *Jamahiriyyah* had alienated and enraged many constituencies in Libya, particularly in the wrath of its final months in 2011, there were communities that had benefited under Gaddafi's rule, if not profited and advanced, either as the regime's social base of support or as a result of the excessive financial largess with which the state addressed political discontent through housing, jobs, and other appeasement schemes. In the aftermath of the 2011 uprising, a growing divide began to appear. This book has characterized this divide as between those seeking to disenfranchise the agents of the Gaddafi state and to dismantle its institutional structures – *revolutionaries* – and those advocating or demanding the rehabilitation of former regime officials and institutions – *accommodationists*.

As Chapters 3 and 4 explained, these divisions emerged in different regions of the country, intersecting with preexisting and newfound rifts, the latter having been generated by the eight-month civil war in 2011. Chapter 4 then examined how these cleavages held significant consequences for the attempt to reconsolidate national authority in 2012 and 2013, and then the civil war that followed from 2014 onward. A few communities in Libya even remained staunchly loyal to the ousted regime, as did thousands of Libyans in exile in Tunisia, Egypt, Malta, Algeria, and elsewhere. That said, accommodationism and loyalism were not always the same thing in the new Libya. The loyalists' often cult-like obsession with the *Jamahiriyyah* and their desire to achieve the restoration of the regime vis-à-vis Saif Al-Islam alienated many accommodationists, not to mention their adversaries among the moderate and radical revolutionary factions within the post-2011 Libyan polity. That said, it is now clear that the international efforts to help liberate Libya from the Gaddafi regime in 2011 had vastly underestimated two key things: first, the socio-political networks of support underwriting the *Jamahiriyyah*'s durability; and, second, the implacable anger that would be directed toward those networks once the revolution seized power. Just as the Anglo-American occupation of Iraq in 2003 had empowered the marginalized and disempowered the ruling minority, the 2011 NATO–Arab League intervention against the Gaddafi regime ultimately had a similar effect leading to the same outcome – civil war.

Apart from the question of loyalist influence, the revolutionary–accommodationist cleavage was simultaneously exacerbated yet distorted by the growing dominance of Islamist ideals and actors across the political spectrum, phenomena documented in Chapters 4 and 5. To make matters worse, the line between nonviolent political Islamism and its armed militant counterpart had been blurred by the solidarities and violence of the 2011 revolution. As Chapter 5 suggests, it was only with the emergence of the Islamic State in Sirte in 2015 that some degree of nationalistic consensus seemed to exist among Libya's warring elites that Libya should continue to exist as Libya and not as a province of the Islamic State's empire. This consensus seemed to draw a line between acceptable and unacceptable forms of militant Islamism in Libya. It was nonetheless a line largely imagined and imposed by the North Atlantic powers backing

Libya's new interim authority, its fourth in four years: the Government of National Accord headed by Fayez Al-Serraj, which took up residence in Tripoli in early 2016. Up until then and afterward, both the Dawn and Dignity coalitions, which had emerged during the outbreak of civil war in 2014, were equally guilty of instrumentalizing orthodox Salafism and mobilizing jihadi ideas and actors for their own ends. But what Chapter 5 attempts to make clear is that the incentive of North Atlantic politico-military support allowed everyone – domestic and foreign alike – to play along with the international fiction that the Islamic State had become the single greatest threat to Libya's transition. As Libyan dissidents had realized in 2011, the ignorance and fears of the North Atlantic world, properly manipulated, could become a powerful weapon in an emergent civil war.

Lessons Unlearned: Rescuing Libya from Rescue

The Islamic State's brief tenure as the municipal government in Sirte, chronicled in Chapter 5, would indeed galvanize the North Atlantic powers to take action in Libya after several years of apathy and neglect. Their military efforts in 2016 would be their second intervention into a civil war in Libya in five years. Yet unlike the 2011 intervention, the low-intensity and largely covert intervention against the Islamic State came with none of the humanitarian pretensions that had guided NATO's "responsibility to protect" in 2011. The North Atlantic powers' response to the emergence of the Islamic State in Libya came with the full acknowledgment that their 2011 intervention had, as President Obama so delicately put it in his final months in office, turned Libya into a "shit show."[2] The real political circus, however, was much closer to the White House. In the final years of the Obama administration, the US Congress convened countless hearings and investigations into the response to the September 11, 2012, attacks in Benghazi. These investigations proved to be nothing more than vulgar displays of congressional partisanship with the sole intention of sullying the reputation of Secretary of State

Hillary Clinton in advance of her second attempt to become the US President in 2016. The hearings effectively served their purpose and contributed to the election of President Donald Trump. Upon coming into office, Obama's successor made it clear that his administration did not consider Libya a priority. Europe would be left to deal with Libya, and its waves of seaborne migrants, on its own.

What the North Atlantic powers realized all too late – indeed, years after the fact – was the extent to which their policies toward revolutionary and post-revolutionary Libya had been guided by a series of fatal assumptions. One of the most insidious was the assumption that the country's natural wealth, human capital, and infrastructure would quickly stabilize Libya after the fall of the Gaddafi regime. Similar assumptions had guided the United States and Great Britain in their invasion of Iraq in 2003, leading to disastrous results in both cases. And in both cases, these assumptions were just as much used to marginalize concerns that failed states would emerge if regime change was conducted by force. In the case of the NATO–Arab League intervention in Libya, the mantle of humanitarianism was used to justify efforts to *exacerbate* a civil war that was already well underway, not to prevent it or suppress it. Whether out of naïvety, ignorance, or duplicity, Libya's revolutionaries and their foreign backers believed that they could unleash these violent forces and then, just as quickly, democratically contain them within the apparatus of a modern state led by a technocratic elite.

These assumptions were highly problematic for many reasons. First of all, the capacities of the Libyan state – such that it even existed in the final years of the *Jamahiriyyah* – were vastly overestimated. For over forty years, Gaddafi's regime managed to maintain power by systematically elimi-nating the social, economic, and political conditions of possibility for rivals to emerge. His fantasy of a horizontal, bottom-up society was just that, a mirage sustained by sycophants and self-delusion. Libyan society was not simply an edifice dominated and suppressed by the Gaddafi regime; it was a series of survival networks that had evolved over decades to manipulate and evade state power. In 2011, these networks allowed Libyan society to finally challenge state power. They would go on to perform the same tasks in the years to come, viewing state power, and those who would seek to wield it, with deep suspicion. That is to say, the kinds of associative life that had developed in Libya under the *Jamahiriyyah* were suited to surviving authoritarianism, failed socialism, and organizing local armed resistance; such organizations could not be easily transformed into or quickly allied with mass-based political parties.[3] And while it was often difficult to imagine how the institutions and infra-structures of the *Jamahiriyyah* could be quickly repurposed to meet the needs of Libya's new central authorities and the population at large, it turned out that these structures could be just as easily repurposed to serve regional and local needs above national ones.

Though there were indeed many advantages working in the favor of Libyan revolutionaries in 2011, the ability of the country's interim authorities to translate these advantages into a stable post-conflict order were definitively under-mined by the socio-political rifts that were either generated by or amplified during the uprising. Had the international community been as willing to contribute as much to peace as to war in Libya, its fate might have been different. But the contract upon which Libya's revolutionaries and NATO forged a military alliance foreclosed the possibility of a robust UN stabilization force. Such an initiative would have raised questions about the abilities of Libya's transitional authorities to deliver on their promise of a cheap revolution to their North Atlantic sponsors. Western leaders, after all, were still incapable of imagining authoritarianism as arising out of anything other than the force of strong-willed madmen. That there were social roots to the tyranny of the *Jamahiriyyah* would have defied the very narrative that justified regime change in the first place. That malignant social effects would result from Gaddafi's violent removal was also an unthinkable fact that nonetheless came true. Taken altogether, these fatal assumptions would have also raised questions as to whether or not reticent political leaders in the United States and Western Europe had bitten off more than they could politically chew in Libya, though an international stabilization force, if not temporary UN trusteeship, might have spared Libya much turmoil and bloodshed in the preceding years. The political impossibility of either initiative in 2011 and 2012 spoke volumes about the extent to which the crisis in Libya could no longer be disentangled from the crises of war and the Middle East that had been haunting leaders and publics in the North Atlantic world for decades.

Entangled Crises: Libya and the Global

Since 2011, most Libyans had become as weary of their implacable national leaders as they were of the bellicose militia commanders sabotaging the transition. Libyans had also become accustomed to the North Atlantic's vacillating interest in their country. If there was a bright side to all of this, it was perhaps the growing sense of exhaustion with armed violence. By 2017, the levels of violence associated with the armed conflicts in Libya had fallen to numbers far below the homicide rate experienced in many countries around the world. It was said that a degree of normalcy began to return to many areas, including parts of the capital and Benghazi. Even stranger still were the number of small- and large-scale foreign investments and development projects going forward under the auspices of municipal councils, regional authorities, or one of Libya's three putative national-level transitional administrations.

At the same time, this new normal – divided sovereignty, sporadic skirmishes, public and private militias – helped to reproduce pessimistic assessments of the country's prospects. As always, Libya maintained its status as the quintessential pariah state, albeit without an identifiable pariah at the helm. This status served to maintain the country under increasingly passive and indirect forms of international management. All the while, it continued to function as a military and political playground for other states and their agendas, whether geopolitical or ideological. On an annual basis, the UN Security Council's panel of experts on Libya documented clear, gross, and systemic violations of the international arms embargo. The Security Council itself, however, could hardly be bothered to do anything about it. The Council, after all, did little to support the very Government of National Accord it had installed in Tripoli once it had agreed to two things: first, military operations against the Islamic State; second, the extension of Europe's borders into Libya in the fight against Africans and Muslims fleeing poverty and conflict.

Libyans nonetheless found ways to survive, to build, to travel, to trade, to secure their livelihoods and to protect their communities, even in the absence of a single national government. After all, they had endured long periods of erratic, diffuse, and often violent forms of central governance before, as well as the years and decades of international isolation. Some of these strategies of survival in Libya certainly warrant concern from the international community, chief among them human trafficking and arms smuggling. However, rather than assuming that these strategies of survival can be simply subordinated or eradicated by a technocratic leviathan, it is far more important to come to grips with these realities in any analysis that hopes to elucidate the social and economic processes driving the political conflict in Libya today.

It is also important to recognize the entanglement of these processes within larger global forces. If Libya's problems were entirely Libyan, a solution would have certainly emerged by now. A lasting peace and a legitimate national government have not come about for a lack of effort by Libyans. For several years now, the struggle to find solutions to Libya's interlocking local, regional, and national conflicts has been waged by countless politicians, activists, *shaykh*s, citizens, experts, imams, businesspeople, bureaucrats, scholars, youth, elites, associations, journalists, and diplomats. These peacemakers have come from various communities within Libya, from across the Mediterranean, from Libya's neighbors, from the African Union and the United Nations. A growing mantra in the wake of the stillborn Government of National Accord is the need to find Libyan solutions to Libya's problems. This impulse was understandable in the wake of the rushed and compromised UN negotiations that led to the 2015 Skhirat Agreement and the ulterior motives driving its implementation in 2016. This book, however, has struggled to demonstrate that, time and time again, Libya's problems are rarely, in fact, inherently Libyan.

After all, the country's first emergence as an international problem – before Libya was even Libya – was in relation to the decay of the Ottoman Empire, the consolidation of the modern Italian state, and the geopolitical anxieties of late imperial Europe on the eve of World War I. The Libyan dilemma of the late 1940s was one in which the North Atlantic powers struggled to manage and supervise the territory's inchoate right to self-determination vis-à-vis the precedent that an independent Arab state in North Africa would create for the rest of the region. The problem of the Gaddafi regime is likewise incomprehensible without giving due consideration to the ways in which Libya was embedded in the geopolitics of the Cold War and the international political economy of the post-1973 global hydrocarbon regime. The solution to the Gaddafi problem was for Washington and its allies to exacerbate the former to the benefit of the latter. The rapid and intensive militarization of Libya with Soviet arms in the 1970s helped to pattern the Cold War map of northern Africa into a balanced system of Western allies (Morocco, Tunisia, Chad, and Egypt), Soviet armed petro-pariahs (Algeria and Libya), and interlocking conflicts like Western Sahara and the Aouzou Strip. This system of insecurity not only helped to thwart the possibility of North African regional integration (a Cold War legacy that persists into the present), it justified arms transfers from the North Atlantic to states that did not have the financial resources of oil to pay for them.

Even before the collapse of the Cold War, the Gaddafi regime was already being re-problematized according to the new international security paradigm of counterterrorism to emerge in the 1980s. Insofar as terrorism came to be understood as a form of transnational asymmetric warfare in the global information age, the Gaddafi regime, as a "state sponsor of terrorism," contributed to the North Atlantic world's efforts to selectively redefine certain forms of armed resistance as inherently apolitical, immoral, irrational, and ultimately irredeemable. That the Gaddafi regime, if not Gaddafi himself, could be redeemed in the early 2000s after being subjected to decades of diplomatic isolation, sanctions, embargos, and punitive military strikes – the insidious, indirect toolkit for coercive foreign policy in the new world order – demonstrated once again that Libya's problems were not Libya's own. More importantly, the success of NATO's intervention in the 2011 Libyan uprising – regime change as responsibility to protect – vindicated the use of conventional military force in world affairs after the disaster of the Anglo-American occupation of Iraq in 2003.

This survey of the country's history both as a geopolitical agent and as an object of modern geopolitics raises questions as to Libya's role in global affairs after the Arab Spring. It also raises questions about our ability to understand the contemporary global moment through the prism of the various crises that gave gripped Libya since 2011. As noted above, Libya has somehow managed to remain a pariah state though its original pariah figure was murdered over five years ago. This is suggestive of the extent to which there is a deeply seated pathology in global affairs that makes it difficult for states to shake off their historical function in the international system. At the same time, the myriad crises in Libya reveal the extent to which changes are emerging in the global system. As the world adapts to waning US hegemony, the exhaustion of capitalism, a post-hydrocarbon energy regime, and the increasing inability of the environment to bear these burdens, the Middle East and North Africa could be ravaged by endless waves of social, economic, and political disruption. Libya nonetheless instructs us to be wary of confusing new and irregular forms of political order with anarchy. What often appears as disarray could be the shape of things to come.

Notes

Chapter 1 State of the Masses

1 Data compiled from the World Bank website: https://data.worldbank.org/country/libya.
2 Anderson, *The State and Social Transformation*, 44.
3 Minawi, *The Ottoman Scramble for Africa*.
4 See Ahmida, *Forgotten Voices*, Chapter 4.
5 For an early reference, see Allan et al., *Libya: Agriculture and Economic Development*, 9.
6 This is essentially the argument, contrasting political development in Tunisia and Libya, presented in Anderson, *The State and Social Transformation*.
7 See Vandewalle, *Libya Since Independence*, 45–6.
8 Quoted in Gurney, *Libya: The Political Economy of Oil*, 2.
9 See Vitalis, *America's Kingdom*.
10 Anderson, *The State and Social Transformation*, 259; Vandewalle, *Libya Since Independence*, 56.
11 See Kadduri, *Modern Libya*, Chapters 8–10.
12 Vandewalle, *Libya Since Independence*, 51–9.
13 El Mallakh, "The Economics of Rapid Growth."
14 A celebrated narrative of the growing state of fear in 1970s Libya can be found in Matar's novel *In the Country of Men*.
15 Quoted in Simons, *Libya and the West*, 101.

16 Davis, *Libyan Politics*.

17 Niblock, *"Pariah States" and Sanctions*, 61.

18 The logic and consequences of arms and oil nexus in the Middle East and North Africa is explained in Chapter 5 of Nitzan and Bichler, *The Global Political Economy of Israel*.

19 Quoted in Cooley, *Libyan Sandstorm*, 100.

20 For background on US–Libyan relations, see ElWarfally, *Imagery and Ideology*; St. John, *Libya and the United States*.

21 O'Sullivan, *Shrewd Sanctions*, 177.

22 Data compiled from various editions of the US government report *World Military Expenditures and Arms Transfers*, regularly published by the State Department, covering the 1960s through the 1980s.

23 One noteworthy effort to come to grips with this "politics of contradiction" (both domestic and foreign policies) can be found in El-Kikhia, *Libya's Qaddafi*.

24 See Cooley, *Libyan Sandstorm*, 92–100.

25 See St. John, *Qaddafi's World Design*; Ronen, *Qaddafi's Libya*.

26 See Muller, "Frontiers"; Wright, *Libya, Chad, and the Central Sahara*.

27 For detailed accounts of the war until 1980, see Joffe, "Libya and Chad"; Neuberger, *Involvement, Invasion, and Withdrawal*.

28 One of the best accounts of the war, told from the perspective of Chad rather than Libya, can be found in Nolutshungu, *Limits of Anarchy*.

29 See Werfalli, *Political Alienation in Libya*.

30 On property law and its implications for the post-2011 conflicts, see Fitzgerald and Megerisi, *Libya: Whose Land Is It?*

31 Niblock, *"Pariah States" and Sanctions*, 60–3.

32 Niblock, *"Pariah States" and Sanctions*, 63–70, 74–80, 87–90.

33 See Amnesty International, *Violations of Human Rights in the Libyan Arab Jamahiriya*; Amnesty International, *Libya: Summary of Amnesty International's Prisoner Concerns*.

34 Amnesty International, *Summary of Amnesty International's Concerns in Libya.*

35 This was detailed to me in an interview with a former Libyan air force officer in Misrata (July 15, 2012).

36 International Institute for Strategic Studies, *The Military Balance 2002–2003*, 333.

37 Simons, *Libya and the West*, 105.

38 Amnesty International, *Libya: Gross Human Rights Violations.*

39 See Human Rights Watch, *Libya: June 1996 Killings at Abu Salim Prison.*

40 Fitzgerald, "Finding Their Place," 179, 180.

41 See Ashour, "Post-Jihadism," 381–3.

42 See Amnesty International et al., *Off the Record.*

43 See United Nations Development Programme, *Human Development Report 2010.*

44 Simons, *Libya and the West*, 116–19. For background, see Deeb and Deeb, *Libya Since the Revolution*, Chapter 3.

45 Transparency International, *National Integrity Systems Assessment*, 11.

46 United Nations Development Programme, *Arab Human Development Report 2009*, 232.

47 World Bank, *Labor Market Dynamics in Libya*, xii.

48 See Economist Intelligence Unit, *Libya: Country Profile 2008.*

49 This is essentially the argument in Chorin, *Exit the Colonel.*

50 See Springborg, "The Political Economy of the Arab Spring."

51 Simons, *Libya and the West*, 158–64.

52 See Ken Dornstein, "My Brother's Bomber," *Frontline*, PBS, September 29, October 6, October 13, 2015, https://www.pbs.org/wgbh/frontline/film/my-brothers-bomber/; Patrick Radden Keefe, "The Avenger," *New Yorker*, September 28, 2015, https://www.newyorker.com/magazine/2015/09/28/the-avenger.

53 John F. Burns, "BP Faces New Scrutiny in Lockerbie Case," *New York Times*, July 15, 2010, http://www.nytimes.com/2010/07/16/world/europe/16britain.html.

54 London School of Economics, "LSE and Libya," October 17, 2011, http://www.lse.ac.uk/website-archive/ newsAndMedia/newsArchives/2011/02/libya_funding. aspx; Ed Pilkington, "US Firm Monitor Group Admits Mistakes over $3m Gaddafi Deal," *Guardian*, March 3, 2011, https://www.theguardian.com/world/2011/ mar/04/monitor-group-us-libya-gaddafi; John Wiener, "Professors Paid by Qaddafi: Providing 'Positive Public Relations'," *The Nation*, March 5, 2011, https:// www.thenation.com/article/professors-paid-qaddafi- providing-positive-public-relations/; Mohamed Eljahmi, "Libya's Inconvenient Truth," *Washington Post*, January 2, 2008, http://www.washingtonpost.com/wp-dyn/ content/article/2008/01/01/AR2008010101299.html.
55 See Zoubir, "Libya and Europe"; Zoubir, "The United States and Libya."
56 See Braut-Hegghammer, "Libya's Nuclear Turnaround."
57 See Freedom House, "Libya," *Freedom in the World*, https://freedomhouse.org/report/freedom-world/2007/ libya.
58 International Crisis Group, *Trial by Error*, 14–15.
59 Issawi, *Transitional Libyan Media*, 3–7.
60 Ashour, "Post-Jihadism," 383–4.
61 Brahimi, "Islam in Libya."
62 Ashour, *Libyan Islamists Unpacked*.
63 Bugaighis, "Prospects for Women in the New Libya," 114–15.
64 Lacher, "Families, Tribes and Cities"; Hweio, "Tribes in Libya."

Chapter 2 Uprising and Intervention: Libya in Revolt

1 McQuinn, "Assessing (In)security After the Arab Spring," 716.
2 Fitzgerald, "Finding Their Place," 181.
3 Amnesty International, *The Battle for Libya*, 13–16.
4 Amnesty International, *Libya: Detainees, Disappeared and Missing*, 3.

5   Amnesty International, *Writer Detained*; Amnesty International, *Libya: Four Arrested*.
6   Pargeter, *Libya: The Rise and Fall of Qaddafi*, 217–19.
7   Ashour, *Libyan Islamists Unpacked*, 3.
8   Benotman et al., "Islamists," 216.
9   Human Rights Watch, *Libya: Security Forces Kill 84*.
10 Cole and Khan, "The Fall of Tripoli: Part 1," 55–6.
11 Human Rights Watch, *Libya: Commanders Should Face Justice*; Human Rights Watch, *Libya: Governments Should Demand End to Unlawful Killings*.
12 Pargeter, *Libya: The Rise and Fall of Qaddafi*, 221–2.
13 McQuinn, "History's Warriors," 235.
14 See Cole, "Bani Walid," 57.
15 Bartu, "The Corridor of Uncertainty," 36.
16 During interviews conducted by the author in Libya in the summer of 2012, several former rebels said that it was Saif Al-Islam's speech and its patronizing tone – more than anything else – that convinced them there was no alternative to an armed insurrection. For an account of the internal political struggles between Saif Al-Islam and his father during this period, and why the former chose repression over reform, see Pargeter, *Libya: The Rise and Fall of Qaddafi*, 227–30.
17 This is a paraphrase of Gaddafi's now infamous promise to purge Libya of rebels "alley by alley" (*zangah zangah*). He said this during his seventy-five-minute speech on national television on February 22, 2011, after rumors suggested that the Gaddafi family had fled – or were about to flee – to Venezuela. See BBC Worldwide Monitoring, "Libyan Leader Says 'Will Fight Until The Last Drop of Blood'," February 23, 2011.
18 Amnesty International, *Libya: Detainees, Disappeared and Missing*, 5–6.
19 Amnesty International, *The Battle for Libya*, 19–20.
20 Mattes, "Rebuilding the National-Security Forces in Libya," 85.
21 See Pack and Barfi, *In War's Wake*, 1.
22 Bassiouni, *Libya: From Repression to Revolution*, 133–42.

23 United Nations Human Rights Council, *Report of the International Commission of Inquiry on Libya*, 18.
24 Smith, "The South," 183.
25 Bell and Witter, *The Libyan Revolution: Roots of Rebellion*, 21–2.
26 Northern and Pack, "Role of Outside Actors," 130–1.
27 Smith, "The South," 184.
28 Pargeter, *Libya: The Rise and Fall of Qaddafi*, 225.
29 Bartu, "The Corridor of Uncertainty," 46.
30 Pack, "Introduction: The Center and the Periphery," 5–7.
31 McQuinn, "Assessing (In)security After the Arab Spring," 717.
32 See Benotman et al., "Islamists," 191–2, 210–11.
33 United Nations Human Rights Council, *Report of the International Commission of Inquiry on Libya*, 3–7.
34 For example, Marc Lynch, "Intervening in the Libyan Tragedy," *Foreign Policy*, February 21, 2011, http://foreignpolicy.com/2011/02/21/intervening-in-the-libyan-tragedy/; Gareth Evans, "No-Fly Zone Is Only Way to Stop the Carnage," *Financial Times*, February 28, 2011; Timothy Garton Ash, "Libya's Escalating Drama Reopens the Case for Liberal Intervention," *Guardian*, March 3, 2011, https://www.theguardian.com/commentisfree/2011/mar/03/libya-escalating-drama-case-liberal-intervention.
35 Roberts, "Who Said Gaddafi Had to Go?"; for background, see Chivvis, *Toppling Qaddafi*, 48–53.
36 De Waal, "'My Fears, Alas, Were Not Unfounded'," 61–4.
37 See de Waal, "'My Fears, Alas, Were Not Unfounded'," 58, 66–7; Roberts, "Who Said Gaddafi Had to Go?" 14.
38 Chivvis, *Toppling Qaddafi*, 43.
39 Bob Woodward, "Robert Gates, Former Defense Secretary, Offers Harsh Critique of Obama's Leadership in 'Duty'," *Washington Post*, January 7, 2014, https://www.washingtonpost.com/world/national-security/robert-gates-former-defense-secretary-offers-harsh-critique-of-obamas-leadership-in-duty/2014/01/07/6a6915b2-77cb-

11e3-b1c5-739e63e9c9a7_story.html. See also Chivvis, *Toppling Qaddafi,* Chapter 3.

40 Chivvis, *Toppling Qaddafi,* 33.
41 Northern and Pack, "The Role of Outside Actors," 116–17.
42 Kriesberg, *Realizing Peace,* 263.
43 For an analysis of this debate, see Gazzini, "Was the Libya Intervention Necessary?"
44 A particularly insightful look into pro-regime mobilization can be found in Cole, "Bani Walid," 295–6.
45 Chivvis, *Toppling Qaddafi,* 100.
46 Bassiouni, *Libya: From Repression to Revolution,* 234–5.
47 Bassiouni, *Libya: From Repression to Revolution,* 240–3.
48 Interviews, Misrata (July 15, 2012) and Zintan (July 19, 2012). See also Northern and Pack, "The Role of Outside Actors," 136–7; Chivvis, *Toppling Qaddafi,* 154–5.

   In the case of the CIA, it appears that agents were dispatched to Libya in March to help coordinate the air and ground campaigns, and to make an assessment of the revolutionaries, about whom the intervening forces knew little, particularly their Islamist leanings. See Chivvis, *Toppling Qaddafi,* 45.
49 Cole, "Bani Walid," 71–4.
50 International Crisis Group, *Making Sense of Libya,* 28–30.
51 For background, see Campbell, *Global NATO and the Catastrophic Failure in Libya,* Chapter 12.
52 De Waal, "'My Fears, Alas, Were Not Unfounded'," 71–2.
53 See Bartu, *Libya's Political Transition,* 2–7; Roberts, "Who Said Gaddafi Had to Go?" 15.
54 Pargeter, *Libya: The Rise and Fall of Qaddafi,* 238.
55 See Bartu, "The Corridor of Uncertainty," 40.
56 Bassiouni, *Libya: From Repression to Revolution,* 202. See also Roberts, "Who Said Gaddafi Had to Go?" 14–15.

57 Northern and Pack, "The Role of Outside Actors," 117.
58 International Crisis Group, *Making Sense of Libya*, 25.
59 BBC News, "Libya Letter by Obama, Cameron and Sarkozy: Full Text." April 15, 2011, http://www.bbc.com/news/world-africa-13090646.
60 BBC News, "Tony Blair Defends Advice to Colonel Gaddafi During Libya Conflict," December 11, 2015, http://www.bbc.com/news/uk-politics-35069842.
61 Panetta and Newton, *Worthy Fights*, 354.
62 See United States House of Representatives Committee on Foreign Affairs, *Libya's Descent*; United Kingdom House of Commons Foreign Affairs Committee, *Libya: Examination of Intervention*.
63 See Chivvis, *Toppling Qaddafi*, 148–54.
64 Cole, "Bani Walid," 64–6.
65 Bell and Witter, *The Libyan Revolution: Stalemate and Siege*, 17–24.
66 Interviews, Tripoli (June 30, 2012), Zintan and Jadou (July 19, 2012)
67 In the 2000s, the Gaddafi regime was slow to destroy its chemical weapons capacity despite its international commitments; about half of its stockpile and precursor agents had been officially destroyed by the time the uprising started. However, there appear to have been significant quantities of "undeclared" mustard gas munitions, though these were stored in Saharan regions far from Tripoli. See Blanchard, *Libya: Transition and US Policy*, 16–18. For background, see Braut-Hegghammer, *Unclear Physics*.
68 Pargeter, *Libya: The Rise and Fall of Qaddafi*, 241.
69 Lacher and Labnouj, "Factionalism Resurgent," 257.
70 See United Nations Human Rights Council, *Commission of Inquiry on Libya*, 17; Human Rights Watch, *Unacknowledged Deaths*; Bassiouni, *Libya: From Repression to Revolution*, 234–67.
71 Interviews, Sirte (June 27–8, 2012) and Bani Walid (July 17, 2012).
72 Gazzini, "Was the Libya Intervention Necessary?" 3.

Chapter 3 State of the Martyrs

1 Zoubir and Rózsa, "The End of the Libyan Dictatorship."
2 Bartu, "The Corridor of Uncertainty," 37–8, 40.
3 Pack and Barfi, *In War's Wake*, 3.
4 Bugaighis, "Prospects for Women in the New Libya," 108.
5 International Crisis Group, *Making Sense of Libya*, 25.
6 Bell and Witter, *The Libyan Revolution: Stalemate and Siege*, 15–16; Bell et al., *The Libyan Revolution: The Tide Turns*, 17.
7 Bassiouni, *Libya: From Repression to Revolution*, 142, 395–7.
8 Pack and Barfi, *In War's Wake*, 1.
9 Bartu, "The Corridor of Uncertainty," 48–50.
10 Bartu, "The Corridor of Uncertainty," 45–7.
11 Bartu, "The Corridor of Uncertainty," 47.
12 Pack and Barfi, *In War's Wake*, 7–8.
13 Cole and Khan, "The Fall of Tripoli: Part 1," 96–8, 102–3.
14 Engel, *Libya As a Failed State*, 3.
15 International Crisis Group, *Holding Libya Together*, 8.
16 Cole and Khan, "The Fall of Tripoli: Part 1," 100–1.
17 See International Crisis Group, *Holding Libya Together*, 8, n. 53.
18 Cole and Khan, "The Fall of Tripoli: Part 1," 63, 82–3, 87–8.
19 Kane, "Barqa Reborn?" 214.
20 McQuinn, "Assessing (In)security After the Arab Spring," 718.
21 Pack and Barfi, *In War's Wake*, 5.
22 See Amnesty International, *Militias Threaten Hopes for New Libya*; Amnesty International, *"We Are Not Safe Anywhere."*
23 Bassiouni, *Libya: From Repression to Revolution*, 586.
24 McQuinn, "History's Warriors," 232–41.
25 McQuinn, "History's Warriors," 242–9.
26 McQuinn, "History's Warriors," 250–5.

27 See, for example, Del Boca, *Mohamed Fekini*; Ahmida, *The Making of Modern Libya*, Chapter 5.
28 Lacher and Labnouj, "Factionalism Resurgent," 261–2.
29 Cole, "Bani Walid," 291.
30 Lacher and Labnouj, "Factionalism Resurgent," 262–9.
31 Bassiouni, *Libya: From Repression to Revolution*, 647–50.
32 See Cole, "Bani Walid," 291.
33 Bassiouni, *Libya: From Repression to Revolution*, 658, 660.
34 Lacher and Labnouj, "Factionalism Resurgent," 265, 267, 269–76.
35 Human Rights Watch, *Libya: Diplomat Dies in Militia Custody*.
36 Lacher and Labnouj, "Factionalism Resurgent," 276–82.
37 United Nations Human Rights Council, *Report of the International Commission of Inquiry on Libya*, 18, 175–7.
38 Smith, "The South," 184. Here Smith is specifically referring to the Tuareg, though his assessment, as he implies, could be applied to any number of communities within Libya. See also Lacher, *Libya's Fractious South and Regional Instability*.
39 Smith, "The South," 176–7.
40 Cole, "Bani Walid," 291.
41 Wehrey, *Insecurity and Governance*, 14–15; Lacher, *Libya's Fractious South and Regional Instability*.
42 See de Waal, "'My Fears, Alas, Were Not Unfounded'."
43 See Murray, "Libya's Tebu."
44 Amnesty International, *Libya: Rule of Law or Rule of Militias?*, 47–8, 55.
45 Murray, "Libya's Tebu," 316–18; Smith, "The South," 180–1.
46 Wehrey, *Insecurity and Governance*, 15.
47 See Human Rights Watch, *Collapse, Conflict, and Atrocity in Mali*.
48 For more background on the 2012 crisis in Mali and the connection to Libya's revolution, see Yahia H. Zoubir, "Qaddafi's Spawn: What the Dictator's Demise Unleashed

in the Middle East," *Foreign Affairs*, July 24, 2012, https://www.foreignaffairs.com/articles/algeria/2012-07-24/qaddafis-spawn; Guichaoua, "Tuareg Militancy."

49 Cole, "Bani Walid," 291.

50 Smith, "The South," 184–5.

51 Guichaoua, "Tuareg Militancy," 325, 328–9, 331–3.

52 Blanchard, *Libya: Transition and US Policy*, 16–17; *Middle East Journal*, "Chronology."

53 Lacher and Labnouj, "Factionalism Resurgent," 277–8.

54 Wehrey, *The Struggle for Security in Eastern Libya*, 5.

55 Cole, "Bani Walid," 291.

56 A telling fact of Cyrenaican marginalization is that one of Gaddafi's first acts was to move the headquarters of the National Oil Corporation to Tripoli from Benghazi. See Kane, "Barqa Reborn?" 209–10.

57 Kane, "Barqa Reborn?" 210–11.

58 Wehrey, *The Struggle for Security in Eastern Libya*, 6.

59 Cole ("Bani Walid," 288), citing Ahmida (*The Making of Modern Libya*) describes the Sanusi state as so "rudimentary" that its security forces were raised from local militias. In the east, Sanusi power relied on the Sa'da confederation of the largest and most powerful tribes. In the west, the Warfalla and Awlad Sulayman guaranteed Sanusi power, until the Warfalla threw their lot in with Gaddafi in 1969.

60 Wehrey, *The Struggle for Security in Eastern Libya*, 6–7.

61 Fitzgerald, "Finding Their Place," 190–1.

62 Fitzgerald, "Finding Their Place," 187–93.

63 Kane, "Barqa Reborn?" 212–15.

64 Bartu, "The Corridor of Uncertainty," 41.

65 Bartu, "The Corridor of Uncertainty," 50–3.

66 See Gluck, *Extending Libya's Transitional Period*, 1–2; Blanchard, *Libya: Transition and US Policy*, 13.

67 Blanchard, *Libya: Transition and US Policy*, 16.

68 Mattes, "Rebuilding the National-Security Forces in Libya," 89–90.

69 Wehrey, *The Struggle for Security in Eastern Libya*, 17–18.

70 The vote was marred by sporadic violence against polling

locations and against a helicopter ferrying ballots. The *Jaysh Al-Barqah* even went as far as to shut down the three major oil-exporting sites along the eastern Sirtica coast. See Wehrey, *The Struggle for Security in Eastern Libya*, 8.

71 Bugaighis, "Prospects for Women in the New Libya," 109.

72 Wehrey, *The Struggle for Security in Eastern Libya*, 8.

73 Making matters worse, the colors of *Al-Watan* were purple and silver, which many compared to the flag of Qatar. See Fitzgerald, "Finding Their Place," 200.

74 Issawi, *Transitional Libyan Media*, 12–13.

75 See Bugaighis, "Prospects for Women in the New Libya," 110, 109.

76 Carter Center, *General National Congress Elections in Libya*; Project on Middle East Democracy, *POMED Backgrounder: Previewing Libya's Elections*.

77 Fitzgerald, "Finding Their Place," 203.

78 During the August 8 handover of authority from the National Transitional Council to the General National Congress, Abdul Jalil reportedly asked an unveiled woman to get off the stage, an act that reinvigorated post-revolutionary debates about women's new role in society and politics. See Bugaighis, "Prospects for Women in the New Libya," 117.

Chapter 4 Hegemony or Anarchy?

1 Issawi, *Transitional Libyan Media*, 6–7.

2 Mattes, "Libya Since 2011," 59. See also Romanet Perroux, *Libya's Untold Story*; Bugaighis, "Prospects for Women in the New Libya," 111–12; Geha, *Understanding Libya's Civil Society*.

3 Bugaighis, "Prospects for Women in the New Libya," 108.

4 Amnesty International, *Detention Abuses Staining the New Libya*.

5 See Amnesty International, *"We Are Not Safe*

Anywhere"; Amnesty International, *Barred from Their Homes.*

6   Amnesty International, *Libya: Rule of Law or Rule of Militias?*, 8. See also International Crisis Group, *Divided We Stand*, 2.

7   International Crisis Group, *Divided We Stand*, 5–7. See also Cole, *Borderline Chaos*; Lacher, *Libya's Fractious South and Regional Instability.*

8   Human Rights Watch, *"The Endless Wait."*

9   Human Rights Watch, *World Report 2012*; Amnesty International, *Libya: Rule of Law or Rule of Militias?*; Amnesty International, *Militias Threaten Hopes for New Libya.*

10   See, e.g., Amnesty International, *Amnesty International Condemns Benghazi Bombing.*

11   Lacher and Cole, *Politics by Other Means*, 46; Amnesty International, *Libya: The Day Militias Shot at Protesters.*

12   Quoted in Wehrey, *Ending Libya's Civil War*, 5.

13   John Thorne, "In Libya, a Patchwork of Militias Keeping the Peace, and Straining It," *The Christian Science Monitor*, October 5, 2012, https://www. csmonitor.com/World/Middle-East/2012/1005/ In-Libya-a-patchwork-of-militias-keeping-the-peace-and-straining-it. See also Mangan et al., *Security and Justice in Postrevolution Libya*, 17–18.

14   Wehrey, *Libya's Militia Menace.*

15   Wehrey, *Ending Libya's Civil War*, 1, 3–4.

16   Pack et al., *Libya's Faustian Bargains.*

17   Bartu, *Libya's Political Transition*, 13. See also Chivvis and Martini, *Libya After Qaddafi*, 67–76.

18   Quoted in International Crisis Group, *Divided We Stand*, 17, footnote 129.

19   McQuinn, "Assessing (In)security After the Arab Spring," 719.

20   Fitzgerald, "Finding Their Place," 201–2; McQuinn, "Assessing (In)security After the Arab Spring," 717. For background, see International Crisis Group, *Divided We Stand*, 16–18.

21 David Kirkpatrick, "A Deadly Mix in Benghazi." *New York Times*, December 28, 2013, http://www.nytimes.com/projects/2013/benghazi/.

22 United Nations Panel of Experts on Libya, *Final Report of the Panel of Experts*, 40 and Annex 37–41; Hersh, "The Red Line and the Rat Line."

23 On jihad in Libya in the 1990s, see Ashour, "Post-Jihadism" and Ashour, *Libyan Islamists Unpacked*. For background on the Abu Salim massacre, see Human Rights Watch, *Libya: June 1996 Killings at Abu Salim Prison*.

24 Human Rights Watch, *Delivered into Enemy Hands*, 91–102.

25 Fitzgerald, "Finding Their Place," 179.

26 Anderson, "Qaddafi's Islam."

27 Fitzgerald, "Finding Their Place," 179–80, 183.

28 Fitzgerald, "Finding Their Place," 183–4.

29 Quoted in Blanchard, *Libya: Transition and US Policy*, 19–20. Both Al-Qaida's main headquarters in Pakistan and its North African affiliate endorsed the Libyan uprising. One of the organization's top-level officials, Abu Yahia Al-Libi, is actually from Libya.

30 Wehrey, *Ending Libya's Civil War*, 6.

31 Wehrey, *Ending Libya's Civil War*, 19.

32 Ashour, *Libyan Islamists Unpacked*, 7; Zoubir, "Qaddafi's Spawn" (see Chapter 3, n. 48).

33 Cole and Khan, "Fall of Tripoli: Part 1," 66–76, 70, 93. See also Benotman et al., "Islamists," 191.

34 Benotman et al., "Islamists," 214–15.

35 Fitzgerald, "Finding Their Place," 185, 192–3.

36 McQuinn, "Assessing (In)security After the Arab Spring," 718.

37 Belhadj even took to the pages of the *Guardian* ("The Revolution Belongs to All Libyans, Secular or Not," September 27, 2011, https://www.theguardian.com/commentisfree/2011/sep/27/revolution-belongs-to-all-libyans) to express his disenchantment with the National Transitional Council. As noted in Chapter 3, the entire region of Cyrenaica often felt marginalized

(yet again) in the post-Gaddafi order. Yet this was acutely felt among the several thousand Islamist fighters of the Eastern Rebel Association led by Fawzi Bu Katif. For background, see Pack and Barfi, *In War's Wake*, 8.

38 Benotman et al., "Islamists," 192.

39 Ashour, *Libyan Islamists Unpacked*, 6.

40 Benotman et al., "Islamists," 218.

41 Blanchard, *Libya: Transition and US Policy*, 20.

42 Ashour, *Libyan Islamists Unpacked*, 4.

43 Benotman et al., "Islamists," 217. See also Fitzgerald ("Finding Their place," 196–7) on the connections between Libya's *Ikhwan* (Muslim Brotherhood), the organization's spiritual guide (the Qatar-based Shaykh Yusuf Al-Qaradawi), and Qaradawi's International Union of Muslim Scholars, of which Ali Al-Sallabi is a member and under whose wing he stayed during his years in exile in Qatar.

44 Ashour, *Libyan Islamists Unpacked*, 4.

45 Fitzgerald, "Finding Their Place," 195–202; Benotman et al., "Islamists," 215.

46 Benotman et al., "Islamists," 191–2.

47 Ashour, *Libyan Islamists Unpacked*, 6.

48 For background, see Ashour, "Post-Jihadism."

49 Benotman et al., "Islamists," 219–21.

50 Mattes, "Libya Since 2011," 62.

51 On Ghariani's statements before the 2012 elections, see Fitzgerald, "Finding Their Place," 103. See also St. John, *Libya: Continuity and Change*, 89–90.

52 Pack and Barfi, *In War's Wake*, 8; St. John, *Libya: Continuity and Change*, 89.

53 St. John, *Libya: Continuity and Change*, 92.

54 International Crisis Group, *Divided We Stand*, 3. McQuinn, "Assessing (In)security After the Arab Spring," 718.

55 St. John, *Libya: Continuity and Change*, 90.

56 See Transparency International, *National Integrity Systems Assessment*, 11. On the specific weaknesses of the justice and security sector under Gaddafi, see

Mangan et al., *Security and Justice in Postrevolution Libya*, 5, 7–11.

57 International Crisis Group, *Divided We Stand*, 24.

58 International Crisis Group, *Trial by Error*, 30–1.

59 International Crisis Group, *Divided We Stand*, 10.

60 Transparency International, *National Integrity Systems Assessment*, 12–13.

61 International Crisis Group, *Trial by Error*, 3–4, 16.

62 Mangan et al., *Security and Justice in Postrevolution Libya*, 20–2, 12–13.

63 International Crisis Group, *Trial by Error*, i.

64 International Crisis Group, *Trial by Error*, 6–7.

65 International Commission of Jurists, *Challenges for the Libyan Judiciary*.

66 Sayigh, *Crumbling States*, 7.

67 International Crisis Group, *Divided We Stand*, 8–10, 14–15.

68 Pack and Barfi, *In War's Wake*, 10.

69 Martin, *UNSMIL SRSG's Speech at Benghazi University*.

70 Pack et al., *Libya's Faustian Bargains*, 2.

71 Karim Mezran, "A Holistic Approach to Security in Libya," MENAsource, Atlantic Council, July 10, 2013, http://www.atlanticcouncil.org/blogs/menasource/a-holistic-approach-to-security-in-libya.

72 Mattes, "Rebuilding the National-Security Forces in Libya," 94–5.

73 Mangan et al., *Security and Justice in Postrevolution Libya*, 12.

74 Pack et al., *The Origins and Evolution of ISIS in Libya*, 32.

75 Mattes, "Rebuilding," 89, citing McQuinn, *After the Fall*.

76 Lacher and Cole, *Politics by Other Means*, 39–41.

77 See, e.g., Kartas, *On the Edge?*

78 International Crisis Group, *Divided We Stand*, 6, 13, 15–16, 18.

79 International Crisis Group, *Divided We Stand*, 8, 18–19; International Crisis Group, *Trial by*

Error, 1, footnote 1; Borzou Daragahi, "Shadow Army Takes over Libya's Security," *Financial Times*, July 6, 2012, https://www.ft.com/content/8f865f1c-c75a-11e1-849e-00144feabdc0.

80 Lacher and Cole, *Politics by Other Means*, 41.

81 United Nations Panel of Experts on Libya, *Final Report of the Panel of Experts*, 24 and Annex 27.

82 Mattes, "Rebuilding," 93.

83 International Crisis Group, *Divided We Stand*, 8, 12–13.

84 Wehrey, *Ending Libya's Civil War*, 11.

85 Wehrey, *Libya's Militia Menace*.

86 Mattes, "Rebuilding," 95; Wehrey, *Ending Libya's Civil War*, 20.

87 United Nations Panel of Experts on Libya, *Final Report of the Panel of Experts*, 175–6.

88 Mangan et al., *Security and Justice in Postrevolution Libya*, 19; Wehrey and Cole, *Building Libya's Security Sector*, 3; See also Lacher and Cole, *Politics by Other Means*, 35–9.

89 Wehrey and Cole, *Building Libya's Security Sector*, 203.

90 International Crisis Group, *Trial by Error*, 27.

91 Mangan et al., *Security and Justice in Postrevolution Libya*, 23; Wehrey, *Ending Libya's Civil War*, 14–15.

92 Abou-Khalil and Hargreaves, *Perceptions of Security in Libya*, 28–9.

93 Mangan et al., *Security and Justice in Postrevolution Libya*, 22–3.

94 Mattes, "Libya Since 2011," 64.

95 David Samuels, "How Libya Blew Billions and Its Best Chance at Democracy," *Bloomberg Businessweek*, August 7, 2014, https://www.bloomberg.com/news/articles/2014-08-07/libya-waste-fraud-erase-billions-in-national-wealth.

96 Blanchard, *Libya: Transition and US Policy*, 22–5.

97 Engel, *Libya as a Failed State*, 1, 4.

98 Engel, *Libya as a Failed State*, 6.

99 Lacher and Cole, *Politics by Other Means*, 36.

100 Quoted in Samuels, "How Libya Blew Billions and Its Best Chance at Democracy" (see note 95 above).
101 Setser and Frank, *Using External Breakeven Prices to Track Vulnerabilities in Oil-Exporting Countries.*
102 See US Energy Information Administration, *Country Analysis Brief: Libya.*
103 Engel, *Libya as a Failed State*, 2.
104 St. John, *Libya: Continuity and Change*, 92–3.
105 St. John, *Libya: Continuity and Change*, 94; Frederic Wehrey and Wolfram Lacher, "Libya's Legitimacy Crisis: The Danger of Picking Sides in the Post-Qaddafi Chaos," *Foreign Affairs*, October 6, 2014, https://www.foreignaffairs.com/articles/middle-east/2014-10-06/libyas-legitimacy-crisis.
106 Mattes, "Libya Since 2011," 70.
107 Pack et al., *Libya's Faustian Bargains*, 47.
108 Amnesty International, *Vanished Off the Face of the Earth*, 2.
109 Engel, *Libya as a Failed State*, 7. See also, for example, Amnesty International, *Libya: Journalist Killed.*
110 Wehrey, *Ending Libya's Civil War*, 20–1.
111 Frederic Wehrey, "Whoever Controls Benghazi Controls Libya," *Atlantic Monthly*, July 1, 2017, https://www.theatlantic.com/international/archive/2017/07/benghazi-libya/532056/.
112 Amnesty International, *Benghazi's Descent into Chaos*, 27–34.
113 Lacher and Cole, *Politics by Other Means*, 45–6.
114 Wehrey, *Ending Libya's Civil War*, 23.
115 International Crisis Group, *Libya: Getting Geneva Right*, 3.
116 Nearly 50 percent of the national government's budget was consumed by salaries and subsidies. See Pack et al., *Libya's Faustian Bargains*, 22.

Chapter 5 Libya on the Brink

1 St. John, *Libya: Continuity and Change*, 94.

2 Mattes, "Libya Since 2011," 62–3.
3 Zelin, *The Islamic State's Territorial Methodology*.
4 Zelin, *The Islamic State's First Colony in Libya*.
5 See Amnesty International, *Cold-Blooded Murder of Copts in Libya is a War Crime*.
6 Wehrey and Alrababa'h, *Rising Out of Chaos*.
7 Pack et al., *The Origins and Evolution of ISIS in Libya*, 25.
8 On Syria, Iraq, and the Islamic State, see Abboud, *Syria*; Stansfield, *Iraq*, Chapters 9–10.
9 Pack et al., *The Origins and Evolution of ISIS in Libya*, 19.
10 Frederic Wehrey, "Libyans Are Winning the Battle Against the Islamic State," *Foreign Policy*, June 30, 2016, http://foreignpolicy.com/2016/06/30/libyans-are-winning-the-battle-against-the-islamic-state/.
11 Helene Lavoix, "The Islamic State in Libya: When Libyan Tribes Pledge Allegiance to the Khalifa," *The Red (Team) Analysis Society*, May 16, 2016, https://www.redanalysis.org/2016/05/16/islamic-state-libya/; Helene Lavoix, "The Islamic State in Libya: Force, Fighters, and Tribes," *The Red (Team) Analysis Society*, April 25, 2016, https://www.redanalysis.org/2016/04/25/islamic-state-libya-2/.
12 "Hassan" quoted in Human Rights Watch, *"We All Feel Cursed,"* 10.
13 United Nations Panel of Experts on Libya, *Final Report of the Panel of Experts*, 48; Roslington and Pack, "Who Pays for ISIS in Libya?" See also Sudarsan Raghavan, "Inside the Brutal but Bizarrely Bureaucratic World of the Islamic State in Libya," *Washington Post*, August 23, 2016, https://www.washingtonpost.com/world/murders-taxes-and-a-dmv-how-isis-ruled-its-libyan-stronghold/2016/08/22/2ce3b8f4-5e60-11e6-84c1-6d27287896b5_story.html.
14 United Nations Panel of Experts on Libya, *Final Report of the Panel of Experts*, 15–16.
15 Details on these human rights abuses (and more) can be found in Human Rights Watch, *"We All Feel Cursed."*

16 Pack et al., *The Origins and Evolution of ISIS in Libya*, 27, 26.

17 Wehrey and Alrababa'h, *Rising Out of Chaos*.

18 Wehrey, *Ending Libya's Civil War*, 4.

19 Center for Insights in Survey Research, *Libyan Municipal Council Research*.

20 See Lacher, "Libya's Local Elites."

21 Kakar and Langhi, *Libya's Religious Sector and Peacebuilding Efforts*.

22 See Fitzgerald and Megerisi, *Libya: Whose Land Is It?*

23 See Cole and Mangan, *Tribe, Security, Justice, and Peace in Libya Today*.

24 See Elmangoush, *Customary Practice and Restorative Justice in Libya*.

25 Kakar and Langhi, *Libya's Religious Sector and Peacebuilding Efforts*.

26 *The Economist*, "Libya's Mufti: A Comment Too Far?," September 3, 2014, https://www.economist.com/blogs/pomegranate/2014/09/libyas-mufti.

27 See Obeidi, *Political Culture in Libya*.

28 Engel, *Libya's Civil War*.

29 Figures taken from Uppsala Data Conflict Program website: http://ucdp.uu.se/.

30 International Crisis Group, *Getting Geneva Right*, 11–12; International Crisis Group, *The Libyan Political Agreement*, 5–6.

31 International Crisis Group, *The Libyan Political Agreement*, 1–3.

32 International Crisis Group, *The Libyan Political Agreementt*, 9.

33 Randeep Ramesh, "UN Libya Envoy Accepts £1,000-a-Day Job from Backer of One Side in Civil War," *Guardian*, November 4, 2015, https://www.theguardian.com/world/2015/nov/04/un-libya-envoy-accepts-1000-a-day-job-from-backer-of-one-side-in-civil-war.

34 International Crisis Group, *The Libyan Political Agreement*, 5–7, 8.

35 Altai Consulting and IMPACT Initiatives, *Mixed Migration Trends in Libya*, 15.

36 International Organization on Migration, "Displacement Tracking Matrix: Libya," March–April 2016, 12–15; Allen Cone, "Up to 700 Migrants Feared Dead in Shipwrecks off Coast of Libya." UPI, May 29, 2016, https://www.upi.com/Top_News/World-News/2016/05/29/Up-to-700-migrants-feared-dead-in-shipwrecks-off-coast-of-Libya/5521464542080/.

37 Samuel Osborne, "Libya's Coastal Cities Are 'Making Millions from People Smuggling'," *Independent*, December 1, 2016.

38 See Amnesty International, *Vanished Off the Face of the Earth*; Human Rights Watch, *World Report 2016*, 383.

39 Amnesty International, *"Libya Is Full of Cruelty."* More recently, see Emma Graham-Harrison, "Migrants from West Africa Being 'Sold in Libyan Slave Markets'," *Guardian*, April 10, 2017, https://www.theguardian.com/world/2017/apr/10/libya-public-slave-auctions-un-migration.

40 See Altai Consulting and IMPACT Initiatives, *Mixed Migration Trends in Libya*.

41 On security in post-revolutionary Fezzan, see Wehrey, *Insecurity and Governance*.

42 See International Crisis Group, *How Libya's Fezzan Became Europe's New Border*, 5–6.

43 For more in-depth analysis, see Costantini, "Conflict Dynamics in Post-2011 Libya"; Droz-Vincent, "Libya's Tentative State Rebuilding."

44 United Nations Panel of Experts on Libya, *Final Report of the Panel of Experts*, 44–5.

45 Quoted in Colin Freeman, "Libya's Central Bank Causing 'Civil War' by Paying Rival Militias, Says UK Envoy," *Telegraph*, February 8, 2016, http://www.telegraph.co.uk/news/worldnews/africaandindianocean/libya/12146453/Libyas-central-bank-causing-civil-war-by-paying-warring-militias-says-UK-envoy.html.

46 Aidan Lewis, "Backing of Workers, Communities Key to Libya's Oil Revival," Reuters, July 20, 2017, https://

www.reuters.com/article/idUKKBN1A50H3. See also World Bank, *Labor Market Dynamics in Libya.*

47 Haythem Rashed, "Libya Reaches Most Critical Juncture Since Gaddafi's Fall," *Financial Times,* January 11, 2016, https://www.ft.com/content/bf016c28-b5f4-11e5-8358-9a82b43f6b2f; Anjli Raval and Heba Saleh, "War and Strife Have Cost Libya $68bn in Lost Oil Revenues," *Financial Times,* January 24, 2016, https://www.ft.com/content/4dc800de-c27a-11e5-b3b1-7b2481276e45.

48 World Bank, *Libya's Economic Outlook.*

49 International Crisis Group, *The Prize,* 5, footnote 14.

50 Nancy Porsia, "Black Market in Dollars and Diesel Thrives at Libya's Cost," Deutsche Welle, February 15, 2016, http://www.dw.com/en/black-market-in-dollars-and-diesel-thrives-at-libyas-cost/a-19049213.

51 Interview, Tripoli, July 3, 2012; International Crisis Group, *How Libya's Fezzan Became Europe's New Border,* 6–7. See also International Crisis Group, *The Prize*; Kartas, *On the Edge?*

52 Porsia, "Black Market in Dollars and Diesel" (see note 50 above).

53 Damir Kaletovic, "Mafia, Guns and Clans: The Big Libyan Oil Heist," OilPrice.com, February 12, 2017, https://oilprice.com/Energy/Energy-General/Mafia-Guns-And-Clans-The-Big-Libyan-Oil-Heist.html; Francesca Mannocchi, "How Libya's Oil Smugglers Are Bleeding Country of Cash," Middle East Eye, February 9, 2017, http://www.middleeasteye.net/news/how-libyas-oil-smugglers-are-bleeding-country-cash-592024472.

54 Ahmed Elumami and Patrick Markey, "Libyan Naval Forces in Tripoli Say Have Seized Foreign Tanker," Reuters, February 13, 2016, https://www.reuters.com/article/us-libya-security-tanker/libyan-naval-forces-in-tripoli-say-have-seized-foreign-tanker-idUSKCN0VM0RZ.

55 United Nations Panel of Experts on Libya, *Final Report of the Panel of Experts,* 47.

56 United Nations Panel of Experts on Libya, *Final Report of the Panel of Experts*, 25.

57 United Nations Panel of Experts on Libya, *Final Report of the Panel of Experts*, 25–48.

58 International Crisis Group, *The Libyan Political Agreement*, 6.

59 Mohamed Eljarh, "Libya at Another Crossroads," MENASource, The Atlantic Council, March 8, 2016, http://www.atlanticcouncil.org/blogs/menasource/libya-at-another-crossroads.

60 Quoted in Al Jazeera. "Libyan UN-Backed Government Starts Work from Naval Base," April 1, 2016, http://www.aljazeera.com/news/2016/04/libyan-unity-government-starts-work-naval-base-160401041524678.html.

61 Mohamed Elshabik, "Aiding Libya: The View from the Ground," Integrated Regional Information Networks, July 5, 2016, https://www.irinnews.org/opinion/2016/07/05/aiding-libya-view-ground.

62 Decan Walsh, "Libya's UN-Backed Government Ventures Farther into Tripoli," *New York Times*, April 1, 2016, https://www.nytimes.com/2016/04/02/world/africa/libyas-un-backed-government-ventures-farther-into-tripoli.html.

63 David Mack, "Kick-Starting Governance in Libya," Middle East Institute, July 7, 2016, http://www.mei.edu/content/article/kick-starting-governance-libya.

64 International Crisis Group, *The Libyan Political Agreement*, 9–10.

65 Carlotta Gall, "Jihadists Deepen Collaboration in North Africa," *New York Times*, January 1, 2016, https://www.nytimes.com/2016/01/02/world/africa/jihadists-deepen-collaboration-in-north-africa.html.

66 Ulf Laessing, "Boko Haram May Be Sending Fighters to Islamic State in Libya: US Officials," Reuters, May 13, 2016, https://www.reuters.com/article/idUSKCN0Y41QH.

67 Richard Lardner, "The Top American General in Africa Says Libya is a Failed State," *US News and World Report*, March 8, 2016, https://www.usnews.

com/news/politics/articles/2016-03-08/us-commander-in-africa-says-libya-is-a-failed-state; Yeganeh Torbati, "Islamic State Fighters in Libya Doubled But Militias Check Growth: US," Reuters, April 7, 2016, https://www.reuters.com/article/us-islamic-state-libya-usa-idUSKCN0X42IT; Ruth Sherlock, "US Planning to Strike Isil in Libya Based on 'Faulty Intelligence'," *Telegraph*, March 5, 2016, http://www.telegraph.co.uk/news/worldnews/africaandindianocean/libya/12184592/US-drawing-up-plans-for-Libya-air-assault-using-faulty-intelligence.html. See also Porter, "How Realistic Is Libya as an Islamic State 'Fallback'?"

68 Patrick Markey, "Sirte Battle Risks Widening Libya Political Splits," Reuters, July 11, 2016, https://af.reuters.com/article/algeriaNews/idAFL8N19P0AC.

69 See International Institute for Strategic Studies, "Confronting Failed Government and the Islamic State"; Patrick Wintour, "RAF Flying Libyan Missions in Preparation for Helping Unity Government," *Guardian*, February 8, 2016, https://www.theguardian.com/uk-news/2016/feb/09/raf-in-libyan-missions-in-preparation-for-helping-unity-government; Associated Press, "Libya Officials: French Special Forces on Ground Fighting IS," *New York Times*, February 24, 2016, https://apnews.com/bd88bf382b7946ffb9787580e0eb6327; Frances D'Emilio, "Italy to Allow US Armed Drones for Defense Use in Libya," Associated Press, February 22, 2016, https://www.apnews.com/5876ffdb8d8b49f9a2528cc07fb1d918; Paul Taylor, "French Special Forces Waging 'Secret War' in Libya: Report," Reuters, February 24, 2016, https://www.reuters.com/article/idUSKCN0VX1C3; Ruth Sherlock, "British 'Advisers' Deployed to Libya to Build Anti-Isil Cells," *Telegraph*, February 27, 2016, http://www.telegraph.co.uk/news/worldnews/africaandindianocean/libya/12176114/British-advisers-deployed-to-Libya-to-build-anti-Isil-cells.html; Associated Press, "Britain's Defense Minister Says About 20 UK Troops Are Being Sent to Tunisia to Help Stop People Crossing Illegally From Chaotic Libya,"

US News and World Report, February 29, 2016, https://
www.usnews.com/news/world/articles/2016-02-29/
uk-troops-to-advise-tunisia-on-halting-libya-border-
breaches; Randeep Ramesh, "SAS Deployed in Libya
Since Start of Year, Says Leaked Memo," *Guardian*,
March 25, 2016, https://www.theguardian.com/world/
2016/mar/25/sas-deployed-libya-start-year-leaked-
memo-king-abdullah.

70 Sudarsan Raghavan, "A Libyan Arms Dealer Chased
by Gaddafi's Legacy," *Washington Post*, September
15, 2016, https://www.washingtonpost.com/world/
middle_east/chased-by-a-dictators-legacy-an-arms-
dealer-navigates-libyas-chaos/2016/09/14/9fbbcb0a-
63d8-11e6-b4d8-33e931b5a26d_story.html.

71 Hani Amara, "Libyan Forces Clear Last Islamic
State Holdout in Sirte," Reuters, December 6, 2016,
https://www.reuters.com/article/us-libya-security-sirte/
libyan-forces-clear-last-islamic-state-holdout-in-sirte-
idUSKBN13V15R.

72 Wehrey, *Quiet No More?*

73 Quoted in Decan Walsh, "Militias in Libya
Advance on ISIS Stronghold of Surt with Separate
Agendas," *New York Times*, June 1, 2016, https://
www.nytimes.com/2016/06/02/world/africa/militias-
in-libya-advance-on-isis-stronghold-of-surt-with-
separate-agendas.html.

74 Quoted in Aidan Lewis and Ahmed Elumami, "Heavy
Toll Weighs on Misrata After Battle for Libya's Sirte,"
Reuters, October 7, 2016, https://www.reuters.com/
article/idUSKCN1271U7.

75 Tarek Megerisi and Mattia Toaldo, "Russia in Libya,
a Driver for Escalation?" Sada, Carnegie Endowment
for International Peace, December 8, 2016, http://
carnegieendowment.org/sada/66391.

76 Ayah Aman, "Egypt Acts as Middleman for Russia–
Libya Arms Deal," Al-Monitor, February 19, 2015,
https://www.al-monitor.com/pulse/originals/2015/02/
egypt-efforts-libya-army-russia-weapons.html (link no
longer active).

77 Toaldo, *Is the Sky Falling on Libya?*
78 Ahmed Ghaddar, Libby George, and Aidan Lewis. "Libya Oil Exports Threatened As NOC Warns Against Port Deal," Reuters, July 24, 2016, https://www.reuters.com/article/idUSKCN1040DO.
79 Raval and Saleh, "War and Strife" (see note 47 above).
80 Karim Mezran and Mattia Toaldo, "Libya's Future and Haftar's Oil Grab," MENASource, Atlantic Council, September 12, 2016, http://www.atlanticcouncil.org/blogs/menasource/libya-s-future-and-haftar-s-oil-grab; Jason Pack, "Can Libya Find Unity Through Oil?" Al-Monitor, September 20, 2016, https://www.al-monitor.com/pulse/originals/2016/09/libya-oil-unity-government-gna-hifter.html (link no longer active). See also Patrick Markey, "In Sign of Progress, Libya's Rival NOC Oil Companies Agree to Merge," Reuters, July 3, 2016, https://www.reuters.com/article/idUSKCN0ZJ0H7.
81 As the Crisis Group notes, in the context of negotiating the Libyan Political Agreement at the end of 2015, "Western powers gave Haftar an ultimatum: get on board or be marginalised." International Crisis Group, *The Libyan Political Agreement*, 15.
82 Jeremy Binnie, "UAE's Forward Operating Base in Libya Revealed," *Jane's 360*, October 28, 2016; Arnaude Delalande, "Emirati Fighter Jets Could Help Tip the Libyan Civil War," War Is Boring, February 6, 2017, https://warisboring.com/emirati-fighter-jets-could-help-tip-the-libyan-civil-war/; Arnaude Delalande, "Erik Prince's Mercenaries Are Bombing Libya: For-Profit Combat Pilots Fly Emirati Air Tractors," War Is Boring, January 14, 2017, https://warisboring.com/erik-princes-mercenaries-are-bombing-libya/; Jared Malsin, "US-Made Airplanes Deployed in Libya's Civil War, in Defiance of UN," *Time*, May 9, 2017, http://time.com/4746914/libya-civil-war-airplanes-haftar-uae/.
83 Geoff D. Porter, "Why the US Bombed ISIS in Libya," NARCO Analysis, North Africa Risk Consulting, January 19, 2017, http://northafricarisk.com/

analysis/2017-01-19. On the widening war in Libya, see Mezran and Miller, *Libya: From Intervention to Proxy War.*

84 Azza K. Maghur, "The Knockout Punch to the Libyan Political Agreement," Open Democracy, January 9, 2017, https://www.opendemcracy.net/ north-africa-west-asia/azza-k-maghur/knockout-punch-to-libyan-political-agreement.

85 International Crisis Group, *The Libyan Political Agreement*, 10–13.

86 Chris Stephen, "United Nations Condemns Attempted Coup in Libya," *Guardian*, October 15, 2016, https://www.theguardian.com/world/2016/oct/15/ libya-united-nations-condemns-attempted-coup-gna; Ahmed Elumami, "Rival Faction Challenges Libya's UN-Back [*sic*] Government in Tripoli," Reuters, October 15, 2016, https://www.reuters.com/article/ idUSKBN12F051.

87 International Crisis Group, *The Libyan Political Agreement*, 14–17; Wehrey, "'Whoever Controls Benghazi Controls Libya'" (see Chapter 4, n. 111).

88 Mathieu Galtier, "Libya: Why the Gaddafi Loyalists Are Back," Middle East Eye, November 11, 2016, http://www.middleeasteye.net/news/libya-why-gadhafi-loyalists-are-back-2138316983; Mohamed Eljarh, "Are Libyans Abandoning Democracy in Search of Stability?" Al-Monitor, October 10, 2016, https:// www.al-monitor.com/pulse/en/originals/2016/10/ libya-abandoning-democracy-search-stability.html (link no longer active).

89 See International Crisis Group, *The Libyan Political Agreement*, 17, footnote 68. Borzou Daragahi, "Libya's Deep State Is Back and Wants the World to Know It," BuzzFeed, April 2, 2016, https://www. buzzfeed.com/borzoudaragahi/libyas-deep-state-is-back-and-wants-you-to-know-it; Colin Freeman, "Gaddafi's Widow Allowed Back to Libya as Part of 'Reconciliation' Drive," *Telegraph*, May 9, 2016, http://www.telegraph.co.uk/news/2016/05/09/

gaddafis-ex-widow-allowed-to-return-to-libya-after-five-years-in/; Mustafa Fetouri, "Will Gadhafi's Son Be Libya's Next Leader?" Al-Monitor, July 22, 2016, https://www.al-monitor.com/pulse/originals/2016/07/libya-saif-al-islam-son-gadhafi-release-political-role.html (link no longer active); Chris Stephen, "Gaddafi Son Saif Al-Islam Freed by Libyan Militia," *Guardian*, June 11, 2017, https://www.theguardian.com/world/2017/jun/11/gaddafi-son-saif-al-islam-freed-by-libyan-militia.

90 Wehrey, *Quiet No More?*; Ahmed Salah Ali, "Haftar and Salafism: A Dangerous Game," MENASource, The Atlantic Council, June 6, 2017, http://www.atlanticcouncil.org/blogs/menasource/haftar-and-salafism-a-dangerous-game.

91 Agence France-Presse, "Libya Conflict: UN Says All Sides Probably Guilty of War Crimes," *Guardian*, February 25, 2016, https://www.theguardian.com/world/2016/feb/25/libya-conflict-un-says-all-sides-are-probably-guilty-of-war-crimes.

92 Human Rights Watch, *Libya: War Crimes as Benghazi Residents Flee*.

93 Amnesty International, *Amnesty International Report 2016/17*, 233–4.

94 United Nations High Commissioner for Human Rights, *Investigation by the Office of the United Nations High Commissioner for Human Rights on Libya*.

95 International Organization for Migration. "Over 417,000 Internally Displaced in Libya: IOM Report," May 13, 2016, https://www.iom.int/news/over-417000-internally-displaced-libya-iom-report.

96 Amnesty International, *Amnesty International Report 2015/16*, 232.

97 Omer Karasapan, "The Impact of Libyan Middle-Class Refugees in Libya," Brookings, March 17, 2015, https://www.brookings.edu/blog/future-development/2015/03/17/the-impact-of-libyan-middle-class-refugees-in-tunisia/.

98 Amnesty International, *Benghazi's Descent into Chaos*, 5–6.

99 Aidan Lewis, "Hundreds of Fighters from Chad, Darfur Feeding off Libya's Turmoil," Reuters, June 27, 2017, https://www.reuters.com/article/idUSKBN19I2HB. See also Tubiana and Gramizzi, *Tubu Trouble*.

100 Ayman Al-Warfalli and Aidan Lewis, "East Libyan Forces Take Desert Air Base as They Push West," Reuters, June 3, 2017, https://www.reuters.com/article/us-libya-security-idUSKBN18U0MA; Ayman Al-Warfalli and Aidan Lewis, "East Libyan Forces Claim Control Of Disputed Southern Air Base," Reuters, May 25, 2017, https://www.reuters.com/article/us-libya-security-south/east-libyan-forces-claim-control-of-disputed-southern-air-base-idUSKBN-18L1PA.

101 Romanet Perroux, *The Failure to End Libya's Fragmentation*.

102 In a November 2016 interview in London, Serraj suggested as much – that the international community's fixation on the Islamic State and trans-Mediterranean migration was doing little to help Libya. Sami Zaptia, "Serraj Blames Hafter, Saleh, Elkaber and Ghariani for Libya's Problems," *The Libya Herald*, November 2, 2016, https://www.libyaherald.com/2016/11/02/serraj-blames-hafter-salah-elkaber-and-ghariani-for-libyas-problems/.

Conclusion

1 Allansson et al., "Organized Violence, 1989–2016," 577; United Nations High Commissioner for Refugees, *Global Trends: Forced Displacement in 2015*, 5.

2 Quoted in Jeffrey Goldberg, "The Obama Doctrine," *Atlantic Monthly*, April 2016, https://www.theatlantic.com/magazine/archive/2016/04/the-obama-doctrine/471525/.

3 McQuinn, "Assessing (In)security After the Arab Spring," 718.

Chronology

1551
The Ottoman Empire seizes Tripoli, ushering in four centuries of direct and indirect rule.

1840s
Muhammad Al-Sanusi relocates his Sufi religious order to the mountains and deserts of Cyrenaica.

1911
The Italian invasion of Tripolitania and Cyrenaica begins.

1918
Ottomans formally cede Tripolitania and Cyrenaica to Italy; the Tripolitanian Republic is declared by elites from the Nafusa and Misrata.

1920
Italy delegates authority over Cyrenaica to Idris Al-Sanusi, head of the *Sanusiyyah* order, though Idris eventually goes into exile, fearing the fascist regime in Rome.

1921–31
Omar Mukhtar leads armed resistance to the Italian occupation of Cyrenaica; Italy wages a near-genocidal counterinsurgency campaign.

1934
Cyrenaica and Tripolitania are formally annexed as *Libia Italiana.*

1943
Libya is occupied by French, British, and US forces, bringing the fascist colony to an end.

1949
The UN General Assembly calls for the independence of Libya.

1951
Idris Al-Sanusi proclaims the independence of the United Kingdom of Libya, a federal monarchy uniting Fezzan, Tripolitania, and Cyrenaica.

1961
Libya's first oil exports; the country joins OPEC the following year.

1963
King Idris abolishes the federal system, further consolidating his power and control over the country's oil wealth.

1965
Civil war breaks out in Chad, leading to increasing levels of Libyan meddling.

1967
The closure of the Suez Canal for eight years following the Six-Day War, enhancing Libya's position on the European oil market.

1969
September 1: Military officers oust King Idris; Mu'ammar Al-Gaddafi, the leader of the coup, soon demands an end to the British and US military presence.

1970
Nationalization of oil production begins.

1973
Gaddafi's vision for the perfect society, the *Jamahiriyyah* (state of the masses), begins to take shape. The October Arab–Israeli war sees dramatic increases in the price of oil.

1975
Gaddafi's rule is challenged by protests and a failed coup attempt.

1978
Gaddafi tries to annex the Aouzou Strip in northern Chad while generously supplying Chadian proxy forces with arms.

1980
Led by Khalifa Haftar, Libyan forces enter the capital of Chad, N'djamena, to install a friendly regime; the US embassy closes in Tripoli.

1981
Opponents of the regime create the National Front for the Salvation of Libya. US and Libyan fighter jets skirmish over the Gulf of Sidra, leading to the downing of two Libyan aircraft.

1983
French forces are dispatched to Chad to repel a second Libyan intervention.

1986
Libyan involvement in international acts of terrorism prompts US bombing raids, though Gaddafi himself survives. World oil prices collapse.

1988
Pan Am Flight 103 explodes over Lockerbie, Scotland, at the end of the year. A French airliner, UTA 772, explodes over Niger the following September.

1992
A UN sanctions regime is placed on Libya for its failure to hand over the UTA 772 and Pan Am 103 suspects.

1993
Officers from the loyalist stronghold of Bani Walid lead an unsuccessful military coup against Gaddafi.

1995
The Libyan Islamic Fighting Group launches a guerrilla campaign against the regime.

1996
Hundreds of prisoners are massacred in Tripoli's Abu Salim jail; many are suspected Islamist militants.

The Great Man-Made River, reportedly the world's largest water-conveyance scheme, begins delivering water to Tripoli from underground aquifers in the Sahara.

1998
Libya agrees to surrender the suspects in the Lockerbie incident; one is found guilty in 2001. Gaddafi then offers compensation to the victims.

1999
The Organization of African Unity, meeting in Sirte, resolves to become the African Union.

2003
Sanctions are lifted by the UN Security Council; Libya discloses and abandons its limited chemical, biological, and nuclear weapons programs.

2004
British Prime Minister Tony Blair meets with Gaddafi in Tripoli.

2006

Libyan forces violently disperse crowds in Benghazi protesting defamatory cartoons of the Prophet Muhammad in European news publications.

2008

US–Libya relations are normalized. Italy apologies for the colonial period and offers compensation in the form of investment. Gaddafi promises to help clamp down on migration to the EU.

2010

Libya and Russia reach nearly $2 billion in weapons agreements.

2011

January–February: Protests across North Africa lead to the collapse of the regimes in Tunisia and Egypt; the Libyan state begins to crack down on dissidents preemptively.

February 17: The Libyan uprising begins in earnest, commemorating the 2006 demonstrations in Benghazi.

February 22: Gaddafi vows to crush the rebellion; repression and resistance increase.

March 10: The National Transitional Council in Benghazi is recognized by France as Libya's legitimate government.

March 17: The UN Security Council authorizes NATO and the Arab League to intervene in the Libyan civil war.

Mid-May: With assistance from foreign military advisors, Misratan rebels break the regime's grip on their city.

Late July: Rebel commander Abdelfatah Younis is killed by unknown assailants.

August 19: An uprising in Tripoli drives out the remnants of the regime as rebel forces from the Nafusa and Misrata converge on the capital.

September–October: Rebel forces search for Gaddafi in Bani Walid and Sirte, leading to a series of bloody street battles in the latter.

September 15: French President Nicolas Sarkozy and British Prime Minister David Cameron visit liberated Tripoli.

October 20: Misratan militias find Gaddafi and his son Mutassim in Sirte, summarily executing them.

October 23: The National Transitional Council formally takes power in Tripoli.

November: Zintani militias capture Saif Al-Islam in the Ubari region of Libya's Sahara.

2012
Early 2012: The Supreme National Council for Revolutionaries is formed to represent the interests of the hundreds of revolutionary militias – *al-thuwar* – that fought for the rebellion in 2011.

April: Rebels in northern Mali, flush with arms smuggled from Libya during the 2011 uprising, declare independence from Bamako; Islamists seize power in the breakaway republic, declaring an Islamic state seated in Timbuktu.

July 7: Peaceful national elections create an interim parliament, the General National Congress, though no single party dominates.

August 8: The National Transitional Council dissolves itself, handing power to the General National Congress.

September 11–12: US diplomatic and intelligence facilities in Benghazi are attacked by Libyan militias, leading to the death of the Ambassador and several other US personnel.

November 14: Ali Zeidan takes the office of Prime Minister.

2013
May 5: The Congress passes the controversial Political Isolation Law, which forbids former Gaddafi-era officials from holding office.

November 15: A Misratan militia in Tripoli opens fire on demonstrators protesting the ongoing presence of armed groups in the capital; some forty are killed.

2014
February 20: Elections are held for Libya's constitutional drafting body; the vote is marred by violence, boycotts, and logistical challenges.

March 14: Ali Zeidan is ousted and flees Libya after he is unable to stop a rogue militia from illegally loading an oil tanker; US special forces seize the tanker and return it to Libya.

May: Global oil prices collapse, further undermining Libya's faltering economy.

May 16: Khalifa Haftar launches Operation Dignity to restore security in Cyrenaica.

June: The Islamic State seizes control of Mosul in Iraq, proclaims the rebirth of the Islamic Caliphate; Libyan Islamists soon affiliate themselves with the organization.

June 25: Poorly attended elections for the House of Representatives, a new interim government, take place amid a brewing civil war.

July: Forces allied to Operation Dignity clash with opponents calling themselves Operation Libya Dawn, the latter composed largely of Islamist and Misratan brigades. Many are killed and the Tripoli airport is destroyed in the ensuing struggle.

August: The House of Representatives relocates to Tobruk in the far east of the country; a rump Congress reconvenes in Tripoli. The exodus of foreigners increases.

October: Islamist militias in Derna pledge themselves to the Islamic State in Iraq and Syria.

November 6: Libya's Supreme Court invalidates the House and restores the Congress. The internationally recognized House aligns itself with Haftar's Dignity Operation; the Congress supports Dawn's militias.

2015
January 27: Islamic State militants attack the Corinthia Hotel in downtown Tripoli.

February 15: Twenty-one Egyptian Coptic Christians are beheaded in Libya by the Islamic State, prompting a round of Egyptian air raids on Derna.

May 31: The Islamic State secures its hold on Sirte, driving out Misrata's militias.

December 17: The UN-backed Libyan Political Agreement is signed in Morocco, creating an interim Government of National Accord headed by Fayez Al-Serraj, chair of the Presidency Council. The House refuses to ratify the agreement, though elements of the Congress work with Serraj.

2016
March 30: Serraj and several cabinet ministers secretly arrive in Tripoli onboard a sea vessel; they begin working from the Abu Sitta naval base.

May 12: Backed by Serraj's administration, the Misratan-led campaign to retake Sirte begins, receiving tactical support from US forces.

June 27: Haftar makes the first of several visits to Moscow, meeting with the Ministers of Defense and Foreign Affairs.

September 11: The Libyan National Army takes control of Libya's largest oil export facilities in the east.

December: Sirte is declared liberated.

2017
January 11: Haftar is received by the Russian Ministry of Defense onboard one of its aircraft carriers off the Libyan coast.

January 19: US bombers and drones attack an Islamic State camp in the Libyan desert south of Sirte, killing dozens.

March–May: Haftar's forces push into central Libya, bringing them closer to allies in Tripolitania and Fezzan.

July 25: Haftar and Serraj publicly meet in France; both say they are committed to a political solution. Little progress is made toward peace and reconciliation by year's end.

December 17: The UN reiterates its support for the Libyan Political Agreement after its second anniversary, though Haftar calls it void. The UN envoy calls for presidential elections by the end of 2018.

References

Abboud, Samer N. 2016. *Syria*. Malden, MA: Polity.

Abou-Khalil, Naji and Laurence Hargreaves. *Perceptions of Security in Libya: Institutional and Revolutionary Actors*. Peace Works No. 108. Washington, DC: United States Institute for Peace, 2015.

Ahmida, Ali Abdullatif. *Forgotten Voices: Power and Agency in Colonial and Postcolonial Libya*. New York: Routledge, 2005.

Ahmida, Ali Abdullatif. *The Making of Modern Libya: State Formation, Colonization, and Resistance*. Second ed. Albany, NY: SUNY Press, 2009.

Allan, John Anthony, K. S. McLachlan, and Edith Tilton Penrose, eds. *Libya: Agriculture and Economic Development*. New York: Routledge, 1973.

Allansson, Marie, Erik Melander, and Lotta Themnér. "Organized Violence, 1989–2016." *Journal of Peace Research* 54, no. 4 (2017): 574–87.

Altai Consulting and IMPACT Initiatives. *Mixed Migration Trends in Libya: Changing Dynamics and Protection Challenges*. New York: United Nations High Commission on Human Rights, 2017.

Amnesty International. *Amnesty International Condemns Benghazi Bombing Targeting Civilians*. AI Index MDE 19/006/2013. London: Amnesty International, May 14, 2013.

Amnesty International. *Amnesty International Report 2015/16*. London: Amnesty International, 2016.

Amnesty International. *Amnesty International Report 2016/17*:

The State of the World's Human Rights. London: Amnesty International, 2017.

Amnesty International. *Barred from Their Homes: The Continued Displacement and Persecution of Tawarghas and Other Communities in Libya*. London: Amnesty International, 2013.

Amnesty International. *The Battle for Libya: Killings, Disappearances and Torture*. London: Amnesty International, 2011.

Amnesty International. *Benghazi's Descent into Chaos: Abductions, Summary Killings, and Other Abuses*. London: Amnesty International, 2015

Amnesty International. *Cold-Blooded Murder of Copts in Libya is a War Crime*. AI Index MDE 19/002/2015. London: Amnesty International, 2015.

Amnesty International. *Detention Abuses Staining the New Libya*. London: Amnesty International, 2011.

Amnesty International. *Libya: Detainees, Disappeared and Missing*. London: Amnesty International, 2011.

Amnesty International. *Libya: Four Arrested Amid Fears of Amazigh Culture Crackdown*. London: Amnesty International, January 6, 2015.

Amnesty International. *Libya: Gross Human Rights Violations Amid Secrecy and Isolation*. AI Index MDE 19/08/97. London: Amnesty International, June 1997.

Amnesty International. *Libya: Journalist Killed for Denouncing Abuses by Armed Group*. AI Index 19/004/2014. London: Amnesty International, May 29, 2014.

Amnesty International. *"Libya Is Full of Cruelty": Stories of Abduction, Sexual Violence and Abuse From Migrants and Refugees*. AI Index MDE 19/1578/2015. London: Amnesty International, 2015.

Amnesty International. *Libya: Rule of Law or Rule of Militias?* London: Amnesty International, 2012.

Amnesty International. *Libya: Summary of Amnesty International's Prisoner Concerns*. AI Index MDE 19/05/87. New York: Amnesty International, October 1987.

Amnesty International. *Libya: The Day Militias Shot at Protesters*. AI Index MDE 19/012/2013. London: Amnesty International, 2013.

Amnesty International. *Libya: Writer Detained After Calling for Demonstrations*. London: Amnesty International, February 5, 2011.

Amnesty International. *Militias Threaten Hopes for New Libya*. London: Amnesty International, 2012.

Amnesty International. *Summary of Amnesty International's Concerns in Libya.* AI Index ed. MDE 19/01/91. London: Amnesty International, March 1991.

Amnesty International. *"Vanished Off the Face of the Earth":* *Abducted Civilians in Libya.* AI Index 19/2178/2015. London: Amnesty International, August 2015.

Amnesty International. *Violations of Human Rights in the Libyan Arab Jamahiriya.* AI Index MDE 19/05/84. London: Amnesty International, November 1984.

Amnesty International. *"We Are Not Safe Anywhere": Tawarghas in Libya.* London: Amnesty International, June 2012.

Amnesty International, Cageprisoners, Center for Constitutional Rights, Center for Human Rights and Global Justice at NYU School of Law, Human Rights Watch, and Reprieve. *Off the Record: US Responsibility for Enforced Disappearances in the "War on Terror."* New York: Human Rights Watch, June 2007.

Anderson, Lisa. "Qaddafi's Islam." In *Voices of Resurgent Islam.* Edited by John L Esposito. New York: Oxford University Press, 1983.

Anderson, Lisa. *The State and Social Transformation in Tunisia and Libya, 1830–1980.* Princeton, NJ: Princeton University Press, 1986.

Ashour, Omar. *Libyan Islamists Unpacked: Rise, Transformation, and Future.* Washington, DC: Brookings Institution, May, 2012.

Ashour, Omar. "Post-Jihadism: Libya and the Global Transformations of Armed Islamist Movements." *Terrorism and Political Violence* 23, no. 3 (2011): 377–98.

Bartu, Peter. "The Corridor of Uncertainty: The National Transitional Council's Battle for Legitimacy and Recognition." In *The Libyan Revolution and Its Aftermath.* Edited by Peter Cole and Brian McQuinn. New York: Oxford University Press, 2015.

Bartu, Peter. *Libya's Political Transition: The Challenges of Mediation.* New York: International Peace Institute, December 2014.

Bassiouni, M. Cherif. *Libya: From Repression to Revolution: A Record of Armed Conflict and International Law Violations, 2011–2013.* Leiden: Martinus Nijhoff Publishers, 2013.

Bell, Anthony and David Witter. *The Libyan Revolution: Roots of Rebellion.* Washington, DC: Institute for the Study of War, 2011.

Bell, Anthony and David Witter. *The Libyan Revolution: Stalemate and Siege.* Washington, DC: Institute for the Study of War, 2011.

Bell, Anthony, Spencer Butts, and David Witter. *The Libyan*

Revolution: The Tide Turns. Washington, DC: Institute for the Study of War, 2011.

Benotman, Noman, Jason Pack, and James Brandon. "Islamists." In *The 2011 Libyan Uprisings and the Struggle for the Post-Qadhafi Future*. Edited by Jason Pack. New York: Palgrave Macmillan, 2013.

Blanchard, Christopher M. *Libya: Transition and US Policy*. Washington, DC: Congressional Research Service, 2016.

Brahimi, Alia. "Islam in Libya." In *Islamist Radicalisation in North Africa: Politics and Process*. Edited by George Joffé. New York: Routledge, 2012.

Braut-Hegghammer, Målfrid. "Libya's Nuclear Turnaround: Perspectives from Tripoli." *The Middle East Journal* 62, no. 1 (2008): 55–72.

Braut-Hegghammer, Målfrid. *Unclear Physics: Why Iraq and Libya Failed to Build Nuclear Weapons*. Ithaca, NY: Cornell University Press, 2016.

Bugaighis, Wafa. "Prospects for Women in the New Libya." In *Arab Spring and Arab Women: Challenges and Opportunities*. Edited by Muhamad S. Olimat. New York: Routlegde, 2014.

Campbell, Horace. *Global NATO and the Catastrophic Failure in Libya: Lessons for Africa in the Forging of African Unity*. New York: Monthly Review Press, 2013.

Carter Center. *General National Congress Elections in Libya: Final Report*. The Carter Center, Atlanta, GA, July 7, 2012.

Center for Insights in Survey Research. *Libyan Municipal Council Research*. Washington, DC: International Republican Institute/ USAID, 2016.

Chivvis, Christopher S. *Toppling Qaddafi: Libya and the Limits of Liberal Intervention*. New York: Cambridge University Press, 2014.

Chivvis, Christopher S. and Jeffrey Martini. *Libya After Qaddafi: Lessons and Implications for the Future*. Santa Monica, CA: RAND Corportation, 2014.

Chorin, Ethan Daniel. *Exit the Colonel: The Hidden History of the Libyan Revolution*. New York: Public Affairs, 2012.

Cole, Peter. "Bani Walid: Loyalism in a Time of Revolution." In *The Libyan Revolution and Its Aftermath*. Edited by Peter Cole and Brian McQuinn. New York: Oxford University Press, 2015.

Cole, Peter. *Borderline Chaos: Stabilizing Libya's Periphery*. Washington, DC: Carnegie Endowment for International Peace, October 2012.

Cole, Peter and Umar Khan. "The Fall of Tripoli: Part 1." In *The Libyan Revolution and Its Aftermath*. Edited by Peter Cole and Brian McQuinn. New York: Oxford University Press, 2015.

Cole, Peter and Fiona Mangan. *Tribe, Security, Justice, and Peace in Libya Today*. Peaceworks 118. Washington, DC: United States Institute for Peace, February 2016.

Cooley, John K. *Libyan Sandstorm*. New York: Holt, Rinehart, and Winston, 1982.

Costantini, Irene. "Conflict Dynamics in Post-2011 Libya: A Political Economy Perspective." *Conflict, Security & Development* 16, no. 5 (2016): 405–22.

Davis, John. *Libyan Politics: Tribe and Revolution. An Account of the Zuwaya and Their Government*. London: I.B. Tauris, 1987.

de Waal, Alex. "'My Fears, Alas, Were Not Unfounded': Africa's Responses to the Libyan Conflict." In *Libya, the Responsibility to Protect and the Future of Humanitarian Intervention*. Edited by Aidan Hehir and Robert W. Murray. New York: Palgrave Macmillan, 2013.

Deeb, Marius and Mary Jane Deeb. *Libya Since the Revolution: Aspects of Social and Political Development*. New York: Praeger, 1982.

Del Boca, Angelo. *Mohamed Fekini and the Fight to Free Libya*. Translated by Antony Shugaar. Basingstoke: Palgrave Macmillan, 2011.

Droz-Vincent, Philippe. "Libya's Tentative State Rebuilding: Militias' 'Moral Economy,' Violence, and Financing (In)Security." In *Businessmen in Arms: How the Military and Other Armed Groups Profit in the MENA Region*. Edited by Elke Grawert and Zeinab Abul-Magd. Lanham, MD: Rowman & Littlefield, 2016.

Economist Intelligence Unit. *Libya: Country Profile 2008*. London: Economist Intelligence Unit, 2008.

El-Kikhia, Mansour O. *Libya's Qaddafi: The Politics of Contradiction*. Gainesville, FL: University Press of Florida, 1997.

El Mallakh, Ragaei. "The Economics of Rapid Growth: Libya." *Middle East Journal* 23, no. 3 (1969): 308–20.

Elmangoush, Najla. *Customary Practice and Restorative Justice in Libya: A Hybrid Approach*. Special Report 374. Washington, DC: United States Institute of Peace, June 2015.

ElWarfally, Mahmoud G. *Imagery and Ideology in US Policy Toward Libya, 1969–1982*. Pittsburgh, PA: University of Pittsburgh Press, 1988.

Engel, Andrew. *Libya's Civil War: Rebuilding the Country from the*

Ground Up. Research Notes 25. Washington, DC: Washington Institute for Near East Policy, April 2015.

Engel, Andrew. *Libya as a Failed State: Causes, Consequences, Options.* Research Notes 14. Washington, DC: Washington Institute for Near East Policy, November 2014.

Fitzgerald, Mary. "Finding Their Place: Libya's Islamists During and After the Revolution." In *The Libyan Revolution and Its Aftermath.* Edited by Peter Cole and Brian McQuinn. New York: Oxford University Press, 2015.

Fitzgerald, Mary and Tarek Megerisi. *Libya: Whose Land Is It?* London: Legatum Institute, April 2015.

Gates, Robert Michael. *Duty: Memoirs of a Secretary at War.* New York: Alfred A. Knopf, 2014.

Gazzini, Claudia. "Was the Libya Intervention Necessary?" *Middle East Report,* no. 261 (2011): 2–9.

Geha, Carmen. *Understanding Libya's Civil Society.* Washington, DC: Middle East Institute, December 2016.

Gluck, Jason. *Extending Libya's Transitional Period: Capitalizing on the Constitutional Moment.* Peace Brief 104. Washington, DC: United States Institute of Peace, September 2011.

Guichaoua, Yvan. "Tuareg Militancy and the Sahelian Shockwaves of the Libyan Revolution." In *The Libyan Revolution and Its Aftermath.* Edited by Peter Cole and Brian McQuinn. New York: Oxford University Press, 2015.

Gurney, Judith. *Libya: The Political Economy of Oil.* New York: Oxford University Press, 1996.

Hersh, Seymour M. "The Red Line and the Rat Line." *London Review of Books* 36, no. 8 (2014): 21–4.

Human Rights Watch. *Collapse, Conflict, and Atrocity in Mali.* New York: Human Rights Watch, 2014.

Human Rights Watch. *Delivered into Enemy Hands: US-Led Abuse and Rendition of Opponents to Gaddafi's Libya.* New York: Human Rights Watch, 2012.

Human Rights Watch. *"The Endless Wait": Long-term Arbitrary Detentions and Torture in Western Libya.* New York: Human Rights Watch, 2015.

Human Rights Watch. *Libya: Commanders Should Face Justice for Killings.* New York: Human Rights Watch, February 22, 2011.

Human Rights Watch. *Libya: Diplomat Dies in Militia Custody.* New York: Human Rights Watch, February 2, 2012.

Human Rights Watch. *Libya: Governments Should Demand End*

to Unlawful Killings. New York: Human Rights Watch, February 20, 2011.

Human Rights Watch. *Libya: June 1996 Killings at Abu Salim Prison*. New York: Human Rights Watch, 2003.

Human Rights Watch. *Libya: Security Forces Kill 84 Over Three Days*. New York: Human Rights Watch, February 18, 2011.

Human Rights Watch. *Libya: War Crimes as Benghazi Residents Flee*. New York: Human Rights Watch, March 22, 2017.

Human Rights Watch. *Unacknowledged Deaths: Civilian Casualties in NATO's Air Campaign in Libya*. New York: Human Rights Watch, 2012.

Human Rights Watch. *"We All Feel Cursed": Life Under ISIS in Sirte, Libya*. New York: Human Rights Watch, 2016.

Human Rights Watch. *World Report 2012*. New York: Human Rights Watch, 2012.

Human Rights Watch. *World Report 2016: Events of 2015*. New York: Human Rights Watch, 2016.

Hweio, Haala. "Tribes in Libya: From Social Organization to Political Power." *African Conflict and Peacebuilding Review* 2, no. 1 (2012): 111–21.

International Commission of Jurists. *Challenges for the Libyan Judiciary: Ensuring Independence, Accountability and Gender Equality*. Geneva: International Commission of Jurists, July 2016.

International Crisis Group. *Divided We Stand: Libya's Enduring Conflicts*. Middle East/North Africa Report 130. Brussels: International Crisis Group, September 2012.

International Crisis Group. *Holding Libya Together: Security Challenges After Qadhafi*. Middle East/North Africa Report 115. Brussels: International Crisis Group, December 2011.

International Crisis Group. *How Libya's Fezzan Became Europe's New Border*. Middle East/North Africa Report 179. Brussels: International Crisis Group, July 2017.

International Crisis Group. *Libya: Getting Geneva Right*. Middle East/North Africa Report 157. Brussels: International Crisis Group, February 2015.

International Crisis Group. *The Libyan Political Agreement: Time for a Reset*. Middle East/North Africa Report 170. Brussels: International Crisis Group, November 2016.

International Crisis Group. *Making Sense of Libya*. Middle East/North Africa Report 107. Brussels: International Crisis Group, June 2011.

International Crisis Group. *The Prize: Fighting for Libya's Energy Wealth*. Middle East/North Africa Report 165. Brussels: International Crisis Group, December 2015.

International Crisis Group. *Trial by Error: Justice in Post-Qadhafi Libya*. Middle East/North Africa Report 140. Brussels: International Crisis Group, April 2013.

International Institute for Strategic Studies. "Confronting Failed Government and the Islamic State in Libya." *Strategic Comments* 22, no. 1 (2016): i–iii.

International Institute for Strategic Studies. *The Military Balance 2002–2003*. New York: Oxford University Press, 2002.

Issawi, Fatima. *Transitional Libyan Media: Free at Last?* Washington, DC: Carnegie Endowment for International Peace, May 2013.

Joffe, George. "Libya and Chad." *Review of African Political Economy*, no. 21 (1981): 84–102.

Kadduri, Majid. *Modern Libya: A Study in Political Development*. Baltimore, MD: Johns Hopkins University Press, 1963.

Kakar, Palwasha and Zahra Langhi. *Libya's Religious Sector and Peacebuilding Efforts*. Peaceworks 124. Washington, DC: United States Institute of Peace, 2017.

Kane, Sean. "Barqa Reborn? Eastern Regionalism and Libya's Political Transition." In *The Libyan Revolution and Its Aftermath*. Edited by Peter Cole and Brian McQuinn. New York: Oxford University Press, 2015.

Kartas, Moncef. *On the Edge? Trafficking and Insecurity at the Tunisian–Libyan Border*. Working Paper 17. Geneva: Small Arms Survey, December, 2013.

Kriesberg, Louis. *Realizing Peace: A Constructive Conflict Approach*. New York: Oxford University Press, 2015.

Lacher, Wolfram. "Families, Tribes and Cities in the Libyan Revolution." *Middle East Policy* 18, no. 4 (2011): 140–54.

Lacher, Wolfram. *Libya's Fractious South and Regional Instability*. Dispatch No. 3. Geneva: Small Arms Survey, February, 2014.

Lacher, Wolfram. "Libya's Local Elites and the Politics of Alliance Building." *Mediterranean Politics* 21, no. 1 (2015): 64–85.

Lacher, Wolfram and Peter Cole. *Politics by Other Means: Conflicting Interests in Libya's Security Sector*. Working Paper 20. Geneva: Small Arms Survey, 2014.

Lacher, Wolfram and Ahmed Labnouj. "Factionalism Resurgent: The War in the Jabal Nafusa." In *The Libyan Revolution and Its Aftermath*. Edited by Peter Cole and Brian McQuinn. New York: Oxford University Press, 2015.

Mangan, Fiona, Christina Murtaugh, and Feraouis Bagga. *Security and Justice in Postrevolution Libya: Where to Turn?* Peaceworks No. 100. Washington, DC: United State Institute of Peace, 2014.

Martin, Ian. *UNSMIL SRSG's Speech at Benghazi University.* Tripoli: United Nations Support Mission in Libya, April 10, 2012.

Matar, Hisham. *In the Country of Men.* New York: The Dial Press, 2007.

Mattes, Hanspeter. "Libya Since 2011: Political Transformation and Violence." *Middle East Policy* 23, no. 2 (2016): 59–75.

Mattes, Hanspeter. "Rebuilding the National-Security Forces in Libya." *Middle East Policy* 21, no. 2 (2014): 85–99.

McQuinn, Brian. *After the Fall: Libya's Evolving Armed Groups.* Working Paper 12. Geneva: Small Arms Survey, October, 2012.

McQuinn, Brian. "Assessing (In)security After the Arab Spring: The Case of Libya." *PS: Political Science & Politics* 46, no. 4 (2013): 716–20.

McQuinn, Brian. "History's Warriors: The Emergence of Revolutionary Battalions in Misrata." In *The Libyan Revolution and Its Aftermath.* Edited by Peter Cole and Brian McQuinn. New York: Oxford University Press, 2015.

Mezran, Karim and Elissa Miller. *Libya: From Intervention to Proxy War.* Washington, DC: Atlantic Council, 2017.

Middle East Journal. "Chronology." 66, no. 1 (2012): 111–61.

Minawi, Mostafa. *The Ottoman Scramble for Africa: Empire and Diplomacy in the Sahara and the Hijaz.* Stanford, CA: Stanford University Press, 2016.

Muller, Martine. "Frontiers: An Imported Concept: An Historical Review of the Creation and Consequences of Libya's Frontiers." In *Libya Since Independence: Economic and Political Development.* Edited by John A Allan. New York: St. Martin's Press, 1982.

Murray, Rebecca. "Libya's Tebu: Living in the Margins." In *The Libyan Revolution and Its Aftermath.* Edited by Peter Cole and Brian McQuinn. New York: Oxford University Press, 2015.

Neuberger, Benyamin. *Involvement, Invasion, and Withdrawal: Qadhdhāfi's Libya and Chad, 1969–1981.* Tel Aviv: Shiloah Center for Middle Eastern and African Studies, Tel-Aviv University, 1982.

Niblock, Tim. *"Pariah States" and Sanctions in the Middle East: Iraq, Libya, Sudan.* Boulder, CO: Lynne Rienner, 2002.

Nitzan, Jonathan and Shimshon Bichler. *The Global Political Economy of Israel.* Sterling, VA: Pluto Press, 2002.

Nolutshungu, Sam C. *Limits of Anarchy: Intervention and State Formation in Chad.* Charlottesville, VA: University of Virginia Press, 1996.

Northern, Richard and Jason Pack. "The Role of Outside Actors." In *The 2011 Libyan Uprisings and the Struggle for the Post-Qadhafi Future.* Edited by Jason Pack. New York: Palgrave Macmillan, 2013.

Obeidi, Amal. *Political Culture in Libya.* New York: Routledge, 2001.

O'Sullivan, Meghan L. *Shrewd Sanctions: Statecraft and State Sponsors of Terrorism.* Washington, DC: Brookings Institution Press, 2003.

Pack, Jason. "Introduction: The Center and the Periphery." In *The 2011 Libyan Uprisings and the Struggle for the Post-Qadhafi Future.* Edited by Jason Pack. New York: Palgrave Macmillan, 2013.

Pack, Jason and Barak Barfi. *In War's Wake: The Struggle for Post-Gaddafi Libya.* Washington, DC: The Washington Institute for Near East Policy, February 2012.

Pack, Jason, Karim Mezran, and Mohamed Eljarh. *Libya's Faustian Bargains: Breaking the Appeasement Cycle.* Washington, DC: Atlantic Council, May 2014.

Pack, Jason, Rhiannon Smith, and Karim Mezran. *The Origins and Evolution of ISIS in Libya.* Washington, DC: Atlantic Council, 2017.

Panetta, Leon and Jim Newton. *Worthy Fights: A Memoir of Leadership in War and Peace.* New York: Penguin, 2014.

Pargeter, Alison. *Libya : The Rise and Fall of Qaddafi.* New Haven, CT: Yale University Press, 2012.

Porter, Geoff D. "How Realistic is Libya as an Islamic State 'Fallback'?" *CTC Sentinel* 9, no. 3 (2016): 1–5.

Project on Middle East Democracy. *POMED Backgrounder: Previewing Libya's Elections.* Washington, DC: Project on Middle East Democracy, July 5, 2012.

Roberts, Hugh. "Who Said Gaddafi Had to Go?" *London Review of Books* 33, no. 22 (2011): 8–18.

Romanet Perroux, Jean-Louis. *The Failure to End Libya's Fragmentation and Future Prospects.* Middle East Brief 110. Waltham, MA: Crown Center for Middle East Studies, May 2017.

Romanet Perroux, Jean-Louis. *Libya's Untold Story: Civil Society Amid Chaos.* Middle East Brief 93. Waltham, MA: Crown Center for Middle East Studies, May 2015.

Ronen, Yehudit. *Qaddafi's Libya in World Politics*. Boulder, CO: Lynne Rienner, 2008.

Roslington, James and Jason Pack. "Who Pays for ISIS in Libya?" *Hate Speech International*, August 2016.

Sayigh, Yazid. *Crumbling States: Security Sector Reform in Libya and Yemen*. Washington, DC: Carnegie Endowment for International Peace, June 2015.

Setser, Brad W. and Cole V. Frank. *Using External Breakeven Prices to Track Vulnerabilities in Oil-Exporting Countries*. New York: Council on Foreign Relations, July 2017.

Simons, Geoff L. *Libya and the West: From Independence to Lockerbie*. Oxford: Centre for Libyan Studies, 2003.

Smith, Henry. "The South." In *The 2011 Libyan Uprisings and the Struggle for the Post-Qadhafi Future*. Edited by Jason Pack. New York: Palgrave Macmillan, 2013.

Springborg, Robert. "The Political Economy of the Arab Spring." *Mediterranean Politics* 16, no. 3 (2011): 427–33.

St. John, Ronald Bruce. *Libya and the United States: Two Centuries of Strife*. Philadelphia, PA: University of Pennsylvania Press, 2002.

St. John, Ronald Bruce. *Libya: Continuity and Change*. Revised ed. New York: Routledge, 2015.

St. John, Ronald Bruce. *Qaddafi's World Design: Libyan Foreign Policy, 1969–1987*. Atlantic Highlands, NJ: Saqi Books, 1987.

Stansfield, Gareth. *Iraq: People, History, Politics*. Second Edition. Malden, MA: Polity, 2016.

Toaldo, Mattia. *Is the Sky Falling on Libya?* European Council on Foreign Relations, September 23, 2016.

Transparency International. *National Integrity Systems Assessment: Libya 2014*. Berlin: Transparency International, 2016.

Tubiana, Jérôme and Claudio Gramizzi. *Tubu Trouble: State and Statelessness in the Chad–Sudan–Libya Triangle*. HBSA Working Paper 43. Geneva: Small Arms Survey, June 2017.

United Kingdom House of Commons Foreign Affairs Committee. *Libya: Examination of Intervention and Collapse and the UK's Future Policy Option*. London: United Kingdom House of Commons, September 14, 2016.

United Nations Development Programme. *Arab Human Development Report 2009*. New York: United Nations Development Programme, Regional Bureau for Arab States, 2009.

United Nations Development Programme. *Human Development Report 2010*. New York: United Nations Development Programme, 2010.

United Nations High Commissioner for Human Rights. *Investigation by the Office of the United Nations High Commissioner for Human Rights on Libya.* A/HRC/31/47. New York: United Nations, February 16, 2016.

United Nations High Commissioner for Refugees. *Global Trends: Forced Displacement in 2015.* Geneva: United Nations High Commissioner for Refugees, 2016.

United Nations Human Rights Council. *Report of the International Commission of Inquiry on Libya.* New York: United Nations, March 2, 2012.

United Nations Panel of Experts on Libya. *Final Report of the Panel of Experts on Libya Established Pursuant to Resolution 1973 (2011).* New York: United Nations, March 9, 2016.

United States House of Representatives Committee on Foreign Affairs. *Libya's Descent.* Washington, DC: US Government Printing Office, September 10, 2014.

US Energy Information Administration. *Country Analysis Brief: Libya.* Washington, DC: US Department of Energy, November 19, 2015.

Vandewalle, Dirk J. *Libya Since Independence: Oil and State-Building.* Ithaca, NY: Cornell University Press, 1998.

Vitalis, Robert. *America's Kingdom: Mythmaking on the Saudi Oil Frontier.* Stanford, CA: Stanford University Press, 2007.

Wehrey, Frederic. *Ending Libya's Civil War: Reconciling Politics, Rebuilding Security.* Washington, DC: Carnegie Endowment for International Peace, September 2014.

Wehrey, Frederic. *Insecurity and Governance Challenges in Southern Libya.* Washington, DC: Carnegie Endowment for International Peace, March 2017.

Wehrey, Frederic. *Libya's Militia Menace.* Washington, DC: Carnegie Endowment for International Peace, July 15, 2012.

Wehrey, Frederic. *Quiet No More?* Beirut: Carnegie Middle East Center, October 13, 2016.

Wehrey, Frederic. *The Struggle for Security in Eastern Libya.* Washington, DC: Carnegie Endowment for International Peace, 2012.

Wehrey, Frederic. "'Whoever Controls Benghazi Controls Libya'." *Atlantic Monthly*, 1 July 2017.

Wehrey, Frederic and Ala' Alrababa'h. *Rising Out of Chaos: The Islamic State in Syria.* Washington, DC: Carnegie Endowment for International Peace, March 2015.

Wehrey, Frederic and Peter Cole. *Building Libya's Security Sector.*

Policy Outlook. Washington, DC: Carnegie Endowment for International Peace, August 2013.

Werfalli Al-, Mabroka. *Political Alienation in Libya: Assessing Citizens' Political Attitude and Behaviour.* Reading: Ithaca Press, 2011.

World Bank. *Labor Market Dynamics in Libya: Reintegration for Recovery.* Washington, DC: World Bank Group, 2015.

World Bank. *Libya's Economic Outlook.* Washington, DC: World Bank Group, October, 2016.

Wright, John L. *Libya, Chad and the Central Sahara.* Totowa, NJ: Barnes and Noble Books, 1989.

Zelin, Aaron. *The Islamic State's Territorial Methodology.* Research Note 29. Washington, DC: The Washington Institute for Near East Policy, January 2016.

Zelin, Aaron. *The Islamic State's First Colony in Libya.* Policy Watch 2325. Washington, DC: Washington Institute for Near East Policy, October 2014.

Zoubir, Yahia H. 2009. "Libya and Europe: Economic Realism at the Rescue of the Qaddafi Authoritarian Regime." *Journal of Contemporary European Studies* 17, no. 3 (2009): 401–15.

Zoubir, Yahia H. 2011. "The United States and Libya: The Limits of Coercive Diplomacy." *The Journal of North African Studies* 16, no. 2 (2011): 275–97.

Zoubir, Yahia H. and Erzsébet N. Rózsa. "The End of the Libyan Dictatorship: The Uncertain Transition." *Third World Quarterly* 33, no. 7 (2012): 1267–83.

Index